American
Family Farm
ANTIQUES

A WALLACE-HOMESTEAD PRICE GUIDE

American Family Farm
ANTIQUES

TERRI CLEMENS

Wallace-Homestead Book Company
Radnor, Pennsylvania

Published in Radnor, Pennsylvania 19089, by Wallace-Homestead,
a division of Chilton Book Company

Wagon on the cover is from Creative Clutter, Lexington, Illinois

Designed by Anthony Jacobson

Manufactured in the United States of America

Library of Congress Cataloging-in-Publication Data

Clemens, Terri.
    American family farm antiques / Terri Clemens.
        p.   cm.
    "A Wallace-Homestead price guide."
    Includes bibliographical references (p.   ) and index.
    ISBN 0-87069-690-4
        1. Farm equipment—Collectibles—United States—Catalogs.
    2. Agricultural implements—Collectibles—United States—Catalogs.
    I. Title.
    S676.3.C58   1994
    681'.763'075—dc20   94-13886
                                                            CIP

1 2 3 4 5 6 7 8 9 0   3 2 1 0 9 8 7 6 5 4

To
Grandpa Harry
and
Grandma Pearl

Contents

Introduction

The American family farm is the backbone of American culture. Pioneering farm families settled our country and influenced our values. Few Americans are farmers today, but whether we live in a city, in a small town, or in a rural area, there is likely to be a farm in our roots. We look back at farm life as simple and honest—an old-fashioned way of living with close-knit families, friendly neighbors, and respectable work. When the pressures of modern life seem too heavy, a nostalgic look back at life on the farm can be a welcome solace.

Americans' feelings of nostalgia for farm life are reflected in the popularity of country decorating. "Country antiques" are comfortable and varied antiques, collectibles, and crafts that have become one of America's most popular decorative styles. "Country" can be an individual style, using a wide range of categories of antiques and collectibles. Farm antiques make up one of those categories.

American Family Farm Antiques is a reference guide for people who want to collect or decorate with farm antiques. Established collectors of farm memorabilia learn about their collections from older farmers, from each other, or from experience in the market. Many collectors are not fortunate enough to be able to share in these sources of knowledge. With a picture glossary, descriptions of farm activities, patent information, references, and a value guide, *American Family Farm Antiques* should provide collectors with the information they need to identify, evaluate, and enjoy their farm memorabilia.

This guide concentrates on the farm-related items that are available at country auctions, flea markets, and antiques shops and shows in rural America. Things that were used to do farm work, to benefit from the products of the farm, and to contribute to the self-sufficiency of the farm family are the focus of this guide.

The years between World War I and World War II brought a technological revolution to housekeeping chores. Electricity, which reached even remote rural areas by 1950, is the most obvious element in this revolution, but running water, central heat, and cleaner-burning fuels also made it easier to run a home: from coal- or wood-heated rooms to centrally heated homes warmed by gas, oil, or electricity; from outhouses, pumps, commodes, and Saturday baths to bathrooms, kitchens, and laundry rooms with running hot and cold water; and from candlelight, oil lamps, and early bedtimes to gas and electric lights.

Stores not only took eggs and butter in trade but also accepted such goods as chickens, ducks, turkeys, pheasants, quail, wool, beeswax, honey, cheese, onions, dried beans, tobacco, shelled corn, and nuts.

Peddlers brought brushes, combs, sewing notions, pots and pans, medicines, eyeglasses, clocks, knives, forks, razors, jewelry, toys, shoes, tea, spices, and flavorings. They also repaired things, and picked up scrap iron, rags, and bought produce.

How to Use This Book

As a dealer, appraiser, and collector, I have used price guides for many years. My experience in collecting prices for this guide has taught me much about how guides should be used.

Identification can be a problem with farm antiques. The picture glossary at the back of the book may help you identify common farm tools. The chapter introductions describe the items that were used for different functions on the family farm. The collecting tips and warnings about reproductions included in the introductions should help you judge the desirability of your item compared with those listed in the guide.

Condition is very important in judging the quality of any antique or collectible. Signs of age add to the appeal of an item, but excessive wear and tear or broken or missing parts will decrease its value. Original paint or easily legible stenciled advertising can double the value of an undecorated or worn piece that is a duplicate in every other way.

The value of a refinished item compared with one in its natural state is a matter of opinion. Of course, a pristine original finish is always desirable, but it

is seldom found. Some collectors consider a shiny, newly refinished item to be ruined. However, there are decorators who won't touch that item unless it looks new. Some collectors enjoy doing their own refinishing or polishing. Some will pay more for a refinished item, others will not even consider buying it. Refinishing usually results in higher asking prices and a smaller market. Careful cleaning will usually bring out the qualities of a piece without sacrificing its integrity.

The values in this price guide have been recorded from real prices at shops, shows, flea markets, and auctions and from advertisements. Many of these prices are prices asked and not necessarily prices realized.

As a dealer, I like to think of price guides as a look at my competitors' prices. If I don't know what to ask for an item, I look to see what others are asking. If I can afford to sell at a lower price than my competition, it makes my customers happy.

This guide is a report of what the competition is asking. Sometimes the person who priced the object was just making a guess. Wrong guesses that are too high are more likely to be seen on the market. The low guesses don't last long enough to be recorded. If I saw a price that I knew from my own experience, or from the advice of collectors in that field, was out of line, I did not include it. Unusual pieces are desirable, and the law of supply and demand makes these things seem pricey.

Many farm antiques are regional collectibles. The prices in this guide are based on how regional things are valued in their own area. I am in Illinois, so most of the local advertising items listed are from Illinois. Wherever you are, your local advertising items should sell in the same range.

Supply and demand also makes a difference regionally. I saw hog scrapers and hay hooks selling for $3 to $6 each in the Midwest. In the South, they were each priced at more than $20, and dealers reported that they didn't sell well. As I traveled east, I found little variation in prices. The Midwest has a bigger supply of farm memorabilia than most parts of the country and more collectors of farm memorabilia to balance supply and demand.

Sometimes prices are hard to pin down. While working on a recent appraisal, I found De Laval die-cut tin cow and calf premiums listed in price guides for $8, $25, and $95. I have seen them priced $195 and $285 at shows. I advised my client to price her Guernsey and Holstein sets, in the original envelopes, at $150 each. She was offered $125 at a one-day estate sale. If I had stopped with the $8 suggestion, I would have done my client a disservice. If I had recommended she try for $285, chances are good that she would still have her cow and calf. When I have found a wide range of prices for the same object, I have tried to recommend a middle ground for this guide, just as I would for an appraisal.

The prices in this guide should be only one consideration in a decision about buying or selling. Your own experience, your feelings or needs, the condition of the object, the availability of comparable items, and regional factors should also be taken into account. The antiques market is one in which the free enterprise system still works. No one sets prices except the buyer and seller involved in each transaction.

Sellers, of course, shouldn't expect to realize these prices unless they decide to become involved in the retail market. Dealers must pay expenses to reach the market that will pay retail prices. That market is accessible to anyone who wants to take the trouble to enter it. If you want to sell your farm memorabilia, you can sell to a dealer or at auction and realize from 25% to 75% of retail prices. Or you can pay your own selling expenses, and realize the same 25% to 75% of retail prices. (Many collectors of farm memorabilia are especially fond of trading, so you might consider barter as another avenue of offering or obtaining goods.)

Dairy

Dairy farming is presented in literature and art as an idyllic way of life. Pastoral scenes often include a small herd of dairy cows, grazing in a lush meadow. Milkmaids are remembered as pretty girls with their hair in braids and wearing clean, white aprons over their skirts. The gentle nature of dairy cattle makes them appealing. Unlike beef cattle, milk cows are often named and treated affectionately.

In the 19th century, dairy farming was a slower, more peaceful way to live than other kinds of farming. Milking was done by hand. Production was the same year-round, without a busy harvest, planting, or butchering season. The negative side of this year-round production was the lack of freedom a dairying family had, because of the daily demands of milking.

Milk output was influenced by the mixture of grass, hay, corn, silage, and nutrient supplements fed to the animals and by selective breeding. Many farmers considered each cow's feeding formula to be so important that detailed logs of feed and production were kept. Genetic lines for registered dairy cattle often go back as far as two centuries. All this attention contributed to the individuality of each cow. Contented cows give more milk, and efforts were made to make the milking process pleasant. Because dairy cows weren't raised for slaughter, families grew attached to them, sometimes considering them to be pets.

American dairy cattle are chiefly of five breeds: Holstein, Jersey, Guernsey, Brown Swiss, and Ayrshire. Holsteins are large black-and-white spotted animals. Jerseys and Guernseys are fawn colored. Guernseys and some Jerseys have white markings, and Jerseys are smaller than Guernseys. Brown Swiss are silver to dark brown with a black nose and tongue. Ayrshires are red and white or brown and white. Goats and sheep are also good producers of dairy products.

At the turn of the century, most nondairy farms had one or two cows to supply the family's needs. Dairy farms near population centers worked closely with commercial dairies, which processed and transported the highly perishable milk and cream to supply city dwellers with milk, cream, butter, cheese, and other dairy products.

Louis Pasteur originated the process of pasteurization in the 1860s. Pasteurization destroys harmful microorganisms in raw milk, such as the bacteria that causes tuberculosis, making the milk safe for human consumption and prolonging its shelf life. Before pasteurization, people seldom drank milk; instead it was sometimes made into cottage cheese or could be cooked in chowders or clabber. It was most often used for animal feed. Cream was separated from the milk and used for cheese and butter. The introduction of pasteurization made milk as important a product as cream.

Pasture is the natural food for dairy cattle. Cowbells, hung around the neck of each animal, made it easier to locate the cows to bring them in at milking time. These bells, made of steel, brass, or copper, were worn on a leather collar. They were made in smaller sizes for calves and goats. Cow pokes, large wooden or metal collars with barbs, kept cows from pushing through fences. Calf weaners were used to keep calves from suckling when they were old enough to eat grass. Some poked the cow, causing her to reject the calf. Others poked the calf or were designed to permit grazing, but not suckling.

Special feed formulas for dairy cattle were sold in heavy cotton bags that were decorated with the producer's advertising. Feed bins, scoops, buckets, and scales were used to distribute the feed.

Disease control was important on dairy farms, as milk was very susceptible to contamination. Tin or cardboard containers held remedies for dairy cattle diseases, salves to clean and soften udders, and feed additives.

Milking involved the use of milking stools, which were low to the ground and had one, three, or four legs. Cow kickers were placed on the cow's back legs to keep the cow from kicking the milker. Milking buckets, or pails, held about 2½ gallons of milk and were made of wood, tin, graniteware, or modern stainless steel. They often had a pouring handle or a spout. The buckets could be carried, two at a time, on a wooden yoke, sometimes called a maiden yoke, that fit over the milker's shoulders.

Separating the milk from the cream involved the use of many implements. Milk was strained by pouring it through cheesecloth or metal strainers made to fit over a milk can. The milk had to be cooled before the cream could be separated from the milk. It was poured into cooling bowls (often stoneware) or into milk cans. Milk cans were placed in tubs of cold water or ice and a cooling rod was moved up and down in the can to agitate the milk. These rods are 2 to 2½ feet long and have a perforated, concave disc attached to the end of the rod. Most rods are steel, but some are brass.

The milk cans that were used to transport the milk from one step to the next are most commonly found in 2½-, 5-, 8-, and 10-gallon sizes. They sometimes bear labels that identify the farm or dairy that owned them. Wooden milk sleds made it easier to move heavy cans from the barn. These sleds are usually quite simple, with wooded runners, sometimes reinforced with metal bands. Most were pulled with rope handles. Cream cans, made of tin, steel, aluminum, or graniteware, are smaller than milk cans, hold from 1 quart to 3 gallons, and often have bail handles. Some are shaped like milk cans; some are tall cylinders.

Milk testers measured the butterfat content of samples of raw milk. Fat naturally rises to the top. Skimmers—flat ladles of tin, brass, copper, horn, or graniteware—were used to separate cream manually from an open bowl of milk. Gravity separators are a simple tool that was used on many small farms.

A cylindrical metal container on legs that usually holds 2 to 10 gallons, the gravity separator has a funnel-shaped bottom opening, a brass or galvanized metal spigot, and a glass gauge that offers a view inside the tank. Watching the gauge as the milk was drained from the opening at the bottom, the person using the separator could shut the valve when the cream was reached and use a different container to catch the cream.

The invention of a separator using centrifugal force was an important technological advance in dairy farming. Carl G. P. de Laval, a Swedish inventor, had developed a steam turbine and put it to use powering a cream separator in 1877. The De Laval Separator soon had competition from Sharples, McCormick Deering, Wards Sattley, Sears Economy, and many other brands. Advertising, premiums, and maintenance products for these machines are abundant and highly collectible. By 1910, most farms with more than one or two milk cows had a mechanical separator.

The mechanical separator worked by spinning the whole milk, which moved the heavier milk to the outside. Milk was poured onto spinning discs, powered by a hand crank or a small electric motor. Milk and cream ran through separate channels to their respective spouts where there were platforms to hold containers for each product.

Processing the cream into butter or cheese involved many tools. Butter churns can be found in several forms, from 16-gallon bentwood churns on legs to 1-quart churns made from glass fruit jars. Stoneware churns and cylindrical, staved, wooden churns both worked the cream into butter by the up and down motion of a wooden dasher. Bentwood, glass, and metal churns had wooden or metal paddles that were turned with a crank. Barrel-type churns, made of wood or stoneware, worked the cream by turning the barrel end to end. Rocker churns, large containers that rocked on a stand, agitated the cream with a back-and-forth motion.

Large wooden butter workers on legs smoothed the churned butter with a ridged roller or by the side-to-side action of a wooden arm across a triangular chute. Maple or aluminum butter paddles also were used to smooth the butter. Older paddles have a hooked handle that fit over the edge of a wooden butter bowl. Butter was formed in rectangular or circular molds and was sometimes decorated with a carved plunger, which was built into the mold, or by a separate paddle-shaped butter stamp. Pairs of ridged paddles were used to roll butter into balls.

Skimmed milk was made into cottage cheese by processing the curds and whey. When the milk had coagulated, the whey was drained through sieves made of splint, tin, earthenware, or graniteware.

Most cheeses were made from whole milk or cream. Bacterial enzyme action ripened the curd to the desired body and flavor. Rennet was added to thicken the curds. Rennet was obtained by soaking a dried piece of calf's stomach in water and using the resulting liquid. Curds were chopped or cut with curd choppers or knives and then drained through cheesecloth, which was supported by a cheese ladder. Cheese ladders are mortised wooden ladders or grids that rested on a tray or pot, which caught the dripping liquid from the cheese. The drained curds were then salted and packed into cheese molds or measures with holes around the frame, which allowed further drainage. The molds were then pressed, sometimes with a tool made for that purpose, sometimes with a wooden board that fit the top of the mold. After days of turning and draining, the cheese was trimmed with a cheese knife or cutter, salted, and fit into cheese boxes or sewn into bags. Some farms had a cheese safe, resembling a screened pie safe, but with finer screens, where the supply of cheese was kept.

Many large farms operated their own dairies, contributing milk and cream bottles, cream top spoons, bottle caps, milk cans, cottage cheese containers, and diverse advertising material to the field of farm antiques and collectibles.

Tips for Collectors

Factors that influence the collectibility of dairy-related items include advertising, regional interest, attractiveness of design, and utility. A piece that bears the name of a local farm or dairy is more valuable close to its home. Some collectors specialize in the products related to one company, such as De Laval. Advertising items are valued for their design, condition, age, and rarity. A Purina milk scale is more desirable to most collectors than one that bears no advertising. Some handmade dairy items are unique and very desirable. Butter molds that were hand carved are almost always more desirable than factory-made ones with pressed designs. Some dairy collectibles are more easily used for decorative purposes than others. A bentwood churn with a flat top can be a useful piece of furniture, while a barrel churn is not as convenient.

Churns made by Dazey came in many sizes and styles. Sometimes the original jars have been replaced with unmarked ones. They can be found with wooden or aluminum paddles.

The 4- and 6-gallon glass churns are much more common than other sizes, and prices should reflect this difference. Metal churns are often missing their original stenciled decoration, which makes them much less desirable than well-preserved examples.

Stoneware dairy items as well as many advertising pieces are affected by collectors in other categories. Handmade, cobalt decorated churns and butter crocks are sought after by stoneware collectors, who often value pieces for their design or maker. Blue and blue-and-white stoneware also have a large group of collectors. Colorful signs, cabinets, tins, and premiums are highly valued by advertising collectors.

Reproductions

Butter molds have been reproduced for many years. Most individual-size molds were made for decorating or collecting. A glass and wooden mold with a cow design was sold by the thousands in the 1980s. Old molds are usually out of round, and many have a small crack. Old molds are usually made of maple. New molds often smell like they're new—like wood or varnish. Shiny, perfectly shaped molds were probably never meant to mold butter.

Modern craftspeople have been making splint cheese baskets for decades. Look for wear and staining (often a bleached look) to help determine the age of baskets. Small wooden tabletop churns were used as decorating items during the 1960s, when "Early American" was a popular style. These are varnished and were obviously never used to churn milk, but they are finding their way into the antiques market, often with high prices.

Book

American Dairy Cattle, by Prentice, 1942, 444 pages **12.50**

American Dairying: Butter and Cheese Makers, Rural Home, L. B. Arnold, 1876, slightly soiled **17.00**

Dairylike Majesty Imp. 198188: His Contribution to the Breed, 1929, Jersey bull, 32 pages, 8″ × 11″ **22.50**

James Way, How to Build and Equip an Up-to-Date Dairy Barn, 1919, octavo, blueprints, photos, water stains **8.00**

Modern Methods of Testing Milk and Milk Products, by Van Slyke, 1912, illustrated, 286 pages **20.00**

Milch Cows and Dairy Farming, Flint, 1859, 413 pages, illustrated, ex-library **45.00**

Bowl, milk, blue and white stoneware, Daisy and Lattice, 10″ × 5″ **140.00**

Bucket

cardboard, "Mor-Milk - A Milk Substitute Food - Dixon, Ill.," metal bands top and bottom, 13″ diameter at top, 13″ high **25.00**

enameled white with red edge, bail with wooden handle **17.50**

galvanized metal, oval opening for pouring milk **6.00**

galvanized metal, paper label reads "Mutual Dairy Aid Concentrate - Manufactured and Guaranteed by Mutual Products Co. - Minneapolis, Minn. USA," five gallon lines marked on bucket, 12½″ × 11″ **9.00**

gray graniteware, bail handle **50.00**

tin, tall cylindrical two-gallon size, 8″ diameter, bail with wood handle, missing lid **17.50**

tin, three gallon, with fitted lid and bail handle **25.00**

Cow poke, oak bentwood yoke is 20½″ × 10″ × 2″, two metal prongs protrude into cow's neck from T-shaped, 40″ wooden handle when cow pushes against fence (Illinois Farm Bureau photo/Busch collection), **85.00**

Cream can, galvanized metal (Sharkey collection), **20.00**

Calf weaner, iron, 5¼" × 5", 8.50

Butter churns
Glass
"Dandy" on cast metal lid, unmarked squared gallon glass jar, wood paddles **49.50**
Dazey
Dazey top with wood paddles, jar embossed "4 QT" **47.00**
Dazey top with wood paddles, jar embossed "No. 80" **145.00**
Dazey top with wood paddles, unmarked six quart jar **60.00**
No. 20, wood paddles, jar embossed "Dazey Churn and Manufacturing Co., No. 20," wood paddles **235.00**
No. 30, jar embossed "30 - Dazey Churn and Mfg Co., St. Louis, USA," wood paddles, metal lid and gears are painted dark red **120.00**
No. 40, wood paddles, jar embossed "Dazey No. 40," 4½" square, 12" high **55.00**
No. 60, wood paddles, jar embossed "Dazey No. 60" **75.00**
one quart, embossed jar, wood paddles **1025.00**
Elgin, 6 quart, paper label, metal paddles **70.00**
"Fill to Here" embossed on square one gallon jar, wooden paddles **70.00**

"Gem Dandy Electric Churn," embossed barrel design on two gallon Hazel Atlas jar, bail handle, Alabama Manufacturing Co., Birmingham, Ala., black and beige electric motor powers aluminum paddles, 23" tall **85.00**
No manufacturer's name
one quart, shaped like a barrel, metal paddles **100.00**
two quart, aluminum paddles ..**75.00**
two quart, wood paddles **125.00**
eight quart, wood paddles **85.00**
round jar base, one gallon, red metal top, wood paddles **65.00**
square jar embossed "4 Qt.," aluminum paddles **42.50**
Presto, square half gallon jar, metal paddles **85.00**
"Sunbeam Mixmaster" embossed on four quart jar, wood paddles ...**65.00**
Wards, electric, jar with label, four quart **33.00**
Metal
"Challenge - The Mason Mfg. Co. - Canton, O. - No. 22 - Patd June 23, 1902," base is 6" × 7" × 9", paddles turned by 4" cast iron wheel, wood frame, 10" × 13" × 9" **180.00**
dasher-type, tin, cylinder tapers from 8" bottom to 7" top, 18" high, metal lip and two strap handles, 32" wood dasher **180.00**
Dazey No. 27, rusted, two wooden lids **45.00**
"The Dazey Churn No. 27" painted on side, double wood lid with knob, wood paddles, very good condition **95.00**
Stoneware
Albany glaze, ear handles, four gallon, unglazed lid, old dasher **85.00**
barrel-type, Bristol glaze, ten gallon churn is stenciled "Superior Sanitary Churn - 10 gallon - Northville, Mich. - Pat'd Dec. 13, 1910," metal strap fits into notch around center of churn, holding it in a wooden frame, hole at base of churn for spigot, original glass lid is missing strap **265.00**

Bristol glaze, stenciled "8," no lid or dasher **110.00**
red clay, orangish green glaze, ear handles, incised "6," no dasher or lid **85.00**
Ruckels, Whitehall, Ill., Bristol glaze, four gallon, replaced lid, old wood dasher **115.00**
Ruckels, Whitehall, Ill., tree bark finish **200.00**
salt glazed, five gallon, cobalt flower, wood lid and dasher, ear handles, cracked **200.00**
salt glazed, six gallon, bee sting in cobalt slip, ear handles, no lid or dasher **195.00**
salt glazed, ten gallon, ear handles, worn stenciling "McWard Stoneware Depot - Zanesville, O," no dasher or lid **300.00**
unmarked brown over white, three gallon **50.00**
unmarked, brown over white, five gallon, no lid or dasher **40.00**

Wood

barrel-type, "Dobson Mfg. Co. - Favorite - Pat'd - Rockford, Ill.," 14" diameter, 32" tall **125.00**
barrel-type, top is stenciled "J. McDermaid, Rockford, Ill.," rests in a wooden frame, iron crank with wood handle **160.00**
barrel-type, bentwood handle turns wheels on one side, barrel is 16" × 17" **150.00**
bentwood, on legs, stenciled in black "The Bentwood Churn, Manufd by the M. Brown Co. Wapakoneta, O," 17" × 16" × 33" **235.00**
Blanchard, "Get the Best - The Blanchard Churn" stenciled each side, painted yellow with black trim, wood body with legs, lid opens to wood paddles, front and back are stenciled with a "B" in a scroll design, cast iron crank is embossed "The Blanchard Co.," 22½" × 18½" × 32" **395.00**
dasher-type, cedar staves, wood lid and dasher **125.00**
dasher-type, tapered cylindrical barrel, recently painted and decorated with decals, old dasher **125.00**
dasher-type, tapered cylindrical barrel, two gallon, wood bands with fingers, mustard paint, new lid, no dasher **195.00**
"E.M. Funk's Champion Churn," red and black with white stenciling, wooden pump-type handle, 13" square × 37" high **145.00**
oval barrel, crank at side turns unusual oval wooden paddle unit, wood lid **300.00**
tabletop, "No. 11," maple, circular reservoir with flared wood opening at top **125.00**
tabletop, circular reservoir, crank with wood handle, flat wood base, 13" diameter, 9" deep **165.00**
"16 gallon," bentwood churn on legs, worn black stenciling, no paddles **100.00**

Butter crock, stoneware

blue and gray, embossed hunting scene **245.00**
blue and white, stenciled "Butter," bail with wood handle, new wood lid **150.00**
blue and white, embossed columns and cows, 4½" × 6½" salt glazed, wire bail **75.00**

Milking stool, weathered wood, 8" × 4" × 8½" (Ted Diamond photo/Eisele collection), 15.00

Butter mold, maple

    rectangular, no design, dovetailed corners
....**20.00**

    round, acorn and two leaves, one pound,
small crack **85.00**

    round, carved goat design, one pound,
small crack **150.00**

    round, intersecting ellipses, one pound
....**90.00**

    round, leaf pattern, one pound **85.00**

    round, sheaf of wheat, one pound ..**90.00**

    round, swan, half pound **125.00**

    round, swan, one pound **110.00**

    round, twelve pointed star-shaped design
....**85.00**

Butter paddle

    maple, handmade, carved hook at end of
handle, $8'' \times 4\frac{1}{2}''$ **22.50**

    maple, manufactured **10.00**

Butter stamp, paddle shaped, carved sheaf
of wheat design **45.00**

Butter worker

    "Pride Butter Worker - Philadelphia," 30"
$\times$ 22" wood base with iron gears and
ridged wooden roller **275.00**

    wood, $19'' \times 31'' \times 3\frac{1}{2}''$ box with ridged
wooden roller on iron track, crank with
wood handle **150.00**

Butter-working bowl

    maple, oblong, $18'' \times 9''$ **75.00**

    wood, machine-turned, round, 15" diame-
ter **35.00**

Calf feeder, "Purina Nursing Chow" in
raised letters on metal bracket with black
finish, aluminum bucket fits into wall
mounted bracket, 8" diameter, 5½" tall
....**15.00**

Calf weaner

    galvanized metal, "NuWay Weaner -
Austin Mfg. Round Grove, Ill.," five
barbs point in, chain **9.00**

    galvanized metal, prongs point out, chain
....**7.50**

    metal, knobs hold weaner in calf's nose,
flap covers calf's mouth, $3\frac{1}{2}'' \times 4\frac{1}{2}''$
....**7.50**

Cheese crock, brown stoneware, wire
clamps lid on, 5" diameter, c. 1970 ...**3.00**

Cheese cutter, "Ideal - Anderson, Indiana,"
cuts an 18" round block of cheese
....**125.00**

*Cheese press, myrtle wood, center press and
wedges pull out from top, 38" high,* **175.00**

Cheese ladder, oak, 2 rungs 10" apart, 28" $\times$
12" **55.00**

Cheese mold, wood, Schwab's, 36" $\times$ 8" $\times$
8" **32.00**

Cheese preserver, glass, round

    illegible embossed lid **45.00**

    "Sanitary Cheese Preserver" embossed on
lid, base has projections to hold cheese
off the bottom, made by Cambridge
Glass, 1930s **60.00**

Churn dasher, wood **15.00**

Churn jar, glass, embossed "No. 20," no
paddles or lid **35.00**

Churn lid and paddles, all metal, fits 4 qt. jar
....**20.00**

Cottage cheese crock, stoneware, names
stenciled in blue or black

    Fairmont's Cottage Cheese **40.00**

    Fenley's Tasty Cream Cheese **40.00**

    Maple Leaf Farm Product Co. **25.00**

    Meadow Gold Creamed Cottage Cheese
....**55.00**

    Model Creamery Creamed Cottage
Cheese **30.00**

Wm. H. Roberts & Son Dairy **35.00**
Summe Bros. Dairy **40.00**
Wehr Dairy **35.00**
Cowbell
  brass plated, worn through in patches, polished, 4½″ tall **16.00**
  copper, 4″ × 8″, on new leather strap, unused but old **25.00**
  copper finish, 5½″ × 6½″, on 26″ leather strap **35.00**
  white metal, 3″ × 5″ **10.00**
  white metal, 4½″ × 8″ **20.00**
  white metal, 4″ × 8″ on leather strap **25.00**
Cow kicker **5.00**
Cream can
  graniteware, gray, one quart, graniteware lid, bail handle **90.00**
  "Liq 4 Qt" embossed on front, bail handle, lid **20.00**
  shaded blue graniteware, half gallon, chipped around base **95.00**
  stainless steel, gallon or half gallon, lid **12.00**
  tin, sunken lid, bail with wood handle, one gallon **15.00**
  tin, shiny finish, two gallon, bail handle **20.00**
  white enamel with black edge, quart, lid **20.00**
Cream separator
  gravity
    galvanized metal, 3½′ tall **25.00**
    "Marvel - Superior Sheet Metal - Indianapolis, Ind.," 12½″ diameter blue tank with aluminum label, fine 3″ brass screen at top, window gauge at front and funnel shaped base, brass spigot, wood legs, 40″ **65.00**
    metal tank painted green, wood legs, brass spigot **40.00**
    "Peoria Peerless - Pat. Applied For," stenciled in black on gold painted metal tank, built in spout with cob stopper, two window gauges, metal strap handles, no legs, 16½″ × 18½″ **40.00**
  mechanical
    De Laval, No. S12, with manual ...**50.00**
    De Laval, No. 156, red finish, handle reads "60 turns a minute" **35.00**

    De Laval, hand operated, brass tag **25.00**
    De Laval, electric, rusted **20.00**
    McCormick Deering, electric, good paint, original instruction manual **25.00**
    "Montgomery Ward 33-315," tabletop model, blue base, tin bowl, hand crank, 13″ diameter × 21″ high, working condition **100.00**
    Montgomery Ward, tabletop model, red base **75.00**
    tabletop size, rusted **25.00**
Dehorners, "501 - Other Side Next to Head" at blade, pliers-like action, 38″ **25.00**
Feed sack, heavy cotton, "100 lbs. Master Mix Master Blend 33% Dairy, McMillen Feed Mills, Fort Wayne, Ind.," gray stripes, red and blue logo, Boz bag ...**6.00**
Goat bell, with paper label, "Sargento #2," picture of goat's head **27.50**
Invoice, De Laval, for one cream separator, 1905 ....**7.50**
Milk can
  1 gallon, "Owned and filled by Ogden Dairy - Chicago," no lid **45.00**
  2 gallon, tin, tall cylinder, lid, bail with wood handle **20.00**
  5 gallon, tag reads "The Galva Creamery Co. - Galva, Ill." dented, lid **20.00**
  5 gallon, original finish, lid **17.50**
  10 gallon, fairly new blue paint **15.00**
  10 gallon, original finish, sloped shoulders, lid **35.00**
  10 gallon, side handle and angled opening, "Metal Barrel Corporation - Peoria, Ill." on lid, new paint **22.50**
  10 gallon, "Soldwedel Dairy" embossed on metal tag **22.50**
  10 gallon, worn red paint **20.00**
Milk cooler, metal rod with 4 holes in stirrer **5.00**
Milking machine, "Surge Milker - Babson Bros. Co. No. S148369," 16″ diameter tank, 9″ high, stainless steel **25.00**
Milking stool
  metal, painted black, three iron legs join below seat at a metal disc with a cut-out star design, 9″ round seat, 11″ high **14.00**
  pine, three legs, 2″ thick top, 12″ × 8″ × 10″ **20.00**

three stick legs go through thick, 12"
round top **45.00**
wood, three square legs through 10" × 8"
top, two canted corners, 15" tall
....**85.00**
Milk safe, pine, screened front door, two
screened holes each side, three shelves,
no legs, 17" × 11" × 41" **260.00**
Milk strainer, tin, 9" diameter, fine 2" round
brass screen in base **10.00**

Milk tester, cast iron, "No-Tin Babcock
Tester - Elgin Mfg. Co. — Elgin, Ill.," black
with stenciling and striping, four original
glass containers inside, spins milk to read
butterfat content, 23" diamter **265.00**
Pasteurizer, David Bradley, two gallon, aluminum, electric **15.00**
Print, milkmaid in wooden shoes pouring
milk into tub, three Holstein cows, color,
in painted frame, 20" × 14½" **65.00**

Curd cutter, 8" × 2" iron cutter on 48" wood handle, **45.00**

Calf weaner, galvanized metal, "SO-BOSS - Simonsen Iron Works, Sioux Rapids, Iowa"
(Busch collection), **10.00**

Scale, hanging

brass face with checkerboard reads "Cow Chow Makes More Milk at Less Cost - Don't Guess - Use This Purina Milk Scale," face is 11″ × 4½″, weighs to 30 lb., unpolished, very good condition **125.00**

"Hanson Dairy Scale," 8″ round face, cow logo, weighs to 60 pounds **35.00**

"Purina Feed Saver and Cow Culler - Purina Program," painted on 9″ round metal face, checkers at top, faded and rusted **10.00**

Sign, "Goats for Sale," handmade wooden sign, painted silver with black lettering, 20″ × 9½″ **65.00**

Sled, work, for moving milk cans

all wood, 24″ × 34″ × 5″, rope handle, three-board top, old red paint ...**170.00**

all wood except hinge at 40″ wooden T-handle, three supporting boards are notched into solid sides, two-board top, 21″ × 48″ × 5½″, waxed finish **225.00**

Thermometer, dairy, glass with mercury, registers temperatures for freezing, churning, cheese, and scalding, 7½″ long **2.50**

Tin

De Laval Separator Oil, red, quart, fair condition **20.00**

"Dr. David Roberts Badger Balm," full, orange and black, 2½″ × 2¼″ **12.00**

"Dr. David Roberts Cow Cleaner," full, quart size **25.00**

"Dr. David Roberts Skin Ointment, Waukesha, Wisconsin USA," full **15.00**

"Ohio Dairy Separator Oil," pictures woman pouring milk into separator, 4″ × 3″ × 7″ **30.00**

"Sal-vet Cow Remedy" yellow and black paper label with picture of dairy cow, copyright 1914 ....**24.00**

"Superla Cream Separator Oil," one gallon, blue and white, very good condition **55.00**

"Surge Special Vacuum Pump Oil - Babson Bros.," gold and black, pint, soiled **8.00**

Meat-producing Livestock

Meat-producing livestock include beef cattle, hogs, sheep, and rabbits. Some farms raised only enough livestock for their own needs, while for many, meat was the primary source of income. Animals were fattened on the farm and sent, often by rail, to stockyards for butchering. Butchering for the family's meat was usually done on the farm or at local locker plants.

The two most common American beef cattle varieties are Black Angus and Hereford. Both are stocky animals. The Angus is black, and Herefords are reddish brown with white faces and markings. Charolais, which are white and lankier than the Angus and Hereford, were introduced into America from France in 1936. Longhorns, the cattle of the western ranges, are lanky and can thrive in the heat of the desert.

Bulls and cows are kept for breeding purposes. Beef cattle that are raised for slaughter are heifers and steers. Heifers are cows that have not calved. Steers are bulls that have been castrated with castrators, or emasculators.

Some breeds of cattle are horned, posing a hazard to the farmer who handles them. Horns were removed from young animals with dehorning tools, or the horns were trained to point down-ward, using heavy iron rings that could be tightened over the horns as they grew.

Cow pokes, sometimes called goose yokes, were used to keep cattle from going through fences. Many were handmade, one-of-a-kind inventions, ranging from collars with spikes to yokes attached to a long handle to metal rods bent to form a pointed oval with barbs at each end.

Cattle were fed tonics to enhance growth. These sometimes contained strychnine or arsenic. Among cattle medications are foot-rot remedies and bloat cures.

Animals were marked for identification. Cattle, especially those that grazed on open range, were often branded with branding irons that seared initials or a symbol on the animal's hide.

Hogs' ears were sometimes punched and a metal tag was fastened to mark the animals for shipping and slaughtering. Horses, sheep, hogs, dogs, and rabbits were often marked with notches cut into the flesh of the ear or with ear tattoos, both made with pliers-like pinching tools.

To move animals from one place to another, farmers used pointed or electrified prods, whips, canes, nose leaders, or hog wrenches. A nose leader is a tonglike tool with ball-shaped ends that tightened in the animal's nose when a spring was released. A rope might be attached to the handle of the nose leader. Copper, steel, or brass 2½- to 3-inch rings could also be permanently secured in the animal's nose. The nose rings made it easier to lead the animal; a rope or wooden lead was attached to the ring with a heavy snap. Hogs were sometimes caught by a back leg with a hooked tool, or they might be pulled by the snout with a hog wrench—also called a hog holder, puller, or catcher. The hog wrench is an iron bar with ends fashioned to be put into the hog's mouth and then pulled up against its snout.

Hogs were kept free of blue lice by the use of hog oilers. Metal hog oilers dispensed pine oil and crude oil when the hog rubbed against wheels or chains that had reservoirs for oil at their bases.

Some implements were specific to raising sheep, which were important to the farm family for meat and for wool. When grazing, the sheep sometimes wore bells for protection from predators. A flock of sheep would follow a belled leader. Their ears were sometimes clipped for identification. Sheep were sheared with scissors-type hand shears or with clippers, which could be powered by a crank, treadmill, or windmill; a horsepower, steam, or gas engine; or an electric motor. When sheep were to be exhibited, they were groomed with curry combs and wool carders as well as shearers or clippers.

Butchering was usually done in the late fall, after the crops were harvested. The animals were killed and then scalded in troughs made of heavy wooden planks or of metal. These troughs were supplied with hot water from cast iron, copper, or brass butchering kettles, which held as much as 75 gallons of water and were heated over wood or coal fires. The kettles were hung from wooden or metal tripods or sat in their own footed base. The Sears catalog offered kettles surrounded by embossed panels that pictured heads of cattle and ears of corn as part of a unit that included a coal- or wood-burning stove. Butchering kettles were also used for cooking food for livestock, boiling sap, melting lead, and later in the butchering process for rendering lard.

After a hog was scalded, its hide was scraped free of bristles with hog scrapers: curved discs with wooden handles. Meat hooks—metal hooks with handles—were used to hold the carcass or cuts of meat. Carcasses were hung head down on gambrels, or hog stretchers, which are carved wooden bars with notched ends.

Butchering required knives and cleavers, as well as grindstones, whetstones, and steels to keep them sharp. Knives used to kill animals, sometimes referred to as pig stickers, were sharpened to a double edge at the tip. Boning and skinning knives were needed as well as large butchering knives. Cleavers, in sizes from 1 to 5 pounds, were used to cut through joints on butcher blocks made from a crosscut section of a tree or manufactured from interlocked sections of maple.

Smoked meat can be kept without refrigeration. Smoked beef is jerky; and pork, when cured, becomes ham and bacon. Smokehouses were used to smoke meat. Hams, slabs of bacon, and other cuts were hung on individual hooks; on rows of small, sharp hooks; or on rings with multiple hooks. Meat was also canned or made into sausage.

Grinders and sausage stuffers were

necessary for making sausage. Grinders were made in many sizes. Early grinders or choppers had wooden blades. Large farms might have a grinder powered by a gas engine. Most used smaller, hand-cranked grinders. The ground meat was seasoned and packed in lengths of intestine. Simple sausage stuffers were made up of a metal cylinder and a wooden plunger that forced the mixture through a spout into the casing. Some stuffers operated by a lever action. A popular sausage stuffer — consisting of a cylinder with a pierced liner, a crank- or wheel-driven pressure plate, and a spout — also did duty as a lard or fruit press.

After the meat was cut and pre-served, the lard was obtained from the remaining fat and scraps. The butchering kettles were used for rendering the fat. The fat was skimmed from the boiling kettle, and then excess moisture was squeezed from it in a lard press. Two paddle-shaped boards, often with a leather hinge, squeezed the cheesecloth-encased lard and cracklings, or the lard was put through a lard press. Lard was used for soap, medicine, and cooking.

Horns were used to hold grease for wheels. They were plugged with wood and sometimes banded with metal. They are usually found in pairs on a strap or chain. Hunting horns for signaling dogs or other hunters were open ended, with wooden or metal mouthpieces. Horns were also used for keeping salt and gunpowder. They were made into dippers, furniture, and mounted as trophies.

Tips for Collectors

Butchering kettles with cracks make good planters. The crack allows drainage and the soil-filled kettle can be left out in freezing weather.

Butcher blocks with tops worn down on one side are less valuable than those that have more even wear.

Many animal-care tools are still in use.

Reproductions

Meat hooks arranged on cast-iron rings or half circles have been popular kitchen accessories for many years. Twenty-year-old rings should not be valued as highly as antique meat hangers. Brass rings with hooks are very unlikely to be old.

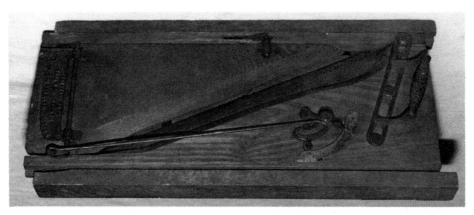

Bacon slicer, oak, cast iron handle, platform and swinging door behind blade, "Arcadia Manufacturing Co. - Newark, New York - Pat'd. 1885 - 1891," 23" × 10½" (Busch collection), **185.00**

Meat hook, wrought iron double hook with wood handle, 8″ (Ted Diamond photo/Eisele collection), **15.00**

Butchering

Bacon hanger, wire coat hanger style, eight hooks project straight out, 10″ × 2½″ × 7½″ **23.00**

Butcher block

cross cut log section, three squared legs, 26″ × 28″ **180.00**

cross cut log section, three thick stick legs, 27″ high, varnished **120.00**

maple, three turned legs, 30″ × 30″ × 12″ top, 27″ high **350.00**

Nose ring, solid copper, 3″ (Ted Diamond photo/Eisele collection), **4.00**

maple, four turned legs, 30″ × 24″ × 15″ top **250.00**

maple, 24″ round top is 14″ thick, three turned legs, very good condition **280.00**

sycamore log section, 20″ diameter, 9″ thick, on three sapling legs, traces of yellow paint, 28″ high **295.00**

Butchering kettle, cast iron

28″ diameter, hanging by two old 36″ wrought iron rods and rings from a new 5′ tall, metal tripod **145.00**

no stand, 30″ diameter **75.00**

with two of four panels, embossed with heads of cattle and ears of corn, that originally surrounded the kettle on top of a stove, sold by Sears in 1908, top of kettle is embossed "60 gallon," one panel is badly damaged **275.00**

with three legged stand, 36″ diameter **175.00**

with three legged stand, mended crack, 30″ diameter **95.00**

Butcher knife, Keen Kutter, inlaid logo **30.00**

Cleaver

"OVB," 20″, wood handle **35.00**

unmarked, 11″, wood handle **10.00**

Winchester, 14″ × 5″ **55.00**

19

Gambrel, hand-carved wood, 27″ **6.00**

Ham hanger, used in a smokehouse, flat wrought iron ring with eight hooks, 14″ diameter, hangs from bent metal rod **45.00**

Hog scraper
    double, 5½″ metal scraper one end of wood handle, 3½″ scraper at other end, 7½″ high **10.00**
    wood handle, 5″ metal scraper, 7″ high **7.00**

Jar, pickled pig's feet, glass, five gallon, bail handle, embossed barrel design, no lid **12.00**

Lard can, five gallon, tin **8.00**

Lard paddle, one piece of wood, stirring end is 6″ wide, 70″ long **8.00**

Lard press, wooden, handmade, bench holds metal strainer, T-shaped wooden handle is turned to push plate down, 36″ × 34″ × 20″ **325.00**

Lard press and sausage stuffer
    iron, Enterprise, screw down press, worn stenciling, 11″ diameter, 20″ high **36.50**
    iron, Enterprise, stenciled "This Cylinder is Bored True - No. 35," excellent condition **65.00**
    tin with iron mechanism **45.00**

Meat hook
    double, 27″ wide, twisted metal, hook each end **7.50**
    wooden handle with a carved design, iron hook, 8″ **8.50**

Sausage stuffer, tin with wood plunger, c. 1870, 21″ (Busch collection), **85.00**

Sausage grinder bench, 27½″ × 8½″ × 13″, c. 1890, **75.00**

20

Cleavers: top, *9″ × 4″ blade, 6½″ handle wrapped with string,* **15.00;** bottom, *10½″ × 7″ blade, trademark illegible, 12″ turned wood handle (Ted Diamond photo/Danenberger collection),* **35.00**

Meat saw, 36″ **10.00**
Sausage grinder, "Enterprise No. 12," mounted on a board **12.00**
Sausage stuffer
   cast iron, new black paint **17.50**
   "Improved Wagner Stuffer - No. 2 - Made by the Salem Tool Co. - Salem, Ohio," painted red, 36″ long **150.00**
Scale
   beam scale, iron, ratchet, no weights, large hooks, 41″ **45.00**
   beam scale, iron, 18″ long, no weights **15.00**
   beam scale, iron, embossed star, no weights **20.00**
   brass face, "Chatillon's," weighs to 100 lb **27.00**
   brass face, "Chatillon's Iron Clad," weighs to 200 pounds, 11″ **22.50**
   brass face, "Warranted Accurate" along side of face, "Pelouse Mfg. Co. - Chicago," large spring below face, weighs to 200 lb, polished **30.00**
   nickel-plated brass face and circular label engraved "Landers, Frary & Clark - New Britain, Ct.," weighs to 300 lb **42.00**
   iron, "Wilson Spring Co. - Newark, N.J. USA - Pat. 25 February," 10½″ long, weighs to 200 pounds **30.00**

Livestock tags: 3″ × 2″ aluminum oval on iron neck chain, **4.00;** *2″ × 2″ brass "#1" tag (Ted Diamond photo/Bloomington, IL, Antique Mall),* **5.00**

21

Scrapple pan, round, no handle **18.00**
Steel, butchering, Keen Kutter **15.00**

Miscellaneous

Bell, sheep
  brass, metal loop at top for strap, *4″* × *4″*
  ....**30.00**
  brass acorn sleigh bell #6 on thin leather
  neck strap **25.00**
Book
  The Blue Book of the Hampshire Breed,
  Vol. 1, 1920 ....**15.00**
  *The Breeds, Management, Structure and
  Diseases of the Sheep*, Canfield, 1848,
  first edition, 366 pages, 26 illustrations,
  ex-library, fair condition **40.00**
  Cattle and their Diseases, by A. J. Murray,
  1877, published by Sanders **15.00**
  Feeds and Feeding, Handbook for the
  Stockman, Madison, Wis., 1910, soiled
  cover **5.00**
  History of Hereford Cattle, by Miller,
  1902 ....**27.50**
  Livestock & Poultry Diseases, by Billings,
  1937, 504 pages with photos, dust
  jacket, excellent condition **10.00**
  *The Successful Stockman and Manual of
  Husbandry*, by Gardenier, 1899, first
  edition, color pop-ups of animals' internal organs, very good condition ..**45.00**
  Swine Husbandry, manual for breeding
  and rearing, by Coburn, 1899, green
  and gilt embossed cover, 311 pages
  ....**10.00**

*Salesman's sample, livestock feeder, wood
and galvanized metal, shiny aluminum
top is hinged over three-section feeder, 14″
× 7″ × 9″, "Martino Mfg. Smidley Feedlot
Equipment - C.H. Ohio Britt, Iowa," in
black lettering on orange, 1950s (Antique
Mall of Chenoa, IL),* **135.00**

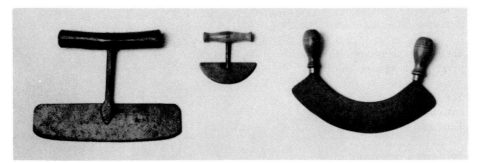

Meat choppers, iron with wood handles: left, *11½″* × *3″ blade, 8½″ high,* **25.00;** center,
kitchen chopper, for vegetables, 4″ × *4½″,* **8.50;** right, *11″* × *2½″ blade, 8″ high, brass
ferrules, (Ted Diamond photo/Eisele collection),* **30.00**

The United States Farriery and Zoological History of Horses, Cattle, Sheep, Hogs, and Bees, 1852, 190 pages, fair condition **13.50**

Wool and the Wool Trade, 1939, 331 pages, very good condition **12.50**

Box, paper

  Dixie Physic Capsules, 1906, orange and black cardboard, 5″ × 3½″ × ¾″ ..**3.00**

  "Dr. Hess Stock Tonic," full, orange and black, 1929, 5 lb. **45.00**

Branding iron

  "W" over a bar, made from one bar of iron, 34″ **45.00**

  "5" on hand wrought 27″ handle ...**15.00**

Bucket

  canvas, folds, metal frame, wire bail with wood handle **15.00**

  galvanized metal, half bushel, ribbed, 18½″ diameter, rope handles **18.00**

  wood, old green paint, 9″ diameter at top, bail with wood handle, lapped wood bands **200.00**

Bull blinders

  all metal **7.50**

  metal and leather **30.00**

  "Russell Mfg. Co., Patent #1912534 and 1925928, Platteville, Wis.," leather and metal **50.00**

Bull come-along, *see nose lead*

Bull whip, plaited leather, 7′ long **15.00**

Clippers, Stewart, metal stand and wheel, electrified, c. 1930 ....**35.00**

Cow poke, loose wood collar with four 5″ spikes at base **25.00**

Dehorner

  Keen Kutter, saw **80.00**

  "Leavitt Mfg. Co. Urbana, Ill. USA," L2, scissors type **24.00**

Ear marker, pliers-type, "CP1" and "CP2" in raised letters each side, cuts a diamond out of ear, 10″ **11.00**

Ear tag, aluminum, number and owner's name, 1″ **0.50**

Emasculator, Appli-Caster, in box, 1950s **5.00**

Feed bag, heavy cotton

  Beacon Feeds, picture of beacon, red, white and blue, 100 lb **22.00**

  "Wayne Rabbit Feed, Allied Mills - Chicago," mounted horseman logo, faded green and red, 100 lb **10.00**

Feed bin

  lid is hinged across back and slants toward the front, slanted lid, interior has three sections, old light blue paint, manufactured hinges and latch, 5½′ × 3′ × 30″ **375.00**

  "Red Top Midget" stenciled in red on yellow wooden box, red metal lids on top and slanted feeder base, 13″ × 23″ × 31″ **60.00**

Fly sprayer, Hudson, 2 quart galvanized reservoir **9.00**

Hay feeder made into a table, boards form X's each end, cross bars held a bale of hay, feeder is 40″ wide × 36″ high, removable pine tabletop is 48″ × 32″ **115.00**

Hog holder

  cast iron, no markings, 15″ **10.00**

  patented Dec. 29, 1874, cast iron, 16″ **15.00**

  hexagonal ends, "Dr. Rinehart Handy Hog Holder - Pat. Nov. 24, 1931, Galesburg, Ill." **15.00**

Hog medicine, "Dr. LeGear's Hog Prescription," 3 lb **20.00**

Hog oiler

  aluminum, "LS2 - Big Midland Mfg. Co.," painted red, vertical chain at side, 26″ high, reservoir is 9″ × 6″ × 5″ **50.00**

  cast iron, "LS2 - Sioux City Livestock Equipment" on one side, "LS3" on other, chain at side, painted blue and white, 26″ high **85.00**

  cast iron, "Model 806-1," two 11″ slotted wheels, orange paint, 12″ × 12″ **30.00**

  cast iron, "Rowe Mfg. - Galesburg, Ill. - Pat. Apr. 11, '16 - Hog Oiler," three rippled, curved posts, 7″ × 9″ top, 32″ tall **100.00**

  cast iron, "Sipe Mfg. Co. - Kansas City, Mo. - Pat. Jan 8, 1918 - No. 1252728," two upright hollow wheels, 8″ and 14″, at right angle from each other, painted blue and silver, 19″ × 14″ **110.00**

  two cast iron wheels each side of wood tank, 20″ wide **70.00**

Hog ringer, "Mills - Pat. Aug. 23, 1872" on

pliers-like handles, turn screw adjusts, 6½" **14.00**

Horn training ring, cast iron
    pair, 2¼" outside diameter, brass adjusting screws **12.50**
    "Stoney - Denver - 1 lb.," adjusting bar **5.00**
    "Weston O - Patntd," brass adjusting screw **4.00**
    "York 1," two brass screws **4.00**

Memo book, Poland China Journal's Service Record, 1919-1920, brown and black, 3" × 6" **2.00**

Nose lead
    tong-type, with rope threaded through holes in handles, cast iron, "123-7" in raised letters, 8½" × 3" **15.00**
    tong-type handles with C-shaped nose gripper **5.00**

Nose ring, solid copper, hinged, 2½" diameter **5.00**

Print, black and white engraving, "Three Views of the Two Year Old Hereford Bull Young Kansas Lad - 85134," oak frame, vertical fold mark at center, 21" × 10½" **57.50**

Sale bill, Duroc Jersey Bred Sow Sale, 1912, Tennessee, Ill., paper, 8" × 13" **9.00**

Salesman's sample, livestock feeder, wood and galvanized metal, shiny aluminum top is hinged over three section feeder, 14" × 7" × 9", "Martino Mfg. Smidley Feedlot Equipment - C.H. Ohio Britt, Iowa," in black lettering on orange, 1950s ..**135.00**

Scoop
    made from a horn **95.00**
    tin with wood handle, 11" × 7" **25.00**

Sheep shearers, scissors-type, 9" **6.00**

Sign
    "We Use Near's Livestock and Poultry Products," porcelain over tin, black on yellow, 10" × 14", chipped **25.00**

Tattooers, rabbit, scissor-type, chrome-plated **5.00**

Tin
    "Bickmorine - Bickmore Powder," for superficial wounds and sores on horses and cattle, 3 ounces, yellow and black **30.00**
    "Dr. LeGear's Gall Salve," red and black, 2 oz, excellent condition **15.00**
    "R & R Carbolized Mutton Tallow Compound," 3" × 1½", yellow and black **10.00**

Wool carders, pair, stenciled "L.S. Watson Mfg. Co. - Leicester, Mass.," horse trademark **22.00**

Poultry

In the 19th century, the extra production of eggs and chickens on the family farm provided the family with a small addition to their income. Poultry products, especially eggs, were often traded for other staples. By the end of the 19th century, though, the demand for poultry products and new scientific methods for increasing production had persuaded many farmers to increase the size of their flocks. A 1910 farm census reported more than 280 million chickens on 5½ million farms. Almost 90% of American farms kept chickens, averaging 80.4 chickens per farm. In towns and cities, a 1906 census showed that there was one chicken for every two people in urban areas.

Poultry farming changed as specialization encouraged farmers to produce chickens, eggs, or chicks. Advances in husbandry produced specialized meat-producing and egg-laying breeds. The introduction of the incubator and the brooder in the 1880s brought division of labor to the hen-house.

The incubator warmed and hatched the eggs, and the brooder provided a warm home and food for the newly hatched chicks, freeing the hens to produce more eggs instead of raising their broods. Hatcheries took over much of the production of chicks, shipping them by rail to chicken ranchers and small farmers. Sometimes chicks were offered through mail-order catalogs like Sears.

The shipping of chicks and eggs created a demand for containers that protected the cargo. Crates made of wooden slats or rungs carried live chickens, chicks were shipped 100 to a box, fertile eggs were mailed in metal egg-mailing boxes, protected by cardboard tubes.

On the new scientific farm, eggs were no longer scattered around the barnyard. The laying hens were confined to nesting boxes in the henhouse and daily collection of eggs was a sure way to avoid fertile eggs. Some broody hens, not interested in setting on an empty nest, were encouraged to lay with nesting eggs that were made of milk glass, wood, or pottery. On small farms, families still gathered eggs in splint baskets or collapsible wire baskets, but on larger farms, rubber-coated, heavy wire baskets took their places.

If eggs weren't gathered daily from a henhouse, they needed to be inspected with a candler to look for a developing chick. Egg candlers were usually made of metal and contained a candle or an alcohol burner. The light from inside the candler was intensified when it shone through a hole in the box. By holding an egg up to this light, the farmer was able to examine the inside of the egg.

Farmers often weighed, graded, and packed their eggs before selling them. Egg scales were used to weigh and grade the eggs. Most scales had a balancing arm that pointed out the weight and grade of each egg. Some had springs or more complicated mechanisms. Wooden egg crates carried eggs by the gross or half gross to and from the farm and market. Eggs were packed between shaped cardboard inserts to protect them inside the crate.

Feeding and watering the chickens involved the use of feeding troughs and bins, which were made of wood or metal. Chicks were fed from chick feeders, which were usually metal containers with several feeding holes around the edge or troughs divided into sections by wire. Watering fountains came in many shapes and sizes, from 1 gallon stoneware containers to 1-pint canning jars upturned on a specially designed base. Chicken feed might be purchased in bulk from feed companies, such as Purina. Green bone grinders were used to make bonemeal for chicks. Many farmers used their own grain mixed with feeding preparations or tonics that enhanced production.

Lice were a constant problem and were fought with many kinds of poisons. Nicotine powders and tobacco flakes were common remedies for lice and roundworms. Gapeworm remedies were sold to fight respiratory problems.

The butchering of chickens required the use of a chicken catcher, a wire crook used to catch the chicken's feet. Cleavers beheaded the chickens, which were then weighed with chicken scales.

The popularity of poultry farming and the proliferation of new scientific methods and products spawned several specialty journals. Among them were *The Golden Egg*, *Profitable Poultry*, *Happy Hen*, *City Farmer*, *Industrious Hen*, and *Poultry Tribune*.

Turkeys, ducks, geese, and guinea fowl were also raised for their meat, eggs, and feathers. Ducks and geese could survive on grass and insects, but they were fed to keep them from wandering. Their feathers were picked at least yearly and sometimes kept in baskets until they were sewn into pillows, ticks for beds, or comforters. Duck and guinea eggs were gathered from the barnyard.

Tips for Collectors

Nineteenth-century items used on small farms command higher prices than the later tools that were used in mass production of poultry products. Splint baskets, hand-painted egg signs, and solid wooden egg boxes are examples of some of the higher-priced poultry-related antiques. Handmade tools or containers are often more desirable than factory-made things, but attractive advertising can add much to the appeal of mass-produced items.

Missing or replaced parts affect the values of many poultry collectibles. Eggs crates without lids and chicken fountains without bases are common. The base of a stoneware chicken fountain is often more valuable than its top. Bases were more subject to breakage and could be easily replaced with substitutes.

The value of collectibles that fit into other collecting categories will vary, depending on their desirability to that group of collectors. For example, Red Wing stoneware collectors might be interested in adding a Red Wing Ko-Rec Feeder chicken fountain to their collection, but they will have no interest in a stoneware fountain without a maker's name. Milk glass nesting eggs are attractive to collectors of Easter memorabilia. Competition from other collecting interests affects prices for stoneware, eggs, advertising, scales, and baskets.

Rarity contributes to the value of poultry collectibles. Small nesting eggs for chickens are much more common and, therefore, less expensive than the larger nesting eggs for ducks.

Museums

Poultry Industry Hall of Fame
1031 Baltimore Boulevard
Beltsville, MD 20705
(301) 344-3875

Situated at the USDA Agricultural Library (Route 1 N, just north of College Park, MD). It's open Mondays through Fridays, free admission

Reproductions

Splint egg baskets, collapsible wire baskets, chicken scales, and egg crates in regular and miniature sizes are all being reproduced and should be examined with care.

Badge, "Chicken Inspector 23," white metal, shield shape, 2″ **10.00**
Book
The American Standard of Perfection, American Poultry Assoc., 1906 ...**15.00**
Commercial Poultry Production, 1955, 415 pages **9.00**
Conkey's Poultry Book, paperback, color picture of boy with hat full of eggs, spotted hen and chick, 1930, 60 pages, 5″ × 7″, fair condition **9.50**

Diseases of Domesticated Birds, 1920, first edition **9.00**
Eggs, 1933 Chicago World's Fair, Progress Publications, 627 pages, includes history, recipes, no dust jacket **18.00**
Geyelin's Poultry Breeding, 1867, new scientific principles, 27 illustrations, ex-library **30.00**
Prairie Farmers Poultry Book, by Osburn, 1922, 243 pages, worn ..**12.00**
Pratt's Poultry Pointers, 1905, soft illustrated covers **8.00**
Purina Poultry Guide, 1933, first edition **6.50**
Standard of Perfection, American Poultry Assoc., 1886, tenth edition, 256 pages **14.00**
  1930 ....**8.00**
Box, cardboard, with hinged lid, top reads "EGGS - Hayes Bros. Hatchery," sides read "Hayes Bros. Supreme Chicks, Decatur, Illinois - 20,000 Chicks Every Morning," two metal latches at front, fair condition, 24″ × 12½″ × 13″ **38.00**
Brooder heater, galvanized metal
  6½″ diameter, front is 4″ high, "Plume & Atwood" on thumbwheel **10.00**
  11″ diameter, 1½″ high, brass burner **8.50**

Chicken fountain, stoneware, "Eureka Poultry Fountain and Feeder - Pat. Pending," two feet, opening at one end, 12″ × 7″ × 8″ (Busch collection), **45.00**

Egg crate maker, "The Champion Egg Case and Box Machine - Chas. K. Ashely Science Hill, Kentucky" (Eisele collection), **225.00**

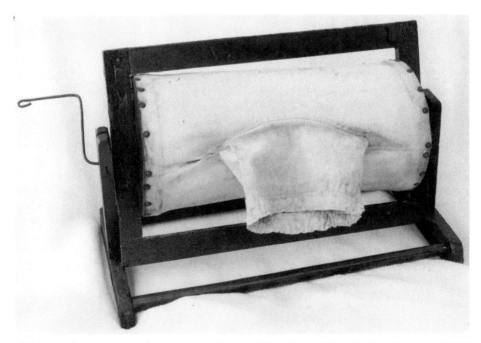

Chicken delouser, canvas bag on wood frame, 28" wide, c. 1900 (Eisele collection), **25.00**

Egg basket, rubber coated wire with cone-shaped center, red, 14″ diameter (Country Hearth, Lexington, IL), **18.00**

Can, "Fancy Fairmount Frozen Fresh Eggs - 30 lbs. Fairmount Creamery - Omaha, Neb.," copyrighted 1928, black on gray, 10″ diameter, 12½″ high **28.00**

Chick feeder

    galvanized metal with red divider, 20″ × 3½″ **10.00**

    galvanized metal, 18″ × 4″ × 3″, 16 round feeding holes **10.00**

    metal, painted red, wires separate feeding sections, 40″ × 4″ **9.00**

    stoneware, jug shape with cut-out half circle near base, "Barteldes Seed Company - Poultry BB Dept" in circle, 6″ diameter, 7″ high **58.00**

    tin, slanted hinged lid is embossed "Hoeft and Company, Inc. HOE's Line Poultry Supplies, Chicago, U.S.A.," divided interior opens to two feeding sections in base, 7″ × 4″ × 9″ **37.50**

    tin, 14″ diameter, 12 feeding holes ..**15.00**

Chicken catcher, wire, wood handle, 40″ long **10.00**

Chicken crate

    wooden rungs, manufactured **25.00**

    wooden slats, manufactured, 40″ × 30″ × 10″ **35.00**

Chicken feeder

    galvanized metal, "Modernized Faultless Feeds" on green and white logo, cylindrical bin clipped into metal base, 6″ diameter, 15½″ tall **30.00**

metal, "Feed Purina Poultry Chows for Big Pullets," faded red and white checkerboard, 8″ diameter, 26″ tall cylindrical bin **20.00**

metal, "Ubiko Life Guard Feeds," life preserver logo, striped border, cylindrical feed container is 10″ diameter × 26″ tall, sits in matching metal pan, feed chart printed on back **22.50**

pine, handmade, two compartments, 24″ × 12″ × 15″, c. 1930 ....**120.00**

sheet metal three-section bin over wood feeder base, 36″ × 9″ × 18″ **48.00**

wood feed bin behind slanted opening divided by wires, handmade, 40″ × 6″ × 8″ **50.00**

Chicken fountain

    galvanized metal, embossed "Makomb," rooster head in circle **20.00**

    glass fruit jar top

        on clear glass base **6.00**

        on enameled blue base (rusty spots), three feet **25.00**

        on galvanized base with 8 feeding holes **24.00**

        on star-shaped galvanized metal base **10.00**

    stoneware

        "Blue Band Sanitary Poultry Buttermilk Feeder - Non-Corrosive," 9″ tall, pie pan-type base has 10″ diameter **60.00**

        "Blue Ribbon Brand - Buckeye Pottery," base is 5½″, pint glass jar is held over base with wire clamp **32.00**

        brown (Albany) glaze, unmarked, gallon cylinder sits on side, two back feet, two embossed birds, outlined in black, at front lip **75.00**

        brown (Albany) glaze, one gallon, unmarked, pie pan base **65.00**

        "A. L. Hyssong, Bloomsburg, Pa.," Albany glaze, half gallon **85.00**

        "Red Wing Poultry Drinking Fount and Buttermilk Feeder," one gallon, on original base **100.00**

        "Red Wing Ko-Rec Feeder - Patent No. 1783790 - Made only by Red Wing Union Stoneware Co. - Red Wing, Minn.," wire handle **80.00**

"Splash Proof Buttermilk Feeder and Poultry Fountain - Western Stoneware Co. - Monmouth, Illinois," base has six feeding holes **175.00**
White Hall, half gallon, with base **50.00**
Uhl Pottery, with matching base **165.00**
Chicken fountain base, stoneware, pie-pan type **15.00**
Chicken fountain top
stoneware, no manufacturer's name **15.00**
stoneware, "Red Wing Poultry Drinking Fount and Buttermilk Feeder," one gallon **45.00**
stoneware, "Splash Proof Buttermilk Feeder and Poultry Fountain/Strictly Acid Proof" in blue **28.00**
Chicken scale
"B & W Co." embossed on brass face, weighs to 25 lb **12.00**
black cylinder with brass face, weighs up to 25 lb **16.00**
"Chatillon's Balance No. 2, New York, Pat'd Dec. 10th, 1867" on brass face, weighs up to 48 lb, 10" **12.50**

Chicken feeder, Faultless Feeds, galvanized metal, two pieces; green, orange, and white; 16" diameter, 17" high(Antique Mall of Chenoa, IL), **35.00**

"Frary's Improved Spring Balance, brass face, weighs up to 50 lb, 13" **15.00**
Corn grinder, "Perfection," new green paint **35.00**
Egg basket
collapsible wire, no handle, 8" diameter **20.00**
collapsible wire, bail handle, 10" diameter **35.00**
splint, handmade, wood handle, 5" diameter, 8½" tall **65.00**
splint, buttocks shape, handmade, wood handle, 10" diameter at top, c. 1900, very good condition **240.00**
splint, 8" diameter, dated 1931 inside wood handle **115.00**
rubber-coated heavy wire, bail handle, 18" diameter; orange, red or yellow ..**15.00**
wire, red rubber coated, cone in center of basket, "Feed Faultless Feeds" metal sign on one side is green and white **34.00**
wire, "Honegger's Big H Feeds - Feeds for Everyone" in red on metal tag, bail handle, slightly rusted **20.00**
wire, worn metal tag "Hens Lay More with Egglac Pellets - Master Mix Feeds," bail handle, 18" **22.50**
wire, "W.E. Roberts - Grand Rapids, Mich. - Pat. Apld. For" on brass label, 13" × 10" **18.00**
Egg candler, tin, kerosene burner, mica window, 8" high **32.50**
Egg carrier, wood, stenciled "Star Egg Carriers and Trays - John Elbs - Rochester, NY," with cardboard insert and sliding wire, 8 ¼" × 6¼" × 2½" **45.00**
Egg carton
formed cardboard, holds one dozen, embossed red rooster, 1940s **5.00**
mold, cast iron, 15" × 4", mounted on board **45.00**
Egg crate
pine, stenciled "Brad's Handy Egg Carrier - Quincy, Ill." in black, reverse reads "Stop & Save at Stroot Hdw. - 12th & Bowy - Quincy, Ill.," wire bail with wood handle, wood lid, 13" × 13" × 13" **55.00**
solid wood sides and lid with bail handle, holds five dozen eggs, old green paint, 1890s **65.00**

solid wood sides, no lid, stenciled "Farmer's Friend Quincy Egg Carrier Co. - When Full Take Me to Shibley & Darr - Shibley, Mo.," dated 1898, bail handle **37.50**

solid wood sides, no lid, "W.H. Geiger - Chatfield Hatchery," bail with turned wood handle **35.00**

tin, sliding top, holds 12 dozen, "Protecto - Crate," cardboard inserts, rusty ..**8.00**

wood slats, one layer **25.00**

wood slats, stenciled "Owosso Mfg. Co. Owosso, Mich.," cardboard inserts, lid with handle, holds five dozen eggs **35.00**

wood slats, cardboard inserts, lid with bail handle, holds 2½ dozen eggs **45.00**

wood slats, no lid, holds five dozen eggs **15.00**

Egg scale

Acme Egg Grading Scale, aluminum, red base, 7" high **17.50**

aluminum number plate, rusted steel body **5.00**

Cyclone, flaking red paint **18.00**

galvanized metal, horizontal beam is weighted at one end, egg sits on curved platform at other **7.50**

horizontal beam, red **10.00**

"Jiffy Way," green **20.00**

"Oakes Egg Scale," decal in very good condition, red **24.00**

"Val-A," gray and silver, red label ...**27.50**

Feed sack, heavy cotton, blue and red on white, **12.00**

Egg scale, aluminum, "Acme Egg Grading Scale - Pat. June 24, 1924 - St. Paul, Minn. USA," numbered 18 through 26, 10" × 4½" × 2½", **27.50**

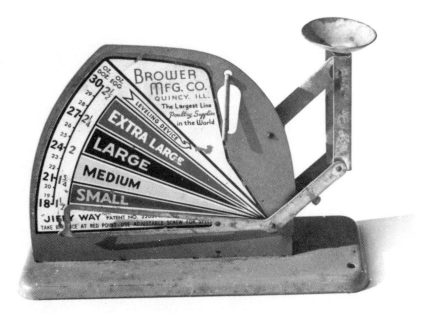

Egg scale, galvanized metal; blue-green with red, yellow, black, and white face; 8″ × 2¾″ × 5½″ (Eisele collection), **30.00**

Egg mailing box
  aluminum, holds 2 dozen, with cardboard
    inserts **20.00**
  aluminum, holds 4 dozen, with cardboard
    inserts **20.00**
  tin, holds 4 dozen **35.00**
Feeding trough, wood, 7″ wide, slanted
  sides are 30″ long **12.00**
Feed sack
  "Murphy's Vig-O-Ray Laying Mash,"
    heavy cotton, 100 lb, Chase Bag Co.,
    faded yellow and red **5.00**
  "Red Comb Growing Mash - Hales &
    Hunter - Chicago - Quality Poultry and
    Eggs in the Making," heavy cotton, 100
    lb, red and blue, picture of cock
    ....**12.00**
  "Usiko Egg Mash with Buttermilk - Cincin-
    nati, O.," 100 lb, logo with corn, faded
    cotton **2.50**
  "Vitacreme Chick Starter Manamar
    Mash," mermaid in circle at center,
    heavy cotton, 100 lb, red and blue on
    white background, "mfd. by J.W.

Bookwalter, Coal City, Ill.," good con-
    dition **10.00**
  "Wayne Mash Concentrate, Allied Mills,
    Inc. Chicago," heavy cotton, 100 lb,
    red stripes and blue horse and rider
    ....**8.00**
Incubator
  "Sure Hatch Incubator Co. - Fremont,
    Nebr." on red decal, pine, thin straight
    legs, car siding top, copper heater at
    right back, 37½″ × 33″ × 30½″
    ....**200.00**
  Victor, pine wainscoting top, glass front,
    turned legs, copper heater at right front
    ....**145.00**
  Wisconsin Incubator Co. Racine, Wis., 24″
    × 28″ top, legs are in poor condition
    ....**100.00**
Incubator heater, red metal kerosene
    burner, 7″ square **10.00**
Laying tonic, "Dr LeGear's Poultry Prescrip-
    tion" 1½ lb. cardboard box, full, colorful
    picture of doctor pointing to laying hens
    ....**20.00**

Louse powder can, "Lee's Louse powder," 2½ lb, paper label **12.00**

Louse powder drum, "Lee's Dri-Rub," cardboard barrel with yellow label, 30″ tall **46.00**

Magazine

The Breeder's Gazette, Mar. 30, 1904 ....**2.00**

Poultry Tribune, Dec. 1935, Art Deco rooster in red and black on cover ..**4.00**

Nesting basket, wire, 14″ diameter, 8″ high, hangs on wall **24.00**

Nesting egg

milk glass, large (for duck or goose) **15.00**

milk glass, small **6.00**

wood, small, worn white paint **3.50**

Poultry inhalant, Dr. LeGear's, full bottle **3.50**

Poultry powder, J. B. L. National Formulae, full box **4.50**

Poultry tablets, Dr. Hess, 45 tablets, 3″ high, orange, black, and yellow **12.00**

Roosting boxes

handmade of pine, 2 rows of 2, 32″ × 10″ × 36″ **35.00**

handmade, heavy pine boards, unit with five sections turned on end to make shelves, 15″ × 12″ × 60″, cleaned and waxed **140.00**

Sign

"Fresh Eggs for Sale," green lettering on white background, alligatored finish, 22″ × 12″ **75.00**

hand lettered, "Eggs for Sale" painted in white on 14″ × 6″ weathered board **30.00**

Worming medicine, cardboard can, "Russell's Large Round Worm Rx," 7 oz, no lid **5.00**

Beasts of Burden

Oxen, horses, and mules were essential to the success of any farm. They were used to pull implements and wagons, to provide transportation for rural people, and to provide energy for jobs that required more than human strength. These animals were often considered to be part of the family, and rural people were often judged by the way they treated the animals that labored for them.

Oxen are steers (castrated bulls) that are used as beasts of burden. Oxen were shod with iron shoes that were like horseshoes but were made of two pieces of iron to fit the ox's cloven hoof. Ox yokes were used to hitch the oxen to an implement. Yokes were usually made of oak and hickory to fit a pair of oxen, but single yokes can be found. Small calf yokes were used to train young animals. Goat yokes are similar to calf yokes. Slow and sure, oxen were ideal for small farms. But as farmers increased their acreage and as new implements became available, oxen were eventually replaced with teams of horses or mules.

Mules are a cross between a horse and an ass, or donkey. They are not considered to be as smart as horses but are less likely to be sick. Horses and mules were hitched to implements that plowed, cultivated, and harvested crops. The horse or mule wore a collar and hames that were attached to a leather harness. The harness was attached to wooden yokes, singletrees, doubletrees, or whiffletrees, which were in turn attached to the implement or vehicle. Horse collars were made of leather or canvas and stuffed with excelsior. They were attached to a wooden or metal pair of hames. Hames with rings or holes for the harness were often topped with brass balls.

Parts of the harness were sometimes decorated. The breast strap and bridle often bore brass studs or other ornaments. Sometimes an extra strap, called a tie-down, connected the bridle to the breast plate and kept the horse from throwing its head. Bridles were decorated with rosettes, circular brass or convex glass ornaments with loops on the back. Glass rosettes might have pictures of flowers or horses mounted on foil behind the convex glass. Tooled leather was used for saddles and stirrup covers. Ornamental strings of brass hearts or celluloid rings sometimes decorated the horse's harness.

Face brasses, or horse brasses, are brass ornaments that hung on the horse's forehead or chest. They date back to Roman times. The earliest brasses were believed to have magical properties and were often decorated with images of the sun or moon. Wrought examples from before the Civil War are scarce. Most were cast between 1860 and 1890. Stamped brasses were made between 1890 and 1910. Victorian brasses can be found with occupational themes.

Reins are used to direct the animal. A rein hold is a wrought-iron spike with two loops to which the driver fastened the reins, freeing his or her hands. Buggies and wagons might be equipped with wooden or metal whip sockets, or holders. Whips were also used to direct animals and came in many sizes, sometimes with ornamental handles. Mule whips had shorter stocks than horse whips.

Many vehicles were pulled by horses. Simple one-horse sulkies carried one passenger, and buckboard wagons carried a large group of people or hauled bushels of grain. Buckboard wagons had spring seats for the driver and a passenger that was separated from the chassis by V-shaped springs. These seats often bear a striped decoration and the name of the manufacturer or owner.

December 1 was once known as Sled Day. Families spent the day polishing sleigh bells and readying sleds and sleighs for the season. Traffic increased during winter months. Heavy hauling was done in winter, because pulling power was increased fourfold when loads could be carried on sled runners over snow instead of on axles and wheels over muddy roads. Most farmers owned more sleds than wagons. Bobsleds made it possible for wagons or buggies to be pulled over snow. Most bobsleds consisted of two sets of metal-reinforced sled runners with a flexible joint between them. They could be interchanged with the wheels and axles of a wagon or carriage.

Sleigh bells alerted approaching traffic of the presence of a vehicle. Some bells were hollow metal (usually bronze) spheres attached to the harness, known as crotals. They also were commonly strung on leather straps that girded the horse. Bells might have one, two, or three slits, or throats. They were made in several shapes, such as apricot, tulip, and acorn. Sleigh bells were made in 20 sizes and are often numbered from 00 (less than 1 inch) to 18 (4 inches). Number 18's, the largest and lowest in tone, were often hung singly on big Percheron or Belgian work horses that were hitched to sledges (heavy sleds). These bells were also called "pung bells." Bell makers sometimes engraved their initials on the bells.

America's sleigh-bell–making center was East Hampton, Connecticut. The Barton family were prolific and innovative bell makers during the Civil War period. Their marked bells are especially prized by collectors. (Watch for bells marked with the initials "W.B.," "H.B.," and "W.E.B.")

Bell makers jealously guarded the formulas for the bronze used in the production of their bells. Copper gave the bell a deep, rich tone, while the zinc or tin in the formula produced a sharp, high sound. Silver bells have a dead sound, and although sleigh bells are sometimes referred to as "silver," they are actually nickel-plated bronze.

Bells could be hung from almost any part of the horse's harness. There were belled body straps, collars, bridles, hames, martingales, rump pads, shaft bells, saddle chimes, and head swingers. Head swingers, with or without plumes, were also called fly terrets. They were carried erect between the ears and had one or more swinging bells attached to an upright frame. Sometimes the frame also carried a plume of dyed horse hair, feathers, fox tails, squirrel tails, ribbon, or yarn. Saddle chimes were similar to head swingers, but were attached to the horse's collar.

Lap robes were necessary to keep the passengers' legs warm while traveling. Buffalo hides were very popular. There were also wolverine, fox, and horsehide robes and plush or felt fabric robes with printed pictures or embroidered designs.

Under the lap robe was invariably a foot warmer. Some foot warmers were made of soapstone blocks that were heated on the stove and wrapped in cloth or paper. Some were stoneware or metal containers that were filled with hot water, and others were metal heaters filled with live coals.

Folding X-shaped metal stools with fabric seats were used for passengers in sleighs.

Farmers used many tools for grooming horses. Horseshoes prevented the hoof from splitting. Blacksmithing tools were used on the farm to make horseshoes. Farriers' tools were used to shoe the horse. The hooves were regularly cleaned and pared with a curved hoof knife, or butteris, and a hoof rasp. Curry combs and brass tail combs groomed the horse's hide, mane, and tail.

Horses wore blankets to protect them from the cold, insects, and saddle sores and to prevent them from cooling too quickly after working. Navajo saddle blankets cushioned the horse's back beneath the saddle. Fly nets—leather or rope strings made into a blanket—were worn alone or over the harness. Ear caps kept insects away from the horse's ears.

If a hitching post was not available, a weight could be used to keep a horse in one place. The reins were attached to a post or weight if a horse was likely to wander. Anticribbers worked like cow pokes to keep horses from chewing fences.

Reproductions

Most horse brasses on the market today are reproductions. Old cast brasses have carefully modeled designs. They have small studs on their backs, which enabled the maker to hold the brass in a vise while it was being finished. The studs were then filed off. Later stamped brasses and recent cast copies are missing these studs.

Full-size horse-drawn sleighs are being cut down and sold as decorating items. They are sometimes represented as miniature sleighs or as large sleds. They are usually about 2 feet high and 5 feet long. The wooden platform is approximately 24 inches by 42 inches. The metal-reinforced runners curve up and curl above the platform.

Cast-iron hitching posts have been reproduced, especially horse's heads and jockeys.

New sleigh bells are common. Sometimes old bells are found on new straps.

Andirons, wrought iron, rearing horses, pair
....**200.00**
Anticribber (keeps horse from chewing on wood fences), leather collar with 9" chromed iron bar inside front, bar pushes in on springs to expose four prongs that poke horse's neck, 48" × 1½" **10.00**
Bank, cast iron, figural horse, still, 5", traces of gilding **55.00**
Bit
   common, two rings linked by bar or chain
   ....**4.00**
   elbow, cast iron **20.00**
   fancy driving bit, 3½" × 3" sides hinged on 7" bit **15.00**
   stallion, hand-forged **10.00**

*Hame, hand made, hand-wrought iron hook and ring, 28", **12.00***

Blinders, leather bridle, fits a horse **12.00**

Bobsled, single runner, from Traverse City, Michigan, c. 1890 ....**425.00**

Book

   Album of Horses, by Marguerite Henry, Rand McNally, 1951, autographed by author, fair condition **20.00**

   Appaloosa Horse, Appaloosa Horse Club stud book and registry, 3rd edition, by Haines, Hatley, and Peckinpah, 512 pgs., c. 1950, very good condition **25.00**

   Crazy about Horses, by Shannon Garst, 1957 ....**15.00**

   Colonel Horns Handy Book on How to Pick High Bred Horses, 1910, 179 pages, printed wrappers **25.00**

   The Family Horse, by Pauline Herman, 1959, dust jacket **12.00**

   Farmer's Veterinary Guide, Beery School of Horsemanship, yellow paper cover, 1940s, 5" × 7" **7.00**

   Gleason's Horse Book, Prof. Oscar Gleason and Leslie MacLeod, Hubbard Publ., 1892, octavo, 496 pages, illustrated **15.00**

   The Horse Owner's Friend: A Treatise on Disease, Dr. Herrick's Family Medicine Co., 1900, 32 pages, very good condition **5.00**

   Official Horse Show Blue Book, Equine Hall of Fame, 1930, 488 pages, leather cover is slightly worn **30.00**

   The Perfect Horse, How to Train Him, Breed Him, Drive Him, Murray, 1873, first edition, 455 pages, 14 plates of famous horses, ex-library, good condition **40.00**

   Practical Horseshoeing, G. Fleming, 1898, first edition, 108 pages, 29 illustrations **45.00**

   Schooling Your Horse, Lattauer, 1956, 177 pages, photos, dust jacket **50.00**

   Special Report on Diseases of the Horse by Dr. D. Salmon, USDA, 1890, fair condition **23.00**

   by Dr. D. Salmon, 1896, stained, 576 pages **14.00**

   by A. D. Melvin, 1911, 614 pages, worn cover **12.00**

   The Stable Book: Management of Horses, Stewart, 1860, octavo, 378 pages, foxed, otherwise very good **65.00**

   A Treatise on the Horse and his Diseases, by Dr. B. J. Kendall, 1896, 96 pages, paperback, good condition **6.00**

   A World of Horses, by Margaret Cabell Self, 1961, first edition, dust jacket, very good condition **25.00**

Box, pine, "Baum's Horse & Stock Food," colored paper label, machine dovetailed corners, 12" × 20" × 9" **25.00**

Bridle

   woven horsehair, made at Deer Lodge Prison **1400.00**

   leather, with copper rosettes embossed with eagles **77.50**

   leather, nickel plated brass studs **35.00**

Bridle rosette, made into pin, picture of horse's head on blue background ...**35.00**

Bridle rosettes, pair

brass backs, blue background with brown running horses, foxed **65.00**

brass backs made into pins, paper roses on beige background **45.00**

Bucket, wood, three metal bands, 20″ tall, 15″ diameter at top **12.00**

Buggy, black body and hood, tufted leather seat for two, 42″ wood wheels, undercarriage, shafts, axles and hubs professionally painted red with black striping, c. 1870, 6′ wide × 8′ long × 8′ tall, very good usable condition **1650.00**

Buggy steps, cast iron, pair **17.50**

Buggy wheel, 40″, refinished, metal reinforced **95.00**

Carriage, phaeton, convertible top, two seats, excellent condition **2500.00**

Celluloid rings, 14 rings on leather strap, marked "Alberite" **1825.00**

Clippers, two handed, chromed head is 3″ wide, 5½″ wood handles, 11″ overall **6.00**

Comb

brass, spring handle, heavy, 11″ **14.00**

brass head is 3½″ long, black wooden handle, 9″ overall **12.00**

Pony collar with mirror, leather stuffed with excelsior, 14″ × 21″ (Country Hearth, Lexington, IL), **85.00**

Curry comb

"Duplex Curry Comb - North & Judd Mfg. Co. - New Britain, Conn. - Anchor Brand - Pat'd June 22 '09," three rows of corrugated ovals, all metal, leather band, 5½″ × 3½″ **20.00**

4″ round comb with 4 rings, red wood handle, 9″ long **5.00**

5″ square comb, red handle, 9″ long ..**5.00**

Doubletree, with two singletrees, each 15″ long, manufactured iron hardware **12.00**

Farrier's box, nail compartments over open work area, on wheels, wood with traces of blue paint, metal strips reinforce top edges, 20″ d. × 15″ h. × 15″ w., c. 1900 ....**130.00**

Farrier's hammer, 3½″ head is marked "Heller - Made in USA - 10 oz." and embossed with horse trademark **25.00**

Figurine, plastic, Breyer

Appaloosa **20.00**

Clydesdale **22.50**

Colt, small size **12.00**

Quarter horse **18.00**

Quarter horse, 6½″ (small size) **15.00**

Fly net

cotton rope, hangs over horse's back **20.00**

for horse's head, with ear covers and fringe, knotted cotton **75.00**

leather strips, covers horse's back ..**40.00**

Foot warmer

charcoal, rounded metal box covered with red and green carpet, wire bail, 13½″ × 8″ **15.00**

stoneware, Logan, Ohio, "OK" **160.00**

Hames

brass covered, brass and iron rings, polished, 25″, pair **110.00**

cast iron with brass knobs, pair, embossed "Welsh" and "6R" on one, "6L" on other **50.00**

pony size, cast iron, curved, 19″, pair **8.50**

pony size, wood with brass rings, no knobs, pair, 21″ high **35.00**

wood, never had knobs, pair, 24″ **6.00**

wood with brass knobs, pair, good condition **15.00**

Hame knobs, iron, pair **6.00**

Pinback buttons, brown and white, made by Whitehead and Hoag, 1896, 1¼" (Ted Diamond photo/Van Dolah collection), each, **22.50**

Harness bench
    with wooden vise, simple, three wood legs and plank seat **79.00**
    with wooden vise, round seat padded and covered in deerskin **120.00**

Harness hanger
    cast iron hook, 8" **7.50**
    eight notches, cast iron, 12" long ...**20.00**
    eleven notches on each of two extensions, cast iron, painted black, 10¾" × 11½" **25.00**
    four cast iron hooks, mounted on old board, 42" long **30.00**

Harness maker's needle pusher, leather half glove with round metal insert at heel of palm **12.00**

Harness strap
    brass covered rectangular iron ornaments with embossed hearts linked to form a strap, celluloid ring at base, 14" long, pair **22.00**
    brass, four graduated circles with embossed hearts at centers, brass ring at bottom, 15½" **46.00**
    breast strap, black leather, decorated with nickel plated hearts, horseshoes, studs and a buckle ornament at center, two loops at back, 2½" × 14" **29.50**
    leather, for mule, chest strap with brass rivets around edges, ring each end, 22" × 5" **32.00**
    leather, four oval brass ornaments and shield on shaped strap, 15" × 3" **55.00**

    leather, pair, two rows of nine brass rivets edge each strap, 32" long **22.00**
    leather, three linked circular ornaments, consisting of circles of brass studs on a leather backing, two have central floral rosettes, celluloid ring at bottom, 17½" × 4¼ at widest point (bottom rosette), buckle at top **35.00**

Harness tightener, embossed leather rectangular cover 4½" × ½" over buckle, 12½" × 2½" **5.00**

Harness vise, wood seat is padded and covered with deerskin, wood clamp **75.00**

Hitching post, finial only, cast iron, horse's head, 10" high, c. 1900 ....**100.00**

Hoof knife, cast iron handle with holes, blade curled at end, "Patented February 3, 1894 - Heller Bros. Co. - Newark, N.J. USA," 8½" **10.00**

Hoof trimmers, iron, "Dasco 314 Cutting Nipper," 14" **5.00**

Horse brass
    cast brass, ten point star in thick crescent **28.00**
    cast brass, stamped "England," hand in scalloped circle, reproduction, 1950s **15.00**
    cast brass, stamped "England," horse's head in horseshoe, 4" high, reproduction, 1950s **15.00**
    stamped brass star design on leather flap **30.00**

Horse collar
    galvanized metal **65.00**

leather, stuffed with excelsior, 23″, very good condition **20.00**

leather, 24″, poor condition **3.00**

leather, 25″, excelsior stuffing, worn **10.00**

leather front, ticking back, excellent condition **35.00**

Horse collar and hames

iron hames with polished brass knobs, leather collar in good condition ..**50.00**

iron hames, painted red with polished brass knobs, leather collar in excellent condition, 21″ × 32″ **95.00**

leather collar in good condition, hames with 14″ of brass trim and knobs **85.00**

wood hames with iron knobs, worn leather collar, 25″ **32.50**

Horse tonic, Dr. David Roberts, pint can and contents **25.00**

Lap robe

horsehide, good condition, scalloped felt trim **35.00**

plush, brown background with a rose motif, satin bound edges, 52″ square, faded **25.00**

plush, purple, yellow, black and white, "Chase" label, 60″ × 54″ **25.00**

plush, red flowers on dark background, yellow geometric border **45.00**

Leather punch, Ideal, chrome plated, 7″ **5.00**

Stirrup, 6½″ × 4½″ × 7″ (Ted Diamond photo/Eisele collection), **15.00**

Mirror, framed with leather horse collar and iron hames with brass knobs **75.00**

Mud shoe, wood with hand wrought iron fastener, 9″ × 11″, refinished **50.00**

Mule collar, woven corn husks, 21″ ...**42.50**

Muzzle, wire basket fits over horse's nose and mouth **5.00**

Neatsfoot Oil Compound, Fiebing's Prime, half pint bottle, orange, black and red paper label **6.50**

Pack saddle, wood, fits mule, c. 1900 ....**65.00**

Plate, 8″, three horses' heads in show bridles, O.P. Co., Syracuse **25.00**

Pony cart, wood with leather-covered side seats **310.00**

Pony collar, leather, excelsior stuffed, very worn, 18″ high **10.00**

Riata, braided rawhide **300.00**

Rings, brass, on leather strap **17.50**

Saddle, western, hand tooled in a floral pattern, worn **300.00**

Saddle bells

brass, nickel plated, three open 2½″ bells, one at center top and one each side, with six clangers outside each, and one smaller bell directly below top one, C-shaped scrolls under bells, 14″ × 10″, c. 1890 ....**325.00**

cast bronze, embossed with stars, three bells on curved metal frame **185.00**

Horseshoer's box, pine, made from a crate, 18″ × 12″ × 14″, old red paint (Ted Diamond photo/Eisele collection), **75.00**

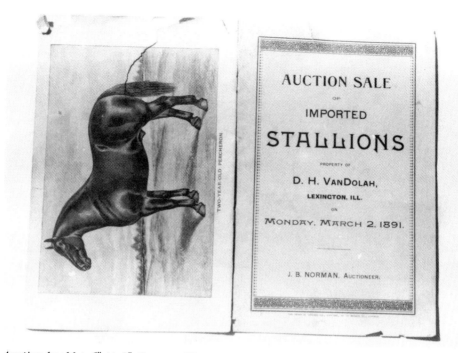

Auction booklet, 6″ × 9″, 8 pages (Van Dolah collection), **20.00**

Sale bill, "Breeders' Sale - 400 Horses," 1912, 9″ × 12″ **8.00**

Side saddle, tooled flaps, iron stirrups, wool seat, poor condition, c. 1940 ....**30.00**

Singletree
  wood, 28″, iron hook each end, ring at center top **5.00**
  hand wrought metal hooks, refinished, 22″ **15.00**
  iron, painted red **7.00**

Sleigh, cutter
  black, two seats, new upholstery ..**400.00**
  black with white striping, one seat, new vinyl upholstery **575.00**
  original condition, one seat, worn upholstery **250.00**

Sleigh bell, bronze
  #13, acorn shape, embossed, polished **22.50**
  #13, acorn shape, embossed, hairline crack **10.00**
  #5, acorn shape, embossed, polished **6.50**
  1¼″, plain closed bell, polished **2.50**

2¼″, acorn shape, polished **16.00**

Sleigh bells, brass or bronze
  body strap
    acorns, 17 graduated bells, numbered 5 through 13, 48″ leather strap **225.00**
    acorns, 20 bells (2 small sizes) on leather strap **185.00**
    acorns, 23 small bells on leather strap **145.00**
    acorns, 23 graduated bells, numbered 6 through 16, 2 large bells are cracked, on leather strap **300.00**
    15 closed bells, numbers 1 through 11, polished, on old leather strap **200.00**
    22 bells, graduated sizes, leather strap **250.00**
  neck strap
    4 closed bells, two 3″, two 2″, on an 18″ strap **99.00**
    6 round bells, Mellotone, two 3″ bells, two 2½″ bells, and two 2″ bells, one bell is cracked **175.00**

14 1" bells, "Pat'd May 14 '78," on leather strap 65.00

shaft bells

2 2½" closed bronze bells mounted on top of curved iron strap, 2" × 14" 65.00

3 2" open bells hang from 10" metal strap 35.00

4 open bells, graduated sizes, on a 15" metal strap 135.00

4 open bells with 2" diameters, nickel-plated brass, on a 13" metal strap 60.00

Stirrup

brass 35.00

cast iron, embossed design at sides 20.00

chromed metal 5.00

side saddle, closed toe section is metal covered with leather, iron stirrup attached at center, flat metal instep support, no heel, 3½" × 7" × 4" 65.00

wood 12.00

wood with brass trim 20.00

wood with tin trim 9.00

Stirrups, pair

brass 42.50

wood, leather bindings 25.00

wood with tooled leather covers 40.00

wood with tooled leather covers, 15" × 8" 50.00

Tether

cast iron, twenty pound flat-bottom ball with loop 27.50

cast iron, rectangular block, 3" × 3" × 4", metal loop on top 30.00

lead ball, 7" diameter, with iron loop 35.00

Tie-down (kept horse from throwing head), breast strap and straps to attach to bit, 5" × 4" heart shaped ornament at breast, leather decorated with studs on all straps, three straps at top and one at bottom of breast strap 20.00

Tin

"Bickmore Gall Salve for Horses and Cattle - Free Sample" 12.00

Bickmorine, Bickmore Powder for superficial wounds and sores on horses and cattle, picture of work horse, 3 ounces, black on yellow 30.00

Tooth rasp, 3" curved cast iron rasp at end of 14½" iron rod, 8" wood handle 10.00

Tripletree, hitches three horses to an implement, a pair of horses with a doubletree and another with a singletree, both attached to one 4' long piece of wood with wrought iron hardware 68.00

Horse bit, iron, pitted, 6½" (Illinois Farm Bureau photo/Busch collection), **5.00**

Umbrella stand, made from hames and
horseshoes, 30″ high, 1950s **40.00**
Whiffletree
painted red with black striping, Pat. Oct.
1, 1885 ....**35.00**
Pat. 1899, refinished **35.00**
Whip
buggy, Stanford Whip Co., 1893 ....**50.00**
fits into a cane, c. 1920 ....**65.00**
plaited leather, 32″, good condition ..**8.00**
Whip holder
metal, holds six whips, "B.T. Crump,
Richmond Va. - Harness - Saddlery," 10″
× 8″ × 2½″ **17.50**

wood, turned, painted black, holds one
whip, 5½″ long **12.00**
Yoke
bentwood hoop, single, 22″ high × 10″
wide **40.00**
for training calf, 33″ **55.00**
goat, single, bentwood **50.00**
horse harness, wood, red paint, iron ring,
32″ **7.50**
ox, double, oak, no hoops, 5′ long ..**50.00**
ox, double, 7″ × 5″ × 53″, two bent
hickory hoops **150.00**
ox, double, curly maple, two bent hickory
hoops **250.00**

Crops

Horse-drawn and steam- and gasoline-powered equipment are described in the machinery chapter.

Hay and Fodder

Hay was a very important cash crop at the turn of the century. Farmers produced hay to feed not only their own horses but also military and city horses. In many areas, hay can be harvested three times a year. Inventions to aid in the production of hay were among the first to be widely sold to farmers.

Before mechanization, the farmer required a scythe, rake, fork, wagon, and perhaps pulleys for the production and storage of hay. When the hay was cut, it was left on the ground to dry. Later, it was gathered and stacked with wooden rakes and forks. It was turned for drying or was loaded onto wagons or elevators with hay forks. Earlier rakes and forks were all wood. Manufactured tools usually had metal support rods, or even metal teeth, or tines.

If the hay was hauled to the barn for storage, special tools were needed to stack the hay in the loft. Grappling forks or double-harpoon hay lifters were suspended by ropes from cast-iron hay carriers, which moved on a track across the peak of the hay loft. The carriers could move large quantities of hay and were used with ropes and pulleys to lift the hay into the loft. Hay knives and forks or harpoons were used to remove manageable bunches of hay from the stack. Harpoons, made of metal or wood, shot a barbed hook into the stack and were pulled away with enough hay for the day's feeding. Hay knives cut through the piled hay. They were made in three basic shapes: scythe, with a deep blade and a wooden handle; saw, with a smooth or serrated edge and two handles; and spade, with a serrated end.

Hay began to be baled by machine in the 1880s. Hay hooks were used to move the bales. The hand-held hooks have handles made of wood or are formed from one piece of metal, bent into a hook at one end and a handle at the other.

An important part of the livestock's feed was fodder, or ensilage. Fodder was made up of hay, straw, chopped stalks, and cobs. Stalks were fed into fodder choppers, wooden troughs on legs with a blade that was operated with a wheel or lever. Green corn was tough and required a chopper run by horse or steam power.

Corn

In 1855, it took 4 hours and 34 minutes of labor to produce 1 bushel of corn. By 1894—with the use of a gang plow, check-row corn planter, and corn picker—a bushel could be produced with 41 minutes of labor.

Corn was first planted with a hoe and dibble stick. By the 1850s, hand corn planters were in use. Some were V-shaped implements, made of wood and metal, and consisted of a tube for the seed and a spring-operated opening to release the seed when the handles were squeezed together. Others had metal rods that opened a sliding release on the seed tube when a handle at the top was pulled. Some planters had an extra tube for fertilizer. A two-row, hand corn planter had a tube at each end of a horizontal handle. Hand-operated planters were later used for small plots and gardens or for replanting.

Harvesting corn is more difficult than harvesting other grain crops, but the time of harvesting was more flexible. The heavy ears and unwieldy stalks were hard to handle. Corn could be cut while green and tied in shocks to dry; the ears were removed later and ground into animal feed, while the stalks were chopped into fodder. Midwestern farmers raised corn for grain as a cash crop instead of for use as animal feed. They were more likely to allow the corn to ripen in the field and to pick the ears late in the year. The ears were usually husked and shelled before storage, but the corn could be left on the cob or even in the husk until it was needed.

Southern farmers were more likely than others to store corn in the husks.

Corn knives were used to harvest corn when it was cut by hand. Later, the knives were used by bean walkers to cut volunteer corn from bean fields. The blades were often made from a scythe blade. During the late 19th century, knives were fashioned that were strapped to the farmer's leg and under the boot. These lessened the need to stoop while cutting. The cut stalks were gathered and tied into shocks. Shock tiers, T-shaped wooden tools, were used to bind each shock. If the corn was cut with the ears intact, the shock had to be retied after the ears were removed.

The husks were removed from the corn with husking pegs, hooks, or spikes. A metal hook or a spike of wood, metal, or bone was attached to a leather strap or half-glove and worn on the hand of the husker while peeling the husk from the ear. The husker's thumb was sometimes protected with a wire mesh covering attached to a leather strap.

Ears of corn were sometimes hung to dry. The most common corn dryers were made of twisted wire with 10 to 16 protruding spikes that each held an ear of corn. Another form was made from a 20-inch strip of iron that had 10 prongs cut and bent at an angle. These had a hole at the top and a hook at the bottom so that they could be hung, one from another. Wire mesh squares held many ears at a time. Ears could be hung by twisting their husks together. Ventilated corn cribs also held drying ears of corn.

When dry, the kernels were often removed from the ears, or shelled. Shelled corn was easier to store than whole ears of corn. Before tools were developed for the purpose, dry corn was scraped from the cobs with sea-shells. Nubbers are small cast-iron fun-nellike devices with knobby inside sur-faces; one ear of corn at a time was twisted through the opening. Shellers with revolving spiked or nubbed iron wheels were available by the mid-19th century. Hand operated shellers were powered by cranks or wheels. The ears were fed into the shellers through a chute, and the kernels dropped into a container below the sheller, while the cobs were ejected. The shelling mecha-nism was sometimes encased in a wooden or metal body on legs. Small iron shellers could be attached to a box or bin with a clamp.

Kernels from the corn were sorted, or graded, so that the largest kernels could be saved for the next year's seed. Corn graders were made in many forms. Some were simple boxes with a grid in the base to separate the kernels by size when shaken. Others worked by turn-ing cylinders of slotted metal or shaking trays with different-size openings. With the introduction of hybrid seed corn, farmers began to purchase seed in heavy cotton bags printed with advertis-ing for the seed company.

Grain was ground into feed or cornmeal in burr mills, cast-iron grinders that are similar to coffee mills. Burr mills were also used to grind rock salt, bone, and bark.

Cobs were burned as fuel or were ground with husks and grain for feed. Husks were fed to pigs or used to stuff mattresses or to make dolls. The Nez Percé people wove them into beautiful bags.

Horse-drawn or steam powered planters, cultivators, binders, shockers, pickers, huskers, and shellers replaced simpler methods and greatly improved production during the late 19th century (see the machinery chapter).

Other Grains (Wheat, Oats, Rye, Barley)

Before mechanization, grain crops had to be cut with reaping hooks, bun-dled into sheaves, threshed, and winnowed. Reaping hooks, elongated C-shaped blades of iron with wooden handles, were replaced by cradle scythes, or grain cradles, by the early 19th century. The cradle scythe is a grass scythe attached to a frame with four or five wooden fingers parallel to the blade. The fingers made the cut stalks easier to gather. The long blade and handle enabled harvesters to cut and bind grain with less bending.

After the grain was harvested, it had to be removed from the head and then separated from the straw and chaff. During the winter, the stalks were piled on the barn floor and pounded with flails. A flail is a wooden tool with a heavy clublike end, called a swiple, attached with leather strips to a long handle, or staff. Grain could also be removed from the heads by leading horses or oxen over the stalks so they trampled it.

After the grain was loosened, it was gathered to be separated from the chaff. Sometimes it was tossed into the air in a winnowing basket. Winnowing baskets are large, semicircular flat baskets with a lip and handles on the back side; they were flipped so that the grain was thrown into the air, where the chaff would blow away. Winnowing was re-placed by the use of fanning mills by the late 19th century. Fanning mills were bulky machines that were crank, wheel, or engine powered. A wooden boxlike frame housed a set of wooden paddles that fanned the grain as it moved down-ward through a series of screens. When the combine made them obsolete, they were used to clean seed before planting.

Tips for Collectors

Grain scythes have longer blades than weed scythes. Reaping hooks have a graceful shape, like a C with one long end, unlike grass scythes, which have a half-circle blade.

Fanning mill parts are showing up as decorative accessories. Colorfully stenciled parts of the frame are mounted with hooks and hung on walls, and "Clipper" hoppers are seen displaying dried flowers.

Recommended Reading

Hurt, R. Douglas. *American Farm Tools from Hand-Power to Steam-Power.* Manhattan, Kans.: Sunflower University Press, 1982.

Grains

Bag, burlap, "Martin's Happy Hour PopCorn," 50 lb, color picture of girl and boy in front of fireplace **15.00**
Bean sorter
    platform is 18″ × 19″ × 3″, 33 slats with two cross bars, copper lever beneath **205.00**
    wood table, 36″ × 14″, wood hopper one end feeds beans onto canvas conveyor belt powered by iron treadle, metal tray each side, 32″ chute takes good beans to container under table **175.00**
Bucket, galvanized metal, two large metal handles, 17″ × 12″ **30.00**
Burr mill
    cast iron, bell shaped hopper is 4″ around top, clamps to table, crank with wood handle, 17″ high **35.00**
    "Wilson Bros. Feed Mill No. 0 - Marion, Pa." **30.00**
Corn dryer
    made from one piece of iron, holds ten ears **10.00**
    twisted wire, 24″ long **6.00**
    wire grid, metal tubular edge, 30″ × 30″ **20.00**

Water bag, linen; blue, red, and green printing on beige; aluminum spout, 12″ × 14½″ (Ted Diamond photo/Danenberger collection), 12.00

Corn grader (or sorter)
    tray, red wood, divider at center, sorts two sizes **32.00**
    tray, wood frame, two galvanized metal screens, one slotted above one with round holes, 12″ × 17″ × 4″, refinished **32.00**
    two cylinders in red wood case on legs **65.00**
    yellow box stenciled in black "Turner's Corn Grader - G.L. Turner, Peoria," three screens, 24″ × 15″ **45.00**
Corn knife
    hooked blade, 28″ long, wood handle **15.00**
    wood handle is 7″ long, 23″ × 3″ **12.50**
Corn nubber, cast iron, embossed "Union Iron Works - Decatur, Ill.," 4″ × 3″ **65.00**
Corn picker, Handy, 1922 ....**25.00**

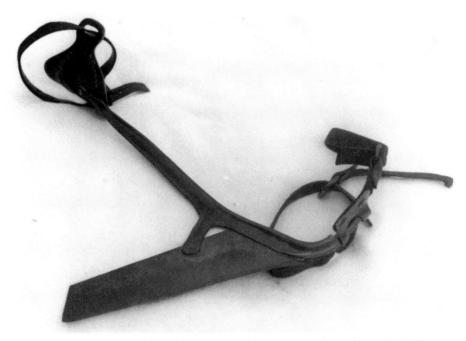

Corn stalk cutter, straps to foot and around calf, cast iron, embossed "Parker's Clipper - Pat'd Sep. 6, Dec. 1, '74," traces of orange paint on blade, **85.00**

Corn planter

    "Acme Corn Planter - Acme Fertilizer Planter Patented - Mf'd by Acmeline Mfg. Co. Traverse City, Mich. USA," one hopper each side of V-shaped planter, 33" **45.00**

    "Acmeline Mfg. Co.," orange **20.00**

    "The American Standard - Sheffield Mfg. - Burr Oak, Mich. USA," patented 1891 and 1893, red wood handle, fancy spring mechanism, tin quart size seed container, 34" **65.00**

    "Empire Rotary" on red wood **32.00**

    "The Triumph - A.K. Kent - Janesville, Wis.," rusted metal, clear stenciling **40.00**

    wood with metal tube **15.00**

Corn sheller

    "Annular - Pat'd Feb. 9, 1897 - Montgomery Wards," cast iron, on metal legs **120.00**

    "Economy - John Deere Plow Co. - St. Louis - Dallas - New Orleans," wood, stenciled in black on red **75.00**

    "Fulton," cast iron, attached to a wooden box, rusty **25.00**

    Hocking Valley, original paint **125.00**

    International Harvester, metal, on legs, rusty **30.00**

    "Little Giant 3," painted red, replaced crank handle, 11" × 11" **25.00**

    "Marseilles - Mfd. in East Moline, Illinois," wood case on legs, painted red ...**65.00**

    McCormick Deering, metal body on metal legs, red paint **50.00**

    "Patch's Black Hawk Sheller 909 - Clarksville, Tenn.," cast iron, mounts on a board, 10" wheel, painted red, 1903 ....**35.00**

    Sears, metal, on legs **25.00**

    wood, clamp-like device with heads of square nails arranged to loosen kernels while ear is squeezed between top and bottom, heavy spring and pin serve as hinge, wood handle on top, 20" × 7" × 4" **275.00**

    wood case, on legs, red **35.00**

Corn slicer, two hole **30.00**

Mug, McCoy Pottery Corn line, 5½" tall, green and creamy yellow, heavily crazed, 1910, **20.00**

Fanning mill

on legs, redwood frame, galvanized metal sides, grain is pushed through slot in wood troughlike top into a rolling cylindrical screen powered by a hand crank **25.00**

"The Winner Mill - Minneapolis, Minn. - No. 24," red, yellow and black, hand cranked, 42" × 31" × 45" **125.00**

Flail, wood

handmade, 60" staff, 33" swiple, excellent condition **75.00**

4' wood staff, heavy 18" swiple, connected with leather strap **35.00**

Grain cradle

five wooden fingers, curved wood handle mended, one missing finger **55.00**

old paint, excellent condition **110.00**

refinished, excellent condition **100.00**

Grain scale, wheelbarrow type

"American Harrow Co. - Detroit, Mich. #2908," rolling metal cylinder covers brass scale, 22" × 60" × 12" **625.00**

no manufacturer's name, wood cover over brass scale, 24" × 60" platform with one 8" wheel **495.00**

Winchester, brass **225.00**

Grain sorter

"Cowan's Dockage Grain Tester - Minneapolis, Minn." stenciled in yellow on three sides of red wood body, hopper, patterned carpet conveying belt feeds grain into series of five screens inside, three tin drawers below, original instructions one side, 27" × 11", body is 16" high, wood hopper is 10" high **500.00**

rectangular redwood frame, two screens **20.00**

Grinder

cast iron, "No. 1½" painted red, 12" wheel, wood handle, 13" high **35.00**

"Perfection Corn Grinder," cast iron, new green paint **35.00**

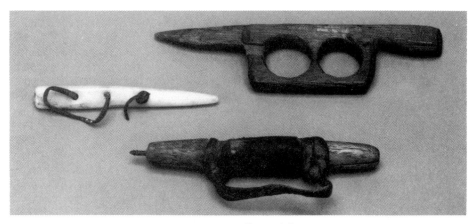

Corn husking pegs: top, hand-carved wood, 6" × 1½", **17.50;** *center, bone with leather strap, 3¾",* **32.50;** *bottom, wood with leather strap, 5" (Illinois Farm Bureau photo/Eisele collection),* **25.00**

Flail, wood, joint carved from one piece of wood, leather strips join staff and swiple, 57" long overall, c. 1850 (Country Hearth, Lexington, IL), 60.00

Hopper, wood
    fanning mill, "Clipper" stenciled in black on red, varnished **45.00**
    seeder, "Eclipse Force Feed Broadcast Seeder," green with yellow stenciling, 22" square at top, tapers to bottom, 24" tall **55.00**
Husking hook
    "Boss" **6.00**
    hook on leather band **3.00**
Husking peg, pointed metal rod, brass fittings, soft leather band **7.50**
Measure
    bentwood, refinished, nailed seam, 9" diameter, 5" tall **55.00**

bentwood, traces of green paint, metal bands at top and bottom, 15" diameter, 8" tall, four-board bottom **65.00**
wood, resembles a pail, one gallon measure one end, half gallon if upturned **70.00**
Plant setter, metal planter, brass tag reads "Master's Little Giant Plant Setter - Pat'd Jan'y 10, 1899 - Chicago, Ill.," 29" long, two tubes, 6" diameter tube dispenses water as plant is set through 3" tube **67.50**

Corn planter, 33" × 8" × 4", c. 1850, (Busch collection), 75.00

Cigar mold, 15″ × 7½″, 27.50

Planter, walk behind, 16″ metal wheel at front, small plow blade behind it is followed by two blades that cover the seed dropped from metal seed hopper embossed "Planter No. 3," smaller concave metal roller behind blades, two wood handles **125.00**

Planter box, wood, yellow with red stripes, stenciled in black, cast iron top embossed "Moline Champion Corn Planter & Check Row and Drill - Patented June 16, Sept. 15, 1885," 10″ × 10″ × 12″ **65.00**

Planter plate, cast iron

for corn or beans, cast iron, John Deere **1.50**

for corn or beans, cast iron, International Harvester **2.50**

for sorghum, cast iron, International Harvester **5.00**

Rake

wood, forked branch handle **45.00**

wood, fourteen wooden teeth, U-shaped metal brace **42.00**

Scythe, curved wood handle, 30″ blade **10.00**

Seed bag

"Lester Pfister '187'"seed corn, heavy cotton **6.00**

"Pride Hybrid Seeds," heavy cotton, red, yellow and blue **7.50**

Fodder chopper, "The Banner" in stenciled yellow letters on red, lever-operated blade, wood, cast iron, and steel, 45″ × 15″ × 29″, c. 1895 (Country Hearth, Lexington, IL), 175.00

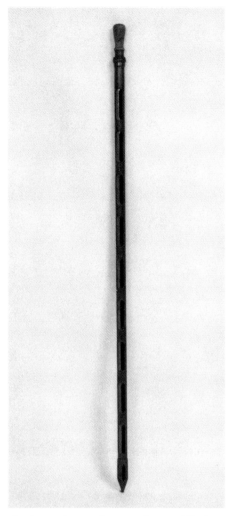

Grain testing probe, two brass cylinders, one rolls inside the other to open and close holes, wood handle, "Manufactured by Dean Gamet - Minneapolis, Minn.," 63" (Illinois Farm Bureau photo/Busch collection), 75.00

Shovel

    hand hewn from one piece of wood, 42" long, scoop is 22" × 12" × 3½" deep **235.00**

    one piece of wood, 44" long, flat shovel end is 10" × 12", repaired with top of a tin can **145.00**

Sieve

    bentwood frame, 18" × 3½", wire screen, refinished **30.00**

    bentwood frame, wire screen, 20" × 4" **25.00**

    horsehair, bent maple frame, woven horsehair band at center seam, 9" × 4½" **85.00**

    brass, three stacking trays, for testing soil, brass label reads "No. 8 - US Standard Sieve Series - .0937 inches - EH Sargent Co.," 8" × 6½" **55.00**

Sign, porcelain over metal, "Producer's Clear Tag Field Seeds - Exclusive Dealer," red, white and blue, fair condition ..**30.00**

Thumb protector, for use with a husking peg, wire mesh thumb guard with a leather wrist strap **16.00**

"Wheat Krinkler," wall mount, green metal, crank with wood knob, made in Columbus, Ohio **35.00**

Hay

Bale fork, double harpoon, U-shaped ..**20.00**

Fork, all wood, four curved tines **115.00**

Grappling fork

    corkscrew-type, iron frame "Pat'd March 6, 1906," painted blue and silver, 32" long **500.00**

    wood with four curved iron teeth, knob handle, 30" wide **85.00**

Harpoon **20.00**

Hay carrier

    "Myers IK Unloader - Ashland, Ohio - N 321," 18" × 12" **35.00**

    "The Ney Mfg Co. - Canton, Ohio - No. 45," two iron wheels, 1 wood wheel **20.00**

Hook

    all iron, loop handle **6.00**

    iron hook, D-shaped handle with wood grip **12.00**

    Keen Kutter, E. C. Simmons **200.00**

Knife

    paper label reads "Wallingford Electric Hay Knife," embossed "EK 40," two red wood handles, original red and silver paint **28.00**

    spade-type, serrated blade **15.00**

two wood handles, straightedge blade **12.00**

wood handle at right angle to offset blade, blade is 21″ × 4″, 12″ handle, 4½″ offset **22.00**

wood handles at side and end, sectioned blade **12.00**

Lifter, double harpoon **10.00**

Loft ladder, 9 rungs, wood **50.00**

Pitchfork

two metal tines, wood handle **27.50**

three metal tines, standard wood handle **10.00**

three metal tines, 8′ long wood handle **25.00**

four iron tines, 14″ wide, wood handle **15.00**

Pulley

iron, 9″ wheel has four curved spokes, iron guard with hook **15.00**

iron with wood wheel **10.00**

iron with iron wheel **8.00**

wood with iron wheel, 9″ × 14″ **25.00**

wood with two iron wheels **12.50**

Rake, wood

had 14 teeth (3 missing), iron supports, 72″ × 29″ **60.00**

handle is one piece of wood split at rake end, 24″ bar had 10 4″ wood teeth, three are broken, 84″ **55.00**

originally attached to machine, Y handle with one long and one short length, two bar supports, 62″ long, fourteen 11″ teeth, 56″ wide, varnished ..**195.00**

16 teeth (3 replaced), two curved wood supports, 64″ long **75.00**

25 teeth on 36″ head, 5′ handle, 2 wood supports **64.00**

Seed sack, heavy cotton

"Grimm Alfalfa," one bushel, green on white **6.00**

"Idaho Alfalfa, Tiger Brand Seeds, Sommer Bros. Seed Co. Pekin, Ill. and Topeka, Kans., one bushel," small hole in bag, bright color picture of tiger's head **10.00**

"Kansas Buffalo Alfalfa Seed," one bushel, picture of buffalo **7.50**

"Mammoth Clover, Kelly's Field & Garden Seeds Always Give Good Results,

Kelly's Best, Kelly Seed Co., Peoria & San Jose, Ill.," color picture of farm with animals and crops, one bushel **10.00**

"Red Clover, Farmers Square Deal Grain Co., Morris, Ill." in black letters **6.00**

Royal Brand Alfalfa, dark green background with red and white design, 50 lb **5.00**

Seeder

canvas bag feeds wood box with spout, wheel controls flow of seed along 36″ shaft **85.00**

"Horn - Patented Sept. 25th, 1923 - The Cyclone Seeder Co. - Urbana, Ind." in red on canvas bag, 20″ metal tube broadcasts seed **35.00**

Miscellaneous

Bag, "Shelled Peanuts - Hancock Peanuts - Courtland, Va.," burlap **4.00**

Basket, cotton-gathering

splint, 25″ diameter, flat bottom ...**185.00**

splint, woven in handles, 23″ diameter, 20″ high, bleached out, fair condition **95.00**

Corn shock tier, oak, 21½″ × 26″ (Busch collection), **95.00**

Book

American Cotton Spinner & Managers' & Carders' Guide, from the papers of Robert Baird, Boston, 1854, 252 pages, fair condition **20.00**

The "Bobbed Wire" Bible, Glover, illustrated, 1972 ....**20.00**

The Book of Ensilage, or The New Dispensation for Farmers, by John Bailey, 1881, tall octavo, embossed covers, gilt edge, 150 pages, very good condition **35.00**

Practical Farm Drainage, by Elliot, 1903, 92 pages **7.00**

Twenty Years Behind the Plough, 1878 ....**20.00**

Yearbook of Agriculture 1953, Plant Diseases, 940 pages, very good condition **15.00**

Bushel basket, with lid stenciled "Chas. Hayashida Farms - Blanca Colo. - 20 lbs. - Mountain Grown Spinach," in green **5.00**

Canteen (for long days on tractor), tin, 12", leather strap **37.50**

Cigar dryer, ten racks in a wood frame, two metal strap handles, 20″ × 8″ × 7″ **65.00**

Cigar mold, wood, 14″ × 8″ **26.00**

Cotton hook, (or hay hook), all metal, 9″ **6.00**

Cotton scales, "Hanson Texas, Model 8916," "Viking," weighs to 160 pounds **35.00**

Cranberry scoop **75.00**

Flax, twisted hank **5.00**

Phosphate spreader, stenciled lettering in white on red, bin only, 12′ long **25.00**

Plow, walking, John Deere 191, repainted **130.00**

Plow share (blade), embossed "Oliver Pat'd Jan. 21, 1908, 19X" **42.00**

Rain gauge, "Compliments of Your Standard Oil Man," red, white and blue metal cylinder with base, 4½″ tall, measures up to 4¼″, rust spots **10.00**

Tobacco bundler, pine, handmade, slots for twine at sides of 40″ × 22″ box with open ends, 30″ tall, weathered **150.00**

Tobacco cutter

"The Champion Knife - Improved," patented 1885 ....**45.00**

Drummond Tobacco Cutter, 1882 ..**45.00**

"P.J. Sorg & Co. - Pat. Dec. 11, 1883" **65.00**

"Reynold's Brown Mule" embossed **60.00**

"Star Tobacco" **65.00**

Tobacco drying basket **50.00**

Water bag, rubber-coated canvas

Desert Company Water Bag **10.00**

"Minnequa Water Bag - Made from Imported Flax - The Pueblo Tent & Awning Co. - Pueblo, Colorado," aluminum clip, plastic cap, 11″ × 15″, stained **12.00**

"The Superior Water Bag," aluminum clip at top, aluminum spout, cork **12.50**

Machinery

In 1835, it took 8 to 12 oxen to pull a wrought-iron and steel plowshare that weighed from 60 to 125 pounds. In 1925, a farmer and a team of oxen, horses, or mules were able to farm 100 acres. Now, with modern equipment, one farmer can efficiently farm 2000 acres.

Early plowshares were made of wood and had an iron strap at the cutting edge. They were not effective against the deep roots of midwestern prairie grasses. In 1837, John Deere invented a highly polished wrought iron plow with a steel share that held a sharp edge. By 1857, Deere was producing more than 10,000 plows a year.

Other varieties of plows performed other functions. There were Eagle plows, with a longer, more curved moldboard. Paring plows, with flat triangular blades, cut roots and left no furrow. There were hillside plows, ditching plows, and subsoil plows. Some plows were horse drawn and guided by a person walking between two wooden arms. Sulky plows had a seat for the driver, and cut two or more furrows.

After the soil was turned by the plow, it was broken up and smoothed with a harrow. Piles of branches served as harrows: they were pulled over the furrows by a team of animals. By the mid-19th century, harrows consisting of spikes arranged along a length of wood, or spring tooth or disc harrows, were common.

Broadcast seeders, wheelbarrow seeders, and horse-drawn grain drills and corn planters were used to plant the fields. Broadcast seeders worked well for crops, such as hay, that didn't need to be planted in rows. Grain drills had furrow openers—planting tubes extending from the seed hopper—and a wheel or blade that closed the furrow. Horse-drawn, check-row corn planters came into use during the late 19th century. These two-row implements allowed farmers to plant at evenly spaced intervals, by first marking the field and then planting at the intersection of the lines. The field could then be cultivated in both directions.

Corn sleds were horse-drawn platforms with a seat and blades on each side. They were manufactured in the 1880s. With a sled, two farmers could cut and shock 4½ acres a day. With a knife, an experienced farmer could cut 1½ acres daily, while another person tied shocks.

The corn picker—invented by Edmund Quincy of Peoria, Illinois, in

1850, and manufactured in 1874—increased production to 7 to 9 acres a day. By the 1880s, the corn picker was able to pick the ears of corn, husk them, and elevate them so that they fell into a wagon alongside the picker. Pickers required so much pulling power that they were not widely used until the labor shortage that was caused by World War I brought gasoline tractors into general use.

In 1830, it took 3 hours and 40 minutes to harvest 1 bushel of wheat. By 1880, that time was reduced to 10 minutes. The McCormick reaper was patented in 1831. Reapers cut the wheat with a cutter bar mounted below a wheel, like a steamboat's paddle wheel. The wheel's paddles forced the stalks against the cutter bar. Horse-drawn binders automatically tied and dumped shocks of wheat. The use of a reaper and binder eliminated the hand work of cutting and tying shocks of wheat. Each implement had numerous inventors and underwent constant improvement and adaptation.

By 1890, the reaper, binder, and thresher had been successfully united in one huge machine, the combine. The entire harvesting process was done mechanically. During combining, the McCormick reaper cut the grain, the twine binder tied the stems into bundles, threshers separated out the grain, fans winnowed away the chaff, and blowers removed the straw. The grain was poured into sacks, sewn up, weighed, and loaded into wagons to be transported to local elevators.

Horse-drawn hay rakes were in use before 1800. Wooden combs that were 10 feet wide with 2-foot-long teeth made windrows of the cut hay. This made it easier to pitch the hay onto a wagon. By the 1820s, revolving rakes, with two interchangeable rakes, left piles of hay in their wake. The first successful hay mower had a reciprocating sickle bar and was introduced in 1831 by William Manning of New Jersey.

The heavy implements used for grain farming required much draft or horsepower. Combines required teams of 20 horses. The steam engine was put to use to supply power for threshing machines as well as cotton gins and mills. The first steam engines were stationary and provided power through belts attached to other implements. By the 1880s, self-propelled steam engines were in use in the fields.

Grain farming required portable engines. Stationary gasoline engines provided power for farm tools and household uses before rural areas received electricity. One-stroke engines were made by many companies in the early 20th century. They ranged in size from huge 35-horsepower engines that could power threshing machines to 1½-horsepower engines that ran small grinders and washing machines. Most can be returned to working condition. Because of the accessibility of the working parts in one-stroke engines, collectors enjoy them as examples of visible technology.

Literature about farm machinery is collected by owners or past owners of various kinds of tractors and implements. Restoring machinery to working condition and repainting it provides a hobby for many individuals. John Deere's *Operation, Care and Repair of Machinery* was printed in 28 editions from 1927 through 1955.

Recommended Reading

Hurt, R. Douglas. *American Farm Tools from Hand-Power to Steam-Power*. Manhattan, Kans.: Sunflower University Press, 1982.

Wagon with seeder, weathered wooden body, 42" wheels in excellent condition, no seat (Creative Clutter, Lexington, IL), **575.00**

Tractors and Implements

Beet seeder, wood hoppers with cast iron sides embossed "Deere Beet Seeder," horse drawn **125.00**

Cart, two 40" wood wheels with metal hubs, 3' × 4", three plank bed, painted red, 7' long with two shafts **225.00**

Corn picker, John Deere No. 25, two row, c. 1934 ....**4250.00**

Corn planter

two row, "Challenge Corn Planter Co., Grand Haven, Michigan" **75.00**

wooden, hand tripped, James Selby seat **150.00**

Corn sled **50.00**

Engine, gas

Bessemer, 35 horsepower, restored, on skid with oilers, good compression **2500.00**

Economy, 1919, 7 horsepower, with underslung wagon, restored **1700.00**

Famous, 10 horsepower, single cylinder, partially restored, new screen cooler, custom cart **3300.00**

Friend, no magneto **175.00**

Fuller and Johnson, 1½ horsepower, excellent original condition **475.00**

John Deere, 1½ horsepower **350.00**

John Deere, 3 horsepower **700.00**

LeRoi, two cylinder, stuck, cracked **50.00**

McCormick Deering, 1½ horsepower **800.00**

National, 5 horsepower, Canadian, looks like an early Stover **475.00**

Novo, 1½ horsepower, good condition **475.00**

Novo, 3 horsepower, vertical, powering double mud sucker, running condition, older restoration **2500.00**

Olins, 15 horsepower, machine work done new rings, all machined areas are recut, stainless steel nuts **2000.00**

Reid, 20 horsepower, runs good, looks good **2500.00**

Sandwich, heavy six, stuck **550.00**

Spang, 15 horsepower, runs, iron skid, restored **2500.00**

Stover, ½ horsepower, clean, complete **500.00**

Westinghouse light plant, stuck **50.00**

Witte, 12 horsepower, single cylinder, hopper cooled, skid, free, complete **1200.00**

Worthington, 15 horsepower, single cylinder, hopper cooled, large custom steel cart, restored **4600.00**

Grain drill, Wards, No. 5, 24 inch **50.00**

Hay rake, wooden, flip over **350.00**

Planter, Hayes, rusted **45.00**

Plow

    International Harvester, two-bottom, trip plow **100.00**

    John Deere, #191, old green paint, horse drawn, 8' **135.00**

    John Deere, two bottom, sulky **450.00**

    Rose Clipper, No. 10, repainted red and green, horse drawn, 8' long **115.00**

    "Syracuse Chilled Plow Co. - Syracuse, N.Y. - A - I Horse - No. 5 - 1878," 20" plowshare **135.00**

Saw, engine mounted Ottawa crosscut, on steel wheeled dolly, runs **450.00**

Snowmobile

    Kellett Blue Goose, 1969 ....**1450.00**

    Polar 200 ....**1450.00**

    Polaris Colt, 1966, unrestored **450.00**

Stalk cutter, horse drawn **100.00**

Surrey, double seat, fringe on top ..**1000.00**

Tractor

    Allis Chalmers C, 5' belly mower, new tines, good condition **2500.00**

    Allis Chalmers WD 45 ....**3000.00**

    Avery, BF, 1948, restored **950.00**

    Bolens, garden tractor, oldest Briggs engine, runs **450.00**

    Case

        C, on steel wheels **850.00**

        CV, 1941 ....**950.00**

        LAI **1100.00**

    Farmall

        regular, 1922, on rubber spoke wheels, with sickle bar, original excellent condition **2450.00**

        regular, 1930, good condition ..**650.00**

        regular, 1932, on steel wheels, excellent running condition, all original, wrenches, grease gun, manual in toolbox **3000.00**

        H, good condition **900.00**

    Ford

        8N, with scraper **2650.00**

        8N, good engine and transmission, tin fair, new front tires, not restored **1800.00**

Corn picker, John Deere No. 25, running condition (Wilkey Auction, El Paso, IL), **7000.00**

NAA, 1953, Golden Jubilee, owner's manual, block heater, hydraulics, front loader **4500.00**

Fordson, 1922, excellent restorable condition **2200.00**

International Harvester, 1927, 15-30, on rubber, engine and rear end overhauled **700.00**

John Deere

  A, High Crop, new engine **7500.00**

  A, unstyled **1500.00**

  A, 1940, narrow front, excellent condition **2000.00**

  A, 1941 ....**950.00**

  AO, Orchard, 8′ snowplow, 1951, runs good **1100.00**

  AR **1600.00**

  AW, 1952, restored **2750.00**

  B, unstyled, flat spoke factory rear steel wheels, round spoke front wheels, repainted new decals, good sheet metal, good running condition **1850.00**

  B, unstyled, factory round spoke wheels on rear, front has solid wheels, both on rubber, needs paint, runs excellent, serial #47920 ....**1295.00**

  B, unstyled, long frame **1500.00**

  B, 1944 ....**500.00**

  B, 1952, excellent tin **1200.00**

  D **2700.00**

  D, 1934, complete, good running condition **3000.00**

  G, unstyled **2000.00**

  G, 1952, will run, partially restored **1500.00**

  H **800.00**

  L, restored **2500.00**

  R **1600.00**

  40 High Crop, restored **4000.00**

  50, serial #5,000,001 ....**2750.00**

  60, doesn't run, rare back rims ..**600.00**

  60 Hi Seat **2450.00**

  60 Standard, power steering ...**5500.00**

  80, excellent **3750.00**

  630 Standard, original paint, runs, excellent condition **5500.00**

  830 ....**3500.00**

Hart Parr

  12-24 ....**3000.00**

28-50, excellent condition **4200.00**

28-50, 1929, two speed, restored **12,000.00**

International Harvester

  600, diesel **2500.00**

  Super W 4, very good condition **2500.00**

  Super WD 6-TA **5000.00**

  Super WD 9 ....**1495.00**

Massey Harris, Pony, with rotary belly mower, plow, disk, cultivator, service manuals **2950.00**

Minneapolis Moline

  2A, wide front, live hydraulics, good condition **550.00**

  Z, standard **800.00**

Oliver

  70, standard **850.00**

  70, standard, rebuilt and painted, new tires **1800.00**

  77, standard **950.00**

  90, running condition **1050.00**

Truck

Ford Model A, 1928, restored, touring quality **7300.00**

Ford Model A, 1929 ....**4100.00**

Wagon

  high wood wheels, spring seat, wood box, very good condition **750.00**

  spring, flared sides, built in 1913 on a Ford Model T chassis, tongue neck yoke, doubletrees, good tires ..**3200.00**

Walking tractor, Walsh, two large and two small metal nubbed wheels, wood handles **125.00**

Literature

Book

Audel's Gas Engine Manual 1907-1908, first edition, 469 pages, illustrated **25.00**

The Century of the Reaper, Cyrus McCormick, 1931, 307 pages, 28 photos, history McCormick reaper, International Harvester, very good condition **32.50**

Farm Engines and How to Run Them, The Traction Engine, James Stephenson, 1903, gilt, 215 pages, ads, engravings **30.00**

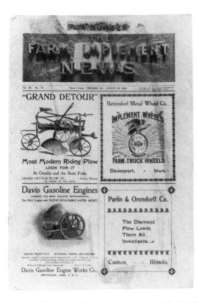

Farm Implement News, *August 10, 1899, Fair Number, 15¾" × 11", 38 pages, many engraved ads, soiled cover (Antique Mall of Chenoa, IL),* **48.00**

Farm Machinery and Equipment, H. Smith, 1929, third edition, 520 pages, 800 photos **65.00**

Farm Mechanics Text and Handbook, 1955, by Lloyd Phipps, 752 pages **12.50**

Farmer's Shop Book, by Louis Roehl, 1924, 429 pages **10.00**

Gas-Gasoline & Oil Engines, by Hiscox/Page, 1897/1918, 640 pages, 435 drawings, very good condition **52.50**

John Deere, by Neil M. Clark, soiled dust jacket, ex-library copy, 1937, 61 pages **45.00**

John Deere's Company: A History of Deere & Company and its Times, W. G. Broehl, Jr., 1984, 880 pages, dust jacket **47.50**

Operation, Care, and Repair of Farm Machinery, John Deere, 1927, first edition **95.00**
fourth edition, very good condition **17.50**
seventh edition, slightly worn cover **12.00**

thirteenth edition, very good condition **15.00**
fourteenth edition, 1930s, stained cover **10.00**
twenty-eighth edition, 1957, very good condition **12.00**

The Red Tractor Book, two issues, 1945 and 1947, ads, photos, soiled **28.00**

Science of Successful Threshing, Dingee-MacGregor, 1915, JI Case Threshing Machine Co., 253 pages, 7th edition, drawings, very good condition ...**25.00**

Shopwork on the Farm, by Jones, 1945, 486 pages **10.00**

Snowmobiler's Companion, by Wimer, 221 pages, 1973, dust jacket, very good condition **8.00**

Stationary, Marine, Gas and Locomotive Engines, N. Hawkins, Theo Audel & Co., 1904, 437 pages, gilded edges **30.00**

Steam Turbines, by Collins, 1909, first edition, tenth printing, 186 pages, 76 drawings and photos, Allis Chalmers, Curtis steam turbine engines, very good condition **26.50**

The Story of John Deere, by Aldrich, privately printed, 1942, 1 of 800 copies, 34 illustrations, good+ condition **36.50**

Tractor Lubrication, from Standard Oil, 1930, 82 pages, brown paper cover with red tractor, 6" × 9" **14.00**

Brochure
Ireland Machine & Foundry, Norwich, N.Y., 1920, 12 pages, 8½" × 11", John Deere distributor, Ireland sawing machines **15.00**
Keystone Hay Loader, Sterling, Ill., trifold, black on yellow, 6" × 8" folded ..**12.50**
Massey Ferguson, Disc Harrow, No. 36 ....**6.00**
Weir Tongueless Cultivators, Made by Weir Plow Co., trifold, color lithograph one side of man with cultivator and two horses, 9½" × 6" **21.00**

Instruction book
Allis Chalmers, WD 4 row Cultivator (40 Series) **20.00**
Allis Chalmers, rear mounted drill planter **20.00**

"Kalke Murphy Grain Stir - Ator," 1969, 8" × 10½", soiled cover 3.50

McCormick Deering All Steel Thresher, 22X38 and 22X36, soiled, 98 pages 20.00

McCormick Deering Farmall F-12, 1934, 64 pages, soiled 25.00

McCormick Deering No. 3, tractor hitches, power drive attachments, 1926 ....5.00

Oliver 70 steel tread tractor, excellent condition 35.00

Instructions and parts list

Allis Chalmers, "66" All Crop Harvester "B" Series, 94 pages, slightly soiled, good condition 22.50

McCormick No. 25-V Tractor Mower 12.50

Magazine

American Thresherman, July 1929 ....10.00

Thresherman's Review and Power Farming, 1913, "Fair edition," worn cover 25.00

Owner's manual

Ford Tractor, 1948 ....17.50

Massey Ferguson No. 82 Combine ..15.00

Parts catalog, Caterpillar Thirty Tractor, 1930, good condition 10.00

Parts list, Rock Island Model G-2 Tractor, 1933, worn 35.00

Parts manual, John Deere, in a binder 20.00

Repairs catalog

John Deere Hay Equipment, 1944 ..40.00

International Harvester No. 29JM ...10.00

Miscellaneous

Binder box

International Harvester logo (intertwined *I* and *H* in *C*) embossed on lid, wood bottom, pitted metal repainted red, 11½" × 5½" × 4¼" 10.00

"McCormick," embossed traces of red paint on slightly rusted metal box, 12" × 5½"x 4¾" 15.00

Wheat drill, horse drawn, five row, cast iron side of wooden hopper is embossed "Manuf'd by the American Seeding Machine Co. - Richmond, Ind.," 31½" × 72" × 32" (Johnson collection), **135.00**

Brochure, John Deere Sagless Elevator, 9″ × 8″, color cover, 31 pages (Antique Mall of Chenoa, IL), 27.00

"McCormick," embossed on lid, with oil can in bracket at side, new red paint **18.00**

"Plano Mfg. Co.- Chicago, Ill. USA" embossed on lid, cast iron, oil can at side **35.00**

"The Superior - B295," oil can bracket at side, cast iron **125.00**

Box, metal, Alemite-Zerk, for grease gun fittings **45.00**

Buggy seat

black leather tufted upholstery, curved metal arm supports, (handmade wooden base makes the seat usable as a bench), 39″ × 20″ × 22″, dry leather, otherwise good condition **245.00**

upholstered, tufted leather, poor condition, wire arm rests **125.00**

Cradle attachment, stenciled "For Milwaukee Junior," picked up hay or wheat, wood **225.00**

Feeder arm from threshing machine, wood with wood teeth, refinished, 48″ × 11″ **25.00**

Funnel, copper, 5″ diameter at top **12.50**

Gas can

one gallon, blue **5.00**

one gallon, Underwriter's Laboratory brass tag **7.50**

three gallon, Standard, clamp down lid, rusted **35.00**

five gallon, "Gasoline" in black on red, bail with wooden handle, 4″ lid, 8″ spout **15.00**

five gallon, for visible pump, Geo. D. Ellis & Sons, Inc. - Philadelphia, Pa. - Ellisco" on embossed tag, galvanized metal **150.00**

Gas engine

Cushman, 1½ horsepower **210.00**

Fairbanks Morse "Z," 4 horsepower **1800.00**

International Harvester, 10 horsepower, Model M, on skid **3000.00**

John Deere, 1½ horsepower **260.00**

Monitor, 6 horsepower, with buzz saw, on truck **2600.00**

Gas pump

Musgo, with matching globe, Indian logo, "Michigan's Mile Maker," green and orange **550.00**

with Red Crown globe, red, Art Deco design **900.00**

Gas pump nozzle

McDonald, brass, polished **20.00**

Morrisson Bros., brass and bronze, polished **25.00**

Glue pot, copper, "Oliver Glue Pot - Oliver Machinery Co. Grand Rapids, Mich. USA" engraved on brass label, copper inner glue pot under domed lid, brass bail with wood handle **58.00**

Harrow, wood with five iron spikes, 44″ long **58.00**

Implement seat

Cast iron

American Harrow - Detroit **75.00**

"Buckeye" in cut out letters, embossed "Akron, O," 16″ × 15″ × 3½″ **75.00**

Champion **35.00**

Deering, 18″ wide **50.00**

Hoosier **95.00**

"J I Case Plow Works, Racine, Wisc" **65.00**

McCormick **45.00**

Milwaukee **55.00**

plain **20.00**

Stoddard **40.00**

Steel, plain, very good condition **5.00**

McCormick Corn Picker and Husker, No. 3, worn stenciling (Wilkey Auction, El Paso, IL), **175.00**

Lamps

pair, from a buggy, oval beveled glass lenses **125.00**

pair, from a Model A, painted black with chrome tops **50.00**

Measurer, fuel tank, McCormick Deering, black lettering on wood measuring stick **47.50**

Oil bottle

"Brookins - Cincinnati" embossed bottle, plain spout **45.00**

"Marquette - St. Paul, Minnesota" embossed bottle, plain spout **38.00**

"Master Mfg. Co. - Litchfield - 1 quart liquid" embossed on bottle, rusted Master spout **25.00**

plain bottle with embossed metal screw-on spout **40.00**

six, plain quart bottles with embossed metal screw-on spouts in wire carrier **190.00**

"Standard" embossed on bottle, plain metal screw-on spout **65.00**

Standard ISA - VIS, colored decal on bottle, metal screw-on spout **95.00**

Standard Polarine, colored decal on bottle, metal screw-on spout **80.00**

Oil bottle carrier, wire, holds eight bottles, twisted wire handle **27.00**

Oil bottle spout, metal, screws on, embossed "The Master Mfg Co. - Litchfield, Ill. - Pat'd Sept. 14, 1926" ..**7.00**

Oil can

galvanized metal, embossed "1 Qt. Liq'd," long spout **9.00**

galvanized metal, embossed "Four Quart Liquid," tube handle, guard behind handle **10.00**

"Goldenrod - Dutton Lainson Co. - Hastings, Nebr.," quart can with worn yellow paint, 12″ curved spout **10.00**

Ornament, "Farmall," chrome, 26″ **12.00**

Planter cover, cast iron

"Deere and Mansur Company, Moline, Ill.," embossed deer in woods **32.50**

"Hayes Four Wheel - No. 44 - Galva, Ill." in circular logo, 8″ × 8″ **22.00**

"The Hayes - Mf'd by Hayes Pump & Planter Co. - Galva, Ill." in raised letters, 8″ × 8″ **28.00**

International, intertwined IHC logo, 9″ diameter, painted green **20.00**

John Deere, leaping deer **32.50**

Plow, arrowhead-shaped cast iron blade, hand hewn wood, shaft is broken off, handles are 5 feet long **200.00**

Reel from a corn planter, wood, original blue paint, with old hemp rope, 20″ wide **170.00**

Seeder, wood bin, traces of orangey red paint, was once stenciled McCormick, wood lid, 96″ × 15″ × 18″ **85.00**

Spring seat

"Acme Harvesting Machine Co. Peoria, Illinois" stenciled on back, green with yellow trim, varnished **285.00**

from horse drawn wagon, old greenish blue paint, poor condition **60.00**

green paint with yellow stenciling, metal arm rests **265.00**

weathered, old red paint **95.00**

Tin

"Empire State 100% Pure Motor Oil," red, green and silver, picture of Empire State Building, airplane, and cars, 2 gallon, c. 1950 ....**36.50**

"Gebhart's 100% Pure Pennsylvania Gold Comet Motor Oil," two gallon, red, white, blue and yellow, sold by Gambels, very good condition **50.00**

"Hoosier Pete Motor Oil," 2 gallons, yellow, black, white and red **45.00**

"Opaline Motor Oil - Sinclair Refining Co. - Chicago," green and silver, two spouts, strap handle, slightly scratched and dented, 8½″ × 5½″ × 5½″ ...**32.00**

Tire pump, Ford, brass, no hose **27.50**

Toolbox, attached to tractor or implement (*see also binder box*)

"AVERY 43," cast iron, rusted, 10½″ × 2″ × 2 ½″ **15.00**

Collins, cast iron **17.50**

Deere, cast iron, cut out lettering "DEERE," pitted, no paint, 10¼″ × 3½″ **15.00**

Deere, cast iron, cut out lettering "DEERE," restored, new green paint, 10¼″ × 3½″ **45.00**

Fordson, gray with embossed lettering painted black **18.00**

Fordson, clear paint finish **8.00**

McCormick, cast iron, new blue paint **20.00**

Toolbox, machinist's, oak, front cover missing **90.00**

Wagon jack

wood, c. 1850, metal gears inside frame, traces of red paint **325.00**

wood, triangular **27.50**

wood, triangular, one jagged side, wood handle, c. 1900 ....**35.00**

Wagon wheel hub **10.00**

Wheel, buggy, refinished, excellent condition, 42″ **95.00**

Wheel, wagon, wood

dry, one outer section missing, wood hub, 43″ **40.00**

dry, metal hub, 36″ **45.00**

painted red, good condition, wood hub, 43″ diameter **95.00**

varnished, good condition, wood hub, 42″ diameter **85.00**

Tools

Farmers were skilled in many trades. When the harvesting was done and the planting was months ahead, the buildings, fences, and machinery needed care. Farmers often built and repaired their own barns and houses. They repaired and maintained their machinery, wagons, and tools. Often they improvised, making do with outdated machinery and tools by using their imagination and whatever resources they had to modify the implements they had.

Every farm had a supply of basic carpenter's tools. These included saws and planes of many types, levels, drills, gauges, and rulers. These were manufactured by Stanley, Keen Kutter, Shapleigh, Hibbard and Spencer, Winchester, and others.

Sharpeners and grinders for butchering and haying equipment ranged from hand held whetstones to large grinding wheels. Wheels might be powered by a hand crank and mounted on a workbench or they could be pedal driven, mounted on a wooden or iron frame with a seat for the operator.

Fencing work called for posthole diggers, rope makers, splicers, and fence stretchers. Wood shingles were made with a mallet and an L-shaped froe. Jacks and wrenches were needed to keep wagons and machinery in working order. Blacksmithing tools and forges were used by many farmers to repair or modify their equipment or to make horseshoes. Leather was used for horse harness, belts for machinery, gaskets, or for wearing apparel or shoes. Leather vises, punches, and strippers were commonly found on farms.

Tips for Collectors

Maker's marks add to the desirability of many tools. Stanley, Keen Kutter, and Winchester tools often command many times more than comparable tools made by other companies.

Keen Kutter has an interesting history. A brand name of the E. C. Simmons Hardware Co., Keen Kutter tools have been produced since the 1870s. A merger with Winchester in the 1920s lasted until the Simmons Co. was purchased by Shapleigh (Diamond Edge) Hardware in 1940.

Planes should have their original blades and the wood should be in good condition. Combination planes' values depend highly on the blades that are included.

Recommended Reading

Barlow, Ronald S. *The Antique Tool Collector's Guide to Value*. El Cajon, Calif.: Windmill, 1991.

Anvil, "Pat'd Nov. 27, 1894 - No. 1" ...**47.50**
Auger, 18″ horizontal wood handle, 36″ long **10.00**
Bellows, blacksmith's, 12″ × 24″ platform, 18″ tall, good original leather **50.00**
Blacksmithing tongs, straight lipped, 18″ long **15.00**
Blow torch
brass **15.00**
polished brass, rubbed wood handle **25.00**
Board rule, Springsteel, "Lufkin Rule Company - Saginaw, USA," probably #52, 3′ long, hardwood handle, oval brass head **105.00**
Book
A Museum of Early American Tools, Eric Sloane, dust jacket, 1964 ....**17.50**
Stanley Tool Guide, Stanley Tools, New Britain, Conn., 1950, detailed instructions for 38 products, holes at top of pages fit three ring binder **26.50**

Broadax
Keen Kutter, with logo **115.00**
Shapleigh Hardware **425.00**
unmarked, old slightly curved handle **55.00**
Broadax head, unmarked **35.00**
Broom cutter, wood frame on legs, steel blade at left side, 34″ wide **140.00**
Bung auger, wooden T-handle, screw tip, 14″ long **14.00**
Calipers, Stanley, wood and brass **21.00**
Clamp, wood with wood screws, 9″ ...**25.00**
Cobbler's bench, pine, handmade, replaced round leather seat, work board, vise and boot form included, originally had a drawer under work area **175.00**
Cultivator wrench **2.50**
Draw knife
folding handle, "A.J. Wilkinson," patented 1895 ....**45.00**
14″ curved blade, two turned wood handles **13.00**
27″ curved blade is 3″ deep, two wood handles **25.00**
Drawer tags, brass ovals, "Allis-Chalmers Co. Tool No. _____ - Springfield Works," from tool drawers at plant, 2½″ × 1¾″ **4.00**
Drill bit holder, cast iron, logo shaped **90.00**
Drill brace, early, wood and brass **120.00**

Blow torch, brass and copper, "Otto Bernz - Pat'd Nov. 15, 1910″, polished, 9″ high (Country Hearth, Lexington, IL), **40.00**

Grinder, stone has 8″-diameter cast iron frame, wood base, c. 1900 (Country Hearth, Lexington, IL), **35.00**

Ice saw, cast iron handle with wooden insert in grip, 42" (Illinois Farm Bureau photo/ Busch collection), **25.00**

Fence stretcher, cast iron, "Rein Lietzke - Hustisford, Wisconsin" **20.00**

Forge, "Buffalo Forge Co. - Buffalo, NY - Bufco USA," 24" across, crank operated bellows **80.00**

Froe

14" wood handle, 13" hand wrought blade **27.50**

18" wood handle, 12" hand wrought blade **22.00**

Gauge

jointer, Stanley #386, adjustable angle guide **60.00**

marking, Stanley #66, rosewood, pat'd. 1873, brass bar and thumbscrew **30.00**

Grinder

cast iron base, 8" diameter stone with a trough at base **35.00**

Keen Kutter, with seat **240.00**

Keystone **27.50**

"Luther Grinder Mfg. Co. - Milwaukee USA - No. 271 Model 2," all metal, bicycle pedals, four legs, iron saddle seat, two small grinding wheels, 30" × 39" h. **85.00**

metal frame and seat, 16" diameter stone **40.00**

wall mount, "Favorite No. 77" **25.00**

Grindstone, 14" diameter wheel only **12.00**

Hatchet, embossed "Winchester," broadax-type head **50.00**

Lathe, foot treadle, all metal, separate jigsaw attachment made of wood and metal, made by Goodell, approx. 24" w., treadle has star pattern **160.00**

Leather punch, Ideal, scissors-type, chrome **5.00**

Leather stripper

iron pistol handle, metal ruler **20.00**

wood and brass pistol handle, "Wm. Brown - Newark, N.J." **40.00**

Level

Disston, brass bound, rosewood ..**225.00**

Keen Kutter, cast iron K624 ....**100.00**

Keen Kutter, KK13, cherry, 12", no port-hole **30.00**

"L.D. Howard - Patent Nov. 5, 1867," level and bevel combination, rosewood, brass and steel, 1" square × 8" long **145.00**

Stanley, dated March 25, 1890, June 2, 1891, and June 23, 1896 ....**35.00**

Stanley #0, hardwood, brass top plate, 28" **15.00**

Stanley #104, hardwood, 16" **8.00**

Bucket, oak staves, wire handle, two metal bands, 7¾" diameter, 9½" high (Klein collection), **27.50**

Paint scrapers, wood handles: left, *"Keen Kutter, E.C. Simmons, Pat. Aug [?], 1910," 4" × 3"* end, *11" long,* **32.00;** center, *brass ferrule, 5" long,* **10.00;** right, *maple handle, 12½" × 2½" × 4" (Illinois Farm Bureau photo/Eisele collection),* **15.00**

Log tongs

    attached to 36" wooden yoke **20.00**

    iron loop handles **15.00**

Machinist's box, wood with tool drawers at

    front **70.00**

Nail carrier, wood, 4 sections, leather strap

    handle, 18" × 18" × 5", cleaned and

    waxed **38.00**

Pipe vise, Keen Kutter **115.00**

Pipe wrench, Keen Kutter **17.50**

Plane

    Diamond Edge, No. 9.5, in original box

    ....**65.00**

    Keen Kutter

        #2 ....**190.00**

        KK4, in original box **105.00**

        wood, coffin shaped, no number, no

        blade **21.00**

    No. 105, metal, 5" × 1¼" × 1¾" **14.00**

    Smith, E., "Warranted," rabbet plane,

    14½", handled **115.00**

    Stanley

        #1, "Bailey," iron, smoothing, 5½", no

        number marking, weighs 1⅛ pounds

        ....**675.00**

        #2, smoothing, Type 13, Type AA mark

        on iron, part of original label on han-

        dle **170.00**

#4, "Bailey," smoothing, 9", japanned

    iron **35.00**

#40, scrub plane, japanned iron, wood

    handle and knob, 9½" long **35.00**

#43, plow plane, nine cutters ..**350.00**

#45, combination plane, Type 2, all

    major parts and 19 cutters, dated

    "March 11, '84" on the skate

    ....**175.00**

#45, combination plane, Type 14, 23

    cutters in two wooden boxes

    ....**150.00**

#46, polished, combination plane

    ....**175.00**

#48, nickel plated tongue and groove

    match plane **75.00**

#55, universal combination plane, with

    four original boxes of cutters and all

    parts except short arms **350.00**

#55, complete with all cutters in origi-

    nal boxes **575.00**

#55, cutters only, four boxes contain-

    ing all 41 special cutters **800.00**

#57, core box plane **135.00**

#71, router, with fence **75.00**

#81, scraper, nickel plated metal, 10"

    ....**17.00**

#113, circular plane **95.00**

#122, smooth plane, no blade **21.00**

#130, double end iron block plane, rosewood handle **45.00**

#144, corner rounding plane ...**275.00**

#148, tongue and groove match plane **80.00**

#190, rabbet plane **17.50**

#193A, complete with attachments **165.00**

#240, excellent condition **240.00**

#444, dovetail plane with two cutters **600.00**

#602, "Bedrock" cast in toe, iron smoothing plane, 7″, rosewood handle and knob, ...**500.00**

Winchester

#5A, corrugated bottom, wooden handle **45.00**

#3010, metal jack plane **95.00**

small **120.00**

#W3 ....**52.50**

Pliers

fence, Keen Kutter **37.50**

Keen Kutter, pistol grip **110.00**

Winchester, 10″ **15.00**

Plumb bob

brass, cone shaped, steel point, 4″ long **10.00**

brass, modified teardrop shape, 7″ long, steel tip **100.00**

Pulley, iron with wood wheel **8.00**

Roof pitch gauge **15.00**

Rope maker

brass, no maker's marks **180.00**

cast iron and wood, "Nov. 1, 1901" embossed in iron **85.00**

cast iron and wood, five hooks, smaller tool also has five hooks **125.00**

Hawkeye, with shuttle twister, cast iron, 1930s **75.00**

"The New Era Rope Machine - Pat'd July 18, 1911 - Mfd. by New Era Mfg. Co. Minneapolis, Minn. - Keep Oiled," 7″ wheel, 8½″ high, mounted on wood **200.00**

Router, Stanley #71, nickel plated cast iron, two turned knobs, 1885–1973 ......**35.00**

Rule, Stanley

#27, plain maple, two feet, folding **12.00**

#36, six inch, two fold, brass square joint **15.00**

#40, ivory and German silver, 1910, folds twice, 12 inches, pull-out calipers, 1870–1910 ....**170.00**

#48, hickory, 36″, stamped numbers **80.00**

#68 ....**10.00**

#69, 12″, folds twice **17.50**

Leather punch, cast iron, embossed "Simmons," 8″ (Sandy's Surplus, Lexington, IL), **7.50**

Rope splicer, 9½″, rosewood handle, tip inscribed "VOOS- Stainless Steel - New Haven, Conn."(Ted Diamond photo/Danenberger collection), **15.00**

Nailer, galvanized metal and iron, handle embossed "Pearson's Nailer - Pat. Jan. 26 - 92, 7 - 88," traces of blue-green paint and gold lettering, 14" × 3½" × 8" (Revelle collection), **85.00**

Saw

    bow, 18" × 30", H-shaped wood frame, tension rod, rotating handles **45.00**

    buck, arched frame, longer side for handle, tension rod and turnscrew, refinished or with old paint (usually red) **22.50**

    clamps to tree with iron mechanism, "Pat. June 3, '02," red paint on wood frame and shield, hinged leg, saw blade is four feet long **75.00**

    coping, Winchester **25.00**

    crosscut

        one man, folding, like new **250.00**

        two man, 4" jagged blade, two wood handles, 6' long **12.00**

        two man, 7" deep blade, two wood handles, 6' long **20.00**

        ice, 6' long, turned wooden lawn mower-type handle **60.00**

        ice, deeply jagged, handles at top and end, 42" **22.50**

    Saw sharpener, cast iron, "I.C. Atkins & Co. - INDPLS, IND," 5½" × 2" **15.00**

    Saw vise, rosewood, 14" × 15½", large brass thumbscrew **155.00**

    Screwdriver, Winchester, #7124 ......**20.00**

Soldering iron, polished copper and iron, wood handle **3.00**

Shovel, brass, embossed "HMPCO - Made in USA - #2," square, no handle, polished **27.50**

Snow pusher, 12" × 18" wood pusher with wood handle **52.50**

Spokeshave, concave, unmarked **15.00**

Surveyor's measurer, wood with brass ends, 7' long, extends to 13', enameled numbers 1-9 and then large foot numbers **35.00**

*Sharpener, hand made, stone wired into wood handle, 7½", **12.50***

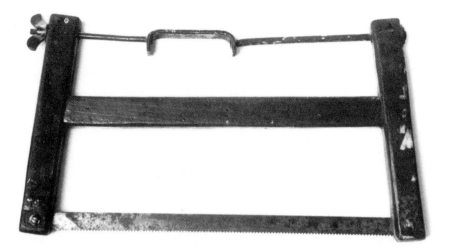

Bow saw, 13½″ × 7½″ (Ted Diamond photo/Eisele collection), **30.00**

Tile spade, old wood handle, 10′ long **15.00**

Tin

  "American Emery - Shapleigh Hardware, 10 lbs.," red with gold, 7″ × 4″ × 8½″ **18.00**

  "The Star Hack Saw," 8″ blades, green and black with stars, contained ½ gross of blades, 8¾″ × 2¼″ × ½″ **15.00**

Tool carrier

  pine, divided, nailed corners, cut out handle in center board parallel to sides, 30″ × 9″ × 16″, cleaned and waxed **53.00**

  pine, straight handle, 36″ × 8″ × 12″ **12.00**

Tool chest, machinist's, oak, front cover over drawers **90.00**

Traveler, wheelwright's, iron, embossed inch marks around 8″ wheel, five curved spokes, iron loop handle, 13″ **90.00**

Weed cutter, twisted metal Y-shaped handle, wood grip, 12″ × 2″ blade, 39″ tall **40.00**

Wrench

  adjustable, thick twisted iron loop handle, 14″ **25.00**

  Avery **12.00**

  Deere and Mansur, 7″ **10.00**

  Edgefield **60.00**

  Ford **3.50**

  Fordson, adjustable, 11″ **15.00**

  International Harvester, fits three sizes of hex nuts **10.00**

  "J.I. Case," for three sizes of hex nuts **10.00**

  John Deere, "JD 50," "JD51," or "JD53" **6.00**

  Keen Kutter, adjustable, 4″ **155.00**

  Keen Kutter, adjustable, alligator **110.00**

  "Mann Bone Cutter," 4½″ **10.00**

  Maytag **17.50**

  Wizard, Aurora, Ill., adjustable, patented May 21, '07 ....**75.00**

Wrenches

  John Deere, group of six **50.00**

  Maytag, complete set of eight shapes **200.00**

Bees and Trees

Bees and trees were the sources of most of the sweets enjoyed by the earliest farm families. Refined sugar has been available for a long time, but production of natural sweets, such as honey, maple syrup, maple sugar, maple candy, and apple butter continued on American farms into the 20th century.

Maple Syrup

Maple syrup is made by boiling sap collected from sugar maple trees or black maples. It takes 30 to 60 gallons of sap to produce 1 gallon of syrup. The syrup can be further boiled to get maple sugar. Maple candy is molded maple sugar.

The sap is obtained on a warm day after a hard freeze in late February or early March. A spile is tapped 3 inches into the tree to drain the sap. Spiles were made of metal or a length of sumac, which had its pithy interior burned out. A wooden bucket or a tin pail collected the sap and would have been hung from the spile itself or set on a flat rock below the spile. These buckets are wider at the bottom than the top and often have a metal cut-out hanger instead of a bail handle. Some wooden buckets have one elongated stave with a hole cut in it from which the bucket could be hung.

Buckets were emptied into barrels or were carried at each end of a wooden shoulder yoke that was often custom carved to fit the bearer. A rope and a strong hickory hook held the bucket on the yoke. Long wooden ladles were used to stir the sap in large troughs or kettles over an open fire. When the sap neared syrup consistency, it was taken to the kitchen to be brought to its syrup or sugar stage.

If the syrup was to be made into candy, it was cooked until it began to crystalize and then was poured into molds. These molds, made of carved wood, tin, iron, or pottery, were often used for other purposes, such as marzipan, muffins, or mints. Most of the molds made especially for maple candy were manufactured in Canada. They are carved from close-grained blocks of wood and often have a cross on their backs.

Fruit Trees

Many farms had fruit orchards in which they grew apples, pears, cherries, peaches, apricots, and plums. Car-ing for the trees involved grafting and pruning tools and sprayers. Grafting knives have curved or hooked blades. They may be as large as 12 inches or as small as a pocketknife. Pruning was done with pruning saws or scissors-like pruners, often on long handles.

Picking the fruit involved the use of tapered ladders, pickers, and baskets or bags. A picker could be handmade or manufactured, with a long wooden handle and a hook for pulling loose the fruit. Below the hook, there might be a wire, canvas, or wooden basket that held several pieces of fruit. Canvas bags could be carried on the picker's back, or the fruit might be placed in splint baskets that held from 1 peck to 1 bushel. These sturdy baskets were handmade or manufactured and had a handle at each side.

Sliced fruits were dried in wooden frames with bottoms of ridged metal with slits or in fruit driers, metal or wooden boxes fitted with several trays for layers of drying fruit. The dried fruits were used in baking.

Vinegar pumps are long wooden shafts that have a second shaft that fits inside and a spigot at the top. They were inserted into barrels to pump vinegar, whiskey, cider, syrup, witch hazel, alcohol, or turpentine.

Cast-iron cherry pitters can seed from 20 to 30 quarts per hour. Some have legs and some are meant to be clamped to tabletops or counters.

Apples

Apples were the most common home grown fruit. Apples were used for eating and baking and for making applesauce, apple butter, sweet and hard cider, vinegar, and white lightning. Apple orchards usually planted in two or three varieties to provide sweet and sour apples and those that would keep well through the winter. Often apples and pears were the only fresh fruits that a farm family could enjoy through the winter.

Apples were processed by pressing them for juice or by slicing and drying them. Windfall, bruised, or misshapen apples were used for cider. If a cider mill wasn't handy, the apples were pressed at the farm in a cider press. Cider presses came in many sizes. The most common consists of two hoppers made of wooden slats that held the apples as they were fed into a grinder and then into a press. The juice came out a spout beneath the press.

Different blends of sweet and sour apples were used for sweet and hard cider, for mincemeat cider, and for vinegar. Within about a week, the cider began to ferment and became hard cider. Sweet cider was boiled down and bottled and corked for mincemeat or was added to the cooking apples in the production of apple butter.

Apples that were made into sauce or butter had to be pared before they were cooked. Sometimes people had apple-paring bees, at which they got together to enjoy each other's company while they pared bushels of apples. The first American patent for an apple parer was issued in 1803. During the next century, 150 patents attempted to improve the invention. Most consist of a crank-driven axle that held the apple and a hinged arm with a blade that was guided over the apple. Gears and pulleys were added by the 1820s. Many early parers have a base and wooden parts; some are handmade. By 1860, most designs included a clamp that attached the parer to a tabletop. Parers offered conveniences like blossom cutters, push-off mechanisms, slicers, and corers.

Apple butter was made in large copper, brass, or iron kettles over an open fire. The copper kettles often had dovetailed seams and iron bails. Long-handled apple butter stirrers with perforated paddles were used to stir the mixture, which helped shield the person stirring from the heat. Stirrers are made of nonacidic wood, such as poplar. Apple butter was kept in crocks of redware or stoneware or in glass jars.

Cider that was to become hard cider, or applejack, was allowed to ferment in stoneware jugs or wooden barrels, kegs, or casks. Utensils such as strainers and funnels—made of copper, pewter, tin, or wood—were used to fill the barrels. Getting the cider out of the barrels made it necessary to make an opening, or bunghole, at the bottom of the barrel for a spigot. The bunghole was made with a tool called a bung auger. Most of these augers have wooden handles that are perpendicular to the pointed metal auger. A wooden stopper, or bung, plugged the hole when the barrel wasn't tapped. Bung starters, heavy wooden mallets, the best of which were made of burled wood, dislodged the bung so that the spigot could be inserted. Wooden bung transformers could be used to make the hole smaller. Spigots are wooden valves that open and close with a wooden handle.

If the hard cider was to become white lightning, its more potent form, it had to be distilled further in a copper still. During Prohibition, most stills were handmade and came in many shapes and sizes, but they were invariably made of copper. Often copper boilers were converted to stills.

Bees

Bees are needed for pollination and are often found near orchards. The first domesticated bees were kept in hollow sections of logs or stumps. Cone-shaped hives, or skeps, of rye straw and oak splint were used before box hives began to be made.

The swarm will stay where the queen is, so special containers were made to hold the queen while moving a swarm. If a swarm got away, the beekeeper could capture the bees in a cone-shaped screen trap, sometimes called a swarm catcher.

To remove the honey from the hives, the bees were stupefied with sulfur smoke from bellowslike or hand-cranked bee smokers. Protective clothing, including veiled hats, was worn while extracting honey from the hive. Tools for assembling and maintaining the removable honey boxes included special bee brushes, knives, wire embedders, and foundation fasteners.

The honey could be marketed in small stoneware jars with bail handles or in glass jars. Square honey dishes served honey in the beeswax honeycomb or it was enjoyed from figural beehive honey dishes. Fermented honey is used to make mead. The beeswax had many uses. It was sometimes used to make candles and process leather. Beeswax was also used for household cleaning.

Nuts

Nutting was done in rural areas near stands of mature trees. Chestnuts, hickory nuts, black walnuts, butternuts, pecans, beechnuts, and hazelnuts were harvested. The nuts were dried and their husks were removed, sometimes in corn shellers. The nuts were then dried for a few weeks before cracking. Nutcrackers, sometimes in figural forms, were used to release the meat from the shell. Chestnut roasters were used to roast nuts over an open fire or in a fireplace or stove.

Tips for Collectors

Make sure apple peelers have all their parts. They are often missing the peeling blade or the clamp that holds them to a work surface.

Some of the most ornate apple peelers, such as the Reading Hardware '78, are fairly common and don't command prices as high as simpler peelers that were not commercially successful. Handmade peelers with wooden parts and peelers that operate in unusual ways are premium collector's items.

Apple basket, all wood, half bushel **90.00**

Apple butter jar, redware, unglazed exterior, glazed interior

    semiovoid, holds approximately one gallon **65.00**

    3½″ high **35.00**

Apple butter kettle, copper

    dovetailed bottom, 30″ wood bar with four 6″ teeth fits across top, wood stirrer in kettle with six teeth turns through top teeth with crank handle, unpolished **350.00**

    dovetailed bottom, iron bail handle, 32″ diameter, clean **275.00**

    dovetailed bottom, iron bail, 22″ diameter, 14″ high, polished **340.00**

    dovetailed bottom, iron bail, 26″ × 17″, polished **300.00**

seamed flat bottom, iron bail, 28″ diameter, polished **175.00**

Apple butter stirrer, wooden, eight feet long, pierced stirrer **16.00**

Apple parer

    cast iron, simple mechanism, dated 1877 ....**40.00**

    cast iron, semicircular, stationary gear rack, gears are moved by moving a wooden handle over gear rack, patented 1868, clamps to work surface **150.00**

    "Hudson Apple Parer Co - Patented Jan. 2, '02" **37.50**

    Keen Kutter **62.00**

    Reading Hardware, cast iron, ornate gears, last patent date, 1878 ....**47.50**

    "Union Apple Parer and Corer - Patented Oct. 10, 1883 - USA," tin, 6″ pointed tube with peeling blade **10.00**

Barrel, wood staves, five metal bands **35.00**

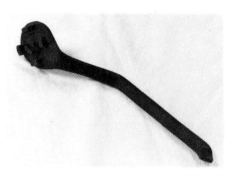

Barrel plug wrench, cast iron, c. 1930, 11″ × 2″, **14.00**

Hack, used to cut groove to make sap flow from pine tree, sap is distilled to make turpentine, 17″, **25.00**

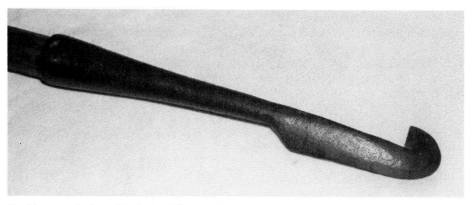

Barking spud, iron blade is 14", c. 1870, used to remove bark from wood (Busch collection), **45.00**

Bee keeper's hat, woven straw, 2" yellow and black striped grosgrain band, 15" × 12" brim, net drops 15" from brim, colored label inside reads "La Vine Yeddo - Made in Switzerland" **35.00**

Bee smoker

bellows recovered with vinyl **6.00**

in handmade pine squeezer, 38" × 6", step on one end to squeeze smoker bellows **34.00**

worn brown bellows, 6" × 5" bellows, 8" × 3" can **15.00**

Book

ABC and XYZ of Bee Culture, A. I. Root, revised by E. R. Root, 1947, 720 pages, good condition **7.50**

The American Fruit Culturalist: Containing Practical Directions for Propagation and Culture of All Fruits, adapted to the U.S., octavo, 1897, 758 pages **20.00**

The Apple: A Practical Treatise Dealing with the Latest Modern Practices of Apple Culture, by Wilkinson, 1915, octavo, first edition, 226 pages **20.00**

The Apples of New York, Beach, 1905, two volumes, color and black and white halftones, very good condition **125.00**

Bee Hunting, by John Lockard, 1936, 4½" × 6½" **4.00**

Day's American Ready Reckoner and Log Measurer, 1866, cardboard cover with lithographed picture of mill, horse, and men measuring log, "Price 50 Cents" **12.50**

First Lessons in Beekeeping, C. P. Dadant, American Bee Journal, 1947, 127 pages **9.00**

Lippincott's Farm Manual, Productive Orcharding, by Fred Sears, 1927, cover soiled **6.00**

Pruning saw, rope was tied to brass rings at each end and saw was thrown over a branch and worked from the ground, 45" (Ted Diamond photo/Danenberger collection), **35.00**

Cherry pitter
  cast iron, on four curved legs **65.00**
  "Enterprise Cherry Stoner," clamps to ta-
    bletop **20.00**
  Goodell, pits two cherries at once, clamps
    to tabletop **22.50**
  "New Standard Corp.- Mt. Joy, Pa.," green
    wood handle, clamps to tabletop,
    rusted **25.00**
  "New Standard Corp. - Mt. Joy, Pa.," pits
    four cherries at a time **125.00**
  "New Std Hdwe. Wks. - Mt. Joy, Pa. - No.
    60 - Pat's Pen.," pits one cherry at a
    time, wood knob on crank, profes-
    sional repair to lip **40.00**
Cider press
  one wood slat barrel is 14″ tall, 16″ diame-
    ter, horizontal cast iron wheel on top
    reads "CP32," press reads "P 3 IN," red
    paint, 47″ tall **125.00**
  two wood slat barrels, cast iron gears and
    wheel with wood handle, last patent
    1874 ....**125.00**
  two wood slat barrels, "P.R. Mast & Co. -
    Springfield, Ohio - Reissued Aug. 24,
    1866," new back legs and tray, repaired
    barrel **150.00**
  Young America, missing big barrel
    ....**30.00**
Cookbook, *Old Favorite Honey Recipes*,
  American Honey Institute, 1941, 6″ × 9″,
  40 pages, soiled cover is decorated with
  cross stitch style pattern **5.00**
Dehydrator, nine shelves **60.00**
Fruit picker, basket handmade from fence
  wire, three loops, 10′ long **45.00**
Fruit press
  "Fruit press, Enterprise Mfg. Co. - Phila-
    delphia, Pat. Sep. 30, '79, No. 1,"
    clamps to table, hopper is 6″ diameter
    at top, wood handle, 13″ high **75.00**
  tin cylinder, cast iron wheel, plate
    embossed "Fruit Press - Brighton Press
    Plate - 10 Qts," "Brighton Press" on
    cross bar, 12″ × 21″ **45.00**
  tin cylinder, supported by three legged
    cast iron stand embossed "JUICY
    FRUIT PRESS - 3 GALLON," press plate
    reads "No. 1 - Mfd. by C.P. Schrever Co.
    - Cincinnati," curved bar turns to push
    press, 12″ × 28″ **65.00**

*Honey pot, stoneware, Bristol glaze, 4¾″
diameter, 6″ high, lid with molded knob
(Illinois Farm Bureau photo/M. Sutter collection),* **25.00**

Honey dish, Frankoma, white glaze ...**12.50**
Honey extractor, metal barrel painted green,
  25″ diameter, 30″ tall, spigot at base, crank
  with wire cage inside barrel, works are
  embossed "The Standard Churn -
  Wapakoneta, Ohio - Patent Allowed"
  ....**57.00**
Jug
  Akron, Ohio, salt glazed, incised "2," bail
    with wooden handle **35.00**
  Blue Ribbon Stoneware, five gallon, blue
    ribbon logo **65.00**
  Buckeye Pottery Co., Blue Ribbon Brand,
    Macomb, Ill., one gallon **30.00**
  "C.L. Williams Co., New Geneva, Pa."
    stenciled in blue, freehand decorated,
    two handled, salt glazed, five gallon
    ....**675.00**
  Eagle Pottery, Macomb, Ill., salt glazed,
    double handles, stenciled eagle and
    pottery name **600.00**
  Louis Tapp and Co., Louisville, Ky., Al-
    bany glaze, incised "4" **145.00**

molded, no manufacturer's name, brown and white, or white

one gallon **13.00**

one gallon, wide mouth **27.50**

two gallon, rounded shoulders ...**22.50**

five gallon, rounded shoulders, stenciled "5" **45.00**

Red Wing

three gallon, Union Stoneware Co., base chips **70.00**

five gallon, with logo **75.00**

five gallon, cracked **15.00**

five gallon, Minnesota Stoneware **87.50**

salt glazed, unidentified manufacturer

one gallon, cobalt on handle, cracked **25.00**

two gallon, semiovoid, undecorated **32.50**

two gallon, tan, stenciled "2," sloped shoulders **55.00**

Peter Welty, Wheeling, W. Va., two gallon, salt glazed, stenciled **225.00**

Tallewanda, five gallon **50.00**

Uhl, Terre Haute, Ind.

blue, no. 161 ....**44.00**

one gallon **17.50**

five gallon, early Evansville mark **70.00**

unmarked

Albany glaze, half gallon **20.00**

Albany glaze, one gallon **15.00**

Bee smoker, tin, wood base reads "Woodman's Famous Bee-Ware - Bingham Bee Smoker - Pat. 1770289 - On the Market over 68 years" (Busch collection), **17.00**

Western Stoneware

one gallon, leaf logo **20.00**

two gallon, maple leaf logo, brown and white **25.00**

three gallon, beehive shape, Bristol glaze, marked "Plant #3" **120.00**

ten gallon, marked "Plant #1" in leaf logo **95.00**

Kettle, copper, for making maple syrup, dovetailed bottom, 22″ diameter, 15″ high, bent and dirty **95.00**

Stereoscope card, black and white, Keystone (Illinois Farm Bureau photo), **4.00**

Barking tool, wood handle, 22½" long, 2½" × 5" blade, traces of red paint on twisted metal handle (Illinois Farm Bureau photo/Eisele collection), **35.00**

Ladder

stepladder, supporting side is shaped like a crutch, 8' tall, 38" wide at base **110.00**

wood, handmade, narrower at top than bottom, 8' tall, old carved initials along sides **95.00**

wood, manufactured, tapers from 25" wide at base to 15" at top, six steps, 80" high **65.00**

Log measure, calculates board feet, "E.T. Lufkin Maker" on metal end, inscribed numbers each side of wood shaft and metal end, 36" **150.00**

Log tongs

cast iron, 28" long **30.00**

cast iron, 26" long, mounted on refinished wooden yoke **38.00**

Nutcracker, cast iron

dog, standing, tail is lever, mouth cracks nut, 11½" **55.00**

"Home Nut Cracker - Schrocter Bros. Hdw Co. - St. Louis" on handle, cast iron with silver finish is 4" × 4", marked "Pecan Nut Cracker - Pat. Aug. 24, 1913," mounted on 8" × 3" board with brass plate reading "Improved Home Nut Cracker, Cracks All Sizes - Pecans, English, Walnuts, Etc." ..**32.50**

"Perfection Nut Cracker - Waco, Texas" **42.50**

squirrel on haunches, black paint, 8½" **62.50**

Pamphlet, *The Story of Honey*, Lloyd Dennis, Ontario Honey Producers, color cover, c. 1940 ....**5.00**

Peach peeler, Sinclair & Booth Hardware, 1895, circular blade, curved prongs hold peach, ornate gears **60.00**

Pecan tree thumper, rubber strip wrapped around wood handle, 19" diameter, 35" long **35.00**

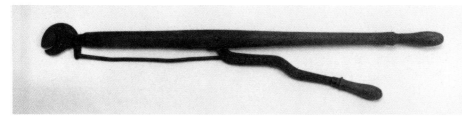

Pruners, oak shaft, iron handle, embossed "American Pruner - Williamsburg, Ohio - Patented Mar. 15, 1872, 38" (Illinois Farm Bureau photo/Danenberger collection), **45.00**

Queen bee holder, wood with wire screen top and end, grooved edges to slide into hive, 3½" × 1¼" **7.50**

Sap bucket

    wood staves with old red paint, 2 metal bands, metal hoop hanger, 12½" tall, 9¼" diameter at top, 12" at base ..**65.00**

    wood staves with red paint, metal bands, metal tab attaches bucket to tree, wider at base than top **48.00**

Spigot, wood **5.00**

Still

    copper cylinder, 18" diameter, with bul- bous top, 30" high, and brass handles, copper tubing extends 30" horizon- tally, then coils downward **425.00**

    made from a copper boiler, no tubing **75.00**

Tin, embossed "Maple Syrup" one side, small wire handle and spout with lid on top, 9½" × 5" × 5" **12.00**

Vinegar pump, wood, 6' long **30.00**

Yoke, shoulder, for carrying buckets, hand carved maple, leather strips each end hold 6" hooked branch, 33" wide **45.00**

Pest Control

Rodents, lice, flies, and small animals were a constant problem on the family farm. Many ingenious methods of ridding the farmyard of these pests were sold to farmers at the turn of the century.

Fly traps were invented by many creative Americans. The Gilbert Fly Trap, patented in 1856, used a rolling cylinder coated with molasses to deliver flies to a dark chamber from which they would pass to a light screened section to await their fate. One inventor suggested that a peck of flies are worth a bushel of corn when feeding the poultry. Another recommended dousing the trapped flies with whiskey and then throwing them into the stove.

Another method of dealing with insects was to scare them away. Fly fans slowly rotated paddles between the source of light and the table, casting shadows to scare off flies. "Shoo-Fly Pies" lured flies and were made with poison. Fly paper and poison bricks also were used to keep houses pest free. Fly swatters proved to be effective and were woven of wire or made from a section of leather.

Small animal traps, especially mouse traps, were produced by many inventors. They trapped live animals or killed them by drowning, dropping a weight on them, or snapping their necks with a spring-loaded wire. Sometimes the trapped animal went through a series of doors or wheels before reaching its destiny. Myriad ideas for building a better mousetrap were patented and produced in as many shapes, sizes, and materials as can be imagined.

Poisons helped farmers control the lice that plagued their livestock and poultry. Most lice powders contained nicotine. Competition between producers of lice and insect remedies was responsible for many colorfully labeled cans, tins, sprayers, and drums.

Tips for Collectors

The manufacturer of a trap is usually identified, often on the trap's pan. The legibility of the maker's name is an important factor in determining condition. Cans, tins, and boxes with interesting or colorful illustrations are more desirable than plain ones. **Note:** Many old poisons contain DDT or other powerful chemicals and are hazardous collectibles if full.

Fly trap, green screen cover, wood base with nails to hold cover, paper label under base, "J.H. Burris - El Paso, IL" (Busch collection), **55.00**

Box, dovetailed, stenciled in red, "Tanglefoot - The Sanitary Fly Destroyer - Non-Poisonous," refinished, 15″ × 9″ × 5½″ **35.00**
Can, cardboard with metal top and bottom, "Pratt's Lice Killer," 2 lb, gold, black, and red paper label, full, 4¼″ × 9″ **20.00**
Crow decoy, wire legs are replaced, Herter's, 22″ long **150.00**

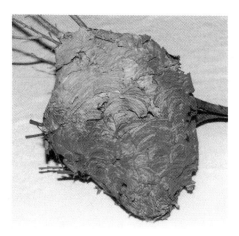

Wasp nest, 14″ × 9″, **25.00**

Crow repellent, "Parsons Seed Saver Crow Repellent," tin, treats one bushel of seed corn, blue and white, half pint **8.50**
Drum, louse powder, "Lee's Dri-Rub," 50 lb, cardboard with yellow label picturing man rubbing pig **45.00**
Fly net
    drapes over horse's back, leather strips, five ribs **45.00**
    drapes over horse's back, knotted cotton rope **15.00**
Fly paper, "Seibert Poison Fly Paper," 8 sheets, in beige envelope with red lettering, 5″ × 8″ **9.00**
Fly swatter
    leather swatter on wood handle **12.50**
    woven wire swatter, red wood handle **5.00**
Fly trap
    cone-shaped wire screen on metal base, hangs from a hook, 14″ high, 7″ base, 5″ top **65.00**

Duster, "D and B Ware Duster for potatoes, tobacco," paper label, 8″ hopper is 14″ high, metal, "Pat. 2-15-21, 11-11-24," 42″ long, **35.00**

Small animal trap, iron, 13½" × 6" (Hintze Auction, Mazon, IL), **20.00**

"Tom's Fly Trap," fits glass fruit jar **20.00**
wire, cone shaped, two piece, 7" × 11" **35.00**
Food cover, dome shaped wire screen, wood knob, 10" **48.00**
Mole trap, Reddick, Niles, Michigan ...**12.00**
Mousetrap
   "Catchemalive," wood and tin **45.00**
   "Easy Setting Choker - Lovell Mfg. Co - Erie Pa USA," three holes in sides of wood block, wire mechanism above each hole, 5½" × 2½" × 1¼" **35.00**
   Kopper Kat, Aurora, Ill., metal **20.00**
   Wigginton, glass **30.00**

5" circular wood platform, four wire traps **15.00**
Poison, "Gopher Corn Poison," by Cenol, orange, blue, and white label pictures gopher, 20 oz, cardboard and tin container **18.50**
Poison container, "Ratter DeMouser - Keep Filled with Warfarin Bait," galvanized metal dome with hole in top and each of four sides, 12½" diameter, 4" high, slightly rusted **10.00**
Powder gun, cardboard, "Metro DDT Insect Powder No. 1," blue and yellow with black lettering, half pound, c. 1950 ....**20.00**

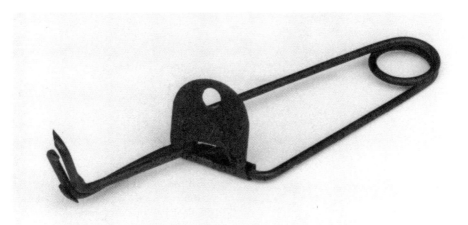

Small animal trap, "Roy-Trap," patented 1917, 9" × 2" (Country Hearth, Lexington, IL), **15.00**

Fly swatter, wire, "Swift - Made by Swift Flyswatter Mfg. Co, Kansas City, Mo. - Pat'd Oct. 14, 1913," 16" × 4½" (Illinois Farm Bureau photo/Eisele collection), **15.00**

Rat trap, "Dead Easy," 7" × 3¼" (Busch collection), **5.00**

Sprayer

    "Acme - Registered Quality - Acmeline Mfg. Co. - Traverse City, Michigan," quart fruit jar attached to bottom of reservoir, 20" × 2" **15.00**

    brass, "Buescher Manufacturing. - Elkhart, Ind.," wood handle, 15" **45.00**

    "Cenol Bed Bug Destroyer - Medium size," orange, blue, and white paper label, 6½" tall **18.50**

    copper reservoir with brass tube, wood handle, 13" **25.00**

    "Dustmaster Powder Duster - No 36D - D.B. Smith, Utica N.Y.," 16 ounce green glass reservoir, 40" long, tube is painted orange **45.00**

    "5DG - Ideal Spray Co. - Pat'd Jan. 18 '27 - Worcester, Mass.," 20" × 13", for fungicide or insecticide, hose attaches below sprayer **32.00**

    "Gulf Surface Sprayer - for applying Gulf Roach and Ant Killer," blue, white and orange **18.75**

    "Lowell Spray Duster," wood handle, red reservoir **10.00**

    "What Is It? Insecticide," tin container with sprayer top, green black, blue and silver, one pint, empty, c. 1910 ...**40.00**

Store display, Moth-ene, three tins in store display, yellow, blue and red, bright colors, excellent condition, 12½" × 7¾" **48.00**

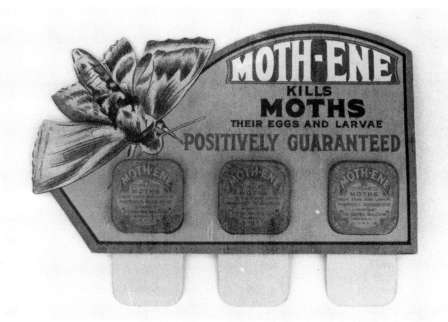

*Store display, cardboard, contains three tins of moth killer; yellow, red and black; 12½″ × 8″ (Antique Mall of Chenoa, IL), **48.00***

Tin

"Crick's Lice Exterminator," black and white lithographed paper label shows hen and rooster, 3 lb, 5″ × 8½″ ...**30.00**

"Daisy Fly Killer," fly trap, lithographed daisies on cover, 6″ × 3½″, 1888 ....**35.00**

"Dill Spray Insecticide," red and yellow with black lettering, half pint, full **10.00**

Dr. Hess Instant Louse Killer, orange, yellow, and black paper label pictures girl with chickens, 1 lb, 3″ diameter, 6½″ high **30.00**

*Mole trap, "Nash Mole Trap - Kalamazoo, Mich.," green paint, 9½″ × 5½″ (Antique Mall of Chenoa, IL), **15.00***

*Mousetrap, "Choker Mouse Trap," traces of red paint, 4″ × 4″ (Illinois Farm Bureau photo/Busch collection), **15.00***

Tin, "Wood's Improved Lollacapop - One of the Greatest Known Antidotes in the World for Mosquitoes, Black Flies and Gnats," made from tallow, beeswax, and camphor, yellow and black, 3½" × 2" (Antique Mall of Chenoa, IL), **14.00**

Kilzum, insecticide and deodorant, one pint **9.50**

"Mabex Insect Powder," yellow and blue, 5" high **8.00**

"Preventol Insecticide," uses for the home on one side, uses for the farm on reverse, yellow, green and black, half pint, full, c. 1915 ....**20.00**

"Rick's Die-U-Rat," rat poison **12.00**

"Wood's Improved Lollacapop - One of the Greatest Known Antidotes in the World for Mosquitoes, Black Flies and Gnats," made from tallow, beeswax, and camphor, 3½" × 2" **14.00**

Trap, small animal

Lovell Sure Catch Rat Trap **5.00**

"Oneida Victor 1," 9" **4.00**

Peerless Rat Trap, paper label on wood side, wire cage **135.00**

snap, Victor rat trap, made by Animal Trap Co. of America, 7¼" × 3½" ..**8.00**

wire, manufactured, 20" × 12" oblong, wire handle, clean **25.00**

wire cage, 26" × 18" × 6", small animal enters and trips door, then is moved into cage section by a rolling wheel **22.50**

Wasps' nest, made by paper wasps, 17" long, egg-shaped, good condition **20.00**

Yard and Garden

The family garden was very important to the self-sufficiency of the rural family. Located near the kitchen, the garden was often tended by children as well as adults. Garden produce was preserved to last all year.

Obsolete farm machinery was often used in the garden. Horse-drawn plows and cultivators were used for many years in small plots.

Seed catalogs were filled with color illustrations of fruit, flowers, and vegetables. The pages were often cut up and used to decorate the pages of scrapbooks. Covers and pages were often framed.

Cranberries grow in sandy marshlands. They are picked from the low-growing bushes with a deep wooden or metal scoop with a comblike edge.

Birdhouses and bird feeders were hung on branches or mounted on poles to attract wrens and other songbirds. Wren houses have small openings to keep larger birds from using the houses. Handmade wooden birdhouses were lavishly decorated or merely functional. Stoneware companies produced birdhouses and birdbaths until the mid-20th century.

The well or pump was usually located as near the house as possible. Well pulleys made of cast iron held a rope from which a bucket or hook was suspended into the water. Sometimes a container of food or liquid was cooled in the well.

By the 20th century, most farms had a yard, or cistern, pump. Wooden pumps with wooden pipes were decorated with striping and stenciled makers' names. Some yard pumps had protective covers of galvanized metal and were chain driven. Cast-iron pumps were operated with a lever handle or could be powered by a windmill. (These pumps differ from kitchen pumps in size and shape. Kitchen pumps are smaller and have bases that mount to a work surface.)

Reproductions

Watch for galvanized sprinkling cans with new brass sprinklers. Cast-iron yard decorations and bootscrapers should be examined for signs of age.

Asparagus buncher, cast iron, "Champion Buncher - Ellers Keystone Agl. Wks. - Pottstown, Pa." in raised letters one end "Champion" on top, old green paint, mounted on 14" × 12" board **85.00**

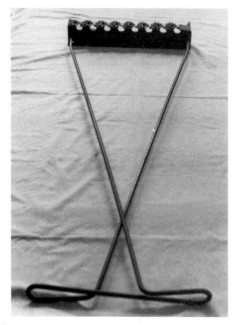

Monta Mower, for mowing slopes, all metal, green with yellow stenciling, 35.00

Basket

    galvanized metal, rectangular, two turned wood handles in cut-out spaces, 20″ × 12½″ × 8″ **17.50**

    gathering, made from a barrel cut lengthwise, cut out handles **145.00**

    splint, ribbed melon style, 10″ opening **90.00**

    thin wood slats, 18″ diameter, 16″ high, bail handle **45.00**

    wire, 14″ diameter, bail handle **15.00**

Berry box, two thin slats of wood, wire rim, pint **3.00**

Berry boxes in carrier, four metal reinforced, thin wood boxes in wood carrier with straight wood handle, 24″ × 6½″ × 11″ **28.00**

Berry pail

    graniteware, turquoise and white marbleized, bail handle, minor chips **85.00**

    gray graniteware, bail handle **35.00**

Bird feeder, weathered wood, 12″ × 8″ × 8″ **26.00**

Birdhouse

    sewer tile, marked "White Hall Sewer Pipe Co" on roof **300.00**

stoneware, unglazed, rubbed brown stain, cylindrical with embossed stone design, round slanted roof has a tile design, one small hole for wren, unmarked, 6½″ diameter, 8″ high ...**95.00**

wood, handmade, alligatored brick red paint over yellow paint, 8″ × 8″ × 10″ **45.00**

wood, white clapboard siding and a red roof, porch, well and watering trough, very good condition, weathered, large, handmade, 1920s **475.00**

wood, white and black, four holes each side, hand made, two red and white chimneys, hole in each gable end, roof of tin strips, 22″ × 18″ × 14″, c. 1950 ....**85.00**

Blueberry picker, 14 fingers, carved wood scoop, 8″ × 8″ × 4″ **55.00**

Horseradish grinder, japanned metal, gold striping, cast iron gears and clamps, 7½″diameter, 16″ long (Busch collection), 145.00

Bluegrass seed picker, red wood handle, back and sides, 9 metal tines at front are angled to form scoop for seed, 12″ × 18″ × 4″ **135.00**

Book

America's Garden Book, 1947, 1241 pages **6.00**

Bush Fruits, Horticultural Monograph, raspberries, blackberries, dewberries, currants, 1907, octavo, 537 pages, illustrations **15.00**

Gardening for Profit, by Peter Henderson, 1888, engravings of fruit, vegetables, implements, worn binding, otherwise good condition **45.00**

The Grape Culturist by Andrew S. Fuller, 1965 ....**45.00**

Master of the Vineyard, by Myrtle Reed, 1910, fancy binding design **30.00**

The New Garden Encyclopedia, Wise publishers, 1946, 1380 pages, very good condition **15.00**

The Practical Fruit, Flower and Vegetable Gardener's Companion, by Neill, 1856, good condition **7.00**

The Standard Cyclopedia of Horticulture, Bailey, 1925, three volumes, 3639 pages, illustrated **95.00**

Vegetable Gardening in Color, by Daniel Foley, 1942, first edition, color illustrations, 256 pages **10.00**

War Gardens Victorious, Charles L. Pack, c. 1920, J. Montgomery Flagg color frontispiece, three color plates, two bound in booklets **34.00**

Sprinkler, "Rain King - Model H," green and silver, 11″ × 9″ (Illinois Farm Bureau photo), 45.00

Booklet, *Henderson's Gardening Guide and Record*, paperback cover with color picture of woman in garden, 64 pages and record keeping pages, c. 1920, 5″ × 8½″ **5.00**

Boot scraper, cast iron
   dachshund, old black paint, red tongue, yellow eyes, 22″ × 8″ × 7″ **225.00**
   horse, full bodied, cast iron, painted white, 10″ standing horse is mounted on a bracket over plain scraper, base is 18″ × 11½″ **450.00**

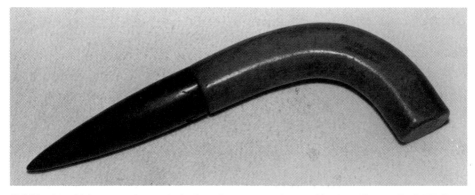

Dibble (or dibber), makes a hole for planting seed, wooden handle marked "William Johnson, Newark, N.J.," 11″ (Busch collection), 22.00

lyre in scalloped base, black, 11″ × 9″ × 7″ **35.00**

reticulated geometric pattern between two posts, 6¼″ × 2″ × 3¾″ **22.50**

retriever, full bodied cast iron doorstop figure mounted on a bracket over a plain scraper, 18″ × 11½″ × 14″ **475.00**

Bucket, pressed fiber, colored paper label is lithographed with picture of woman in field of forget-me-nots, "Great Northern Seed Co. - Rockford, Illinois - USA" **38.00**

Bushel basket, manufactured, rounded bottom is patched **49.00**

Cart, wrought iron, holds a bushel basket behind 12″ metal wheel, 50″ × 16″ tall **85.00**

Catalog

    F. W. Bow Nursery, 1929 ....**7.00**

    Great Northern Seed Co., color picture of onions on cover, 1930 ....**7.50**

    Hiram Sibley, Rochester, N.Y., 1882, 112 pages, 6″ × 9″ **32.50**

"Kellogg's Great Crops of Strawberries" 1923, 32 color pages, cover pictures basket of strawberries, torn cover **9.00**

Peter Henderson & Co., New York, N.Y., 1932, 8″ × 10½″ **20.00**

Stark Year Book, apple trees pictured on cover **15.00**

The Wayside Gardens Co., Mentor, Ohio, 1930, 80 pages **9.00**

Cranberry scoop (or picker)

metal, handmade from a tin can, strap handle, fifteen metal teeth welded to can, 10″ × 5″ **42.00**

metal, sliding lid with illegible patent date and manufacturer, metal T-shaped handle, wire teeth, 13″ × 7½″ × 2½″ **35.00**

wood paddle shaped back is 1½″ thick, 16″ × 8″, metal teeth are mounted to wood at a right angle, handmade **98.00**

wood with metal teeth, short rectangular handle, 12″ × 8″ × 3″ **55.00**

Sprinkling can, galvanized metal, half-gallon size, old brass sprinkler head (Country Hearth, Lexington, IL), 42.00

wood box with metal teeth, metal strap handle across top, 14″ × 9″ × 3½″ **75.00**

wood, painted red, dated 1890 ...... **75.00**

Cranberry shaker, wood handle, 14″ × 3″ round wood holder with screen at base, 40″ long **235.00**

Cultivator

5 curved iron 8″ prongs, two wood handles, 53″ **10.00**

10″ disc reel in front of three cultivators, two curved wood handles **15.00**

one row, newly painted green and yellow **30.00**

Dinner bell, cast iron

No. 3, with yoke and replaced clapper **150.00**

No. 4, with yoke **240.00**

with yoke, embossed "C.S. Bell, Hillsboro, O. #2" **150.00**

with yoke, embossed "Crystal #2" **125.00**

10″ diameter, on yoke and pole **86.00**

Duster, "Dustmaster Powder Duster - No. 36D - D.B. Smith - Utica, N.Y.," 40″ long, wood plunger handle, tube is painted orange, 16 ounce green glass reservoir **45.00**

Fence, cast iron, 200 feet with driveway gates **2900.00**

Garden ornament

cat, concrete, English, 13″ high **48.00**

duck, cast iron, 14″ high **165.00**

frog, Uhl Pottery, large **900.00**

rabbit, cast iron, ears up, 12″ high, white or black **140.00**

squirrel on a stump, Red Wing Stoneware **110.00**

two gophers on a log, Red Wing Stoneware **575.00**

Gate

cast iron, 36″ w., ornate **380.00**

"The Stewart Iron Works Co. - Covington, Ky." on shield-shaped label, seven spindles, two arrows, iron, 36″ wide **125.00**

Asparagus buncher, green cast iron, wood base with worn red stenciling, brass bands inside, 12″ × 15″ (Busch Collection), **75.00**

wire mesh over tubular frame, 36" wide
....**50.00**
Gate posts, pair, tree trunk posts with ear of
corn and leaves as finial, old black finish
on posts, new green and yellow paint on
finial, 42" high **750.00**
Grass catcher, "Rev-O-Noc - No. 8 - Grass
Catcher - Hibbard Spencer," canvas and
galvanized metal, 24" × 30" **25.00**
Herb drying net, 36" square holey cotton net
hangs from four adjustable, folding metal
arms **15.00**
Herb drying rack
three hinged sections, four round rods
each section, 60" **45.00**
three hinged sections, four square slats
each 39" × 57" section **60.00**
four hinged sections, four square slats
each 33" × 51" section, old red paint
....**120.00**
Hoe
blade with two prongs, 7" × 4", at a 75
degree angle from 5' wood handle
....**22.50**
handmade blade **12.00**
Hook, wrought iron
three hooks on one shaft, handmade, 9"
....**20.00**
five hooks at base of center shaft, handmade, 20" **25.00**
Hose, soaker, handmade from canvas, 1930
....**6.00**

*Pump, wood; original green paint with red,
yellow and black hand-painted decoration;
never used, original shipping tag from
Sears, "Not Guaranteed if Vent is Plugged,"
stenciled under handle 73" tall (Busch collection),* **275.00**

Berry box holder, maple, 28" wide, holds 4 boxes, (Mays collection), **40.00**

92

Hose reel

wood, painted red with "Columbia" stenciled in white on handle, iron wheels **60.00**

wood, two metal wheels and push handle, refinished **65.00**

Lawn mower, reel type with clippers in front of reel, "Dixon, Ill. U.S.A. - Clipper Lawn Mower" stenciled on wood handle **140.00**

Plant stand, wire, four shelves, painted white, c. 1900 ....**475.00**

Potato planter, wire and wood, "Potato Implement Co., Traverse City, Michigan," 32", c. 1925 ....**25.00**

Plow, horse drawn, two curved wood handles, one steel blade, weathered **45.00**

Pump, cistern

"Gem" in punched out letters at top of metal pump casing, new red, white and blue paint, rusted base, 11" × 23" × 40" **72.50**

"IXL Galvanized Steel Chain Pump & Tubing - Sold by _____" stenciled in black on galvanized cover each side, black iron spout, mfd. by Shriver, Cincinnati, crank handle, never used, 11" × 23" × 40" **225.00**

"The Red Cross Mfg Co. - Bluffton, Ind." embossed on handle, "Wards" on pump, new red paint, 4½' high ..**75.00**

"Red Jacket, Davenport, Iowa, L35," rusted, with pipe **35.00**

"Red Jacket, FT7," new red paint, 4' tall **57.00**

"Wistrand T 16," black cast iron, triangular lattice design at base, embossed star each side of spigot **60.00**

wooden, green paint with stenciling, 5½' tall, small iron spigot and wood handle **120.00**

wooden, worn red paint, iron spigot is embossed "Grand Rapids," wood handle, 7½' high **60.00**

wooden, "John H. Kelly - Winamac, Ind. - No. 2" stenciled in yellow on red, 5½' tall, made into a lamp **250.00**

wooden, grey and black, 4½' tall, long curved wood handle, wood spout **175.00**

Basket, ash splint, 18" × 13" × 15", notched handle, **85.00**

Rain barrel, oak staves, six metal bands, 34" tall **35.00**

Rake, wood, 18 teeth, refinished, two curved wood supports **85.00**

Salesman's sample, horse drawn push mower **3600.00**

Scythe

grass, 5½' long square wood handle, 26" blade, 19th century **35.00**

24" blade, slightly curved 5½' very weathered wood handle **5.00**

Seed bag, Donley's Super Cleaned Field and Lawn Seeds **7.50**

Seed box, "Rice's Seeds," dovetailed oak box with paper label inside top, chromolithographed pansies and woman's face in oval, 11" × 9" × 4½" **85.00**

Seed box lid, chromo-lithographed label pictures vegetables, reads "There are none better - Rush Park Seed Co. - Unrivalled Garden Seeds - Independence, Iowa," 32" × 18" **100.00**

Seed catalog

"Salzer's Seeds La Crosse, Wisc.," pictures of farm machinery on cover, sixteen color pages, 1920, 9" × 12", very good condition **20.00**

"Vaughan's," 1906 ....**24.00**

Seed catalog cover, "Vaughan's Seed Store," 1895, three hyacinths in pink, blue and white **6.00**

Seed catalog page, color lithography, vegetables, from James Vick's Seeds, 8" × 10½", c. 1930 ....**6.50**

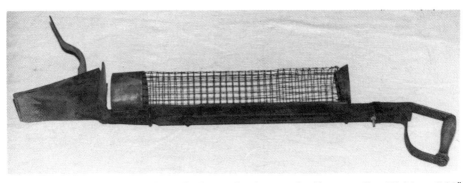

Potato planter, wire cage and wood, "Potato Implement Co - Traverse City, Michigan," 32", c. 1925 (Busch collection), **25.00**

Seed counter, oak, cast iron pulls, 12 drawers, needs some restoration **550.00**
Seed jar, pouring lid with patent #1920131 on glass fruit jar **15.00**
Seed package, 3 ounce, cardboard box with color picture, 1950s **1.50**
Seeder, hangs from a shoulder strap, canvas bag has a wheel at its base that broadcasts seed **17.50**

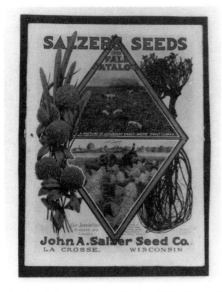

Seed catalog, Salzer's Seeds, 1920 Fall, 15 pages, color front, 8″ × 10½″ (Antique Mall of Chenoa, IL), **22.00**

Spading fork, small, Keen Kutter **90.00**
Sprayer, *see pest control chapter*
Sprinkler
  brass, "Crescent" **12.00**
  cast iron, figural duck, late 1920s ..**170.00**
Sprinkling can
  galvanized metal
    gooseneck spout with no sprinkler is 15″ long, 12″ × 11″ × 7″ oval can **30.00**
    one gallon, old triangular brass sprinkler head **42.00**
    spout has no sprinkler, one gallon **12.00**
    "Tri-Way - Triple Purpose Sprinkling Can" on paper label, two green and yellow plastic sprinkler heads, 2½″ and 1½″, 16″ × 15″, 1950s **15.00**
    with sprinkler, one gallon **20.00**
    gooseneck spout, one gallon, painted red, no sprinkler **42.00**
  metal, painted beige, old brass sprinkler head **35.00**
  "Han-D Sprinkl Can," rectangular, two gallon, green with logo in yellow cloud, 11″ × 14″, c. 1950 ....**35.00**
Stakes, for planting rows, iron, connected with chain, pair **10.00**
Tool, "Barker Weeder, Mulcher & Cultivator - Pat. Nov. 10, 1931 - David City, Nebr." **20.00**
Weed cutter, blade has a hooked end, wood handle **7.50**

Well pulley

    13″ wheel marked "I-906," cast iron, five curved spokes, one large hook …**25.00**

    wood, reel inside two wood sides, 14″ × 9″ …………………………………**125.00**

Wheelbarrow

    old green paint, 16″ metal spoked wheel …………………………………**325.00**

    old red paint over oak, metal spoked wheel …………………………**200.00**

    white paint over green, metal spoked wheel …………………………**110.00**

Wind and Weather

Weather Vanes and Lightning Rods

Weather vanes indicate the direction of the wind. They may or may not have directional arrows to aid the observer. Early weather vanes have made their way into museums as examples of American folk art. These early vanes aren't likely to show up at farm auctions today.

Most of the weather vanes found today in rural areas were factory made at the turn of the century. The best of these are copper vanes that were made by hammering sheet copper into molds. Farm animals are the most common figures represented on these vanes. Some have weighted zinc heads to balance the weight of the longer arrow. Weather took a heavy toll on wooden vanes, making them hard to find. Flat sheet-iron vanes are most commonly found. Weather vanes also decorated lightning rods and are common in the Midwest. Many zinc animal vanes with gilded zinc figures were given as premiums by seed companies.

Lightning rods are still seen on many midwestern barns. The copper or iron rods were mounted on roof peaks and were connected to a grounding wire that was buried in the earth near the building. Lightning rods could be purchased plain or with a variety of decorative copper tips, ornamental glass lightning rod balls or pendants, and weather vanes. Lightning rod balls may have served only as decoration, but some claim that they broke when the lightning rod was struck by lightning, alerting the farmer to look for damage.

Lightning rod balls are usually $3\frac{1}{2}''$ to $4\frac{1}{2}''$ in diameter and have a hole at each end. Sometimes these holes are protected with metal collars. Balls were made in several colors and types of glass. The most common colors are white and blue opaque glass, clear, and amethyst (caused by exposure of clear glass to the sun). Mercury glass, cased glass, flashed glass, and slag glass balls are very desirable. Lightning rod balls have been categorized by collectors into 34 basic patterns.

1. Burgoon or Dot and Dash, round with embossed dots and dashes.

2. Chestnut, like two doorknobs attached face to face (10 colors).

3. D & S, Japanese lantern shape, embossed "D&S" (15 colors).

4. Diddie Blitzen, embossed "Diddie Blitzen" (9 colors).

5. Doorknob, like two doorknobs face to face, indented equator (11 colors plus slag).

6. Ear of Corn, egg-shaped, resembles corn on a cob (6 colors).

7. Electra Cone, like two funnels, embossed "Electra" (10 colors).

8. Electra Round, round, embossed "Electra" (11 colors).

9. Hawkeye, embossed "Hawkeye" (10 colors).

10. JFG, embossed "JFG" (3 colors).

11. K-Ball, initial "K" at base of collar (9 colors).

12. Maher, embossed "Maher Manufacturing Co." (6 colors).

13. Mast, embossed "Trade MAST Mark" (6 colors).

14. Moon and Star, embossed with moon and stars (13 colors).

15. National, Belted, 5″, raised band lettered "National" (6 colors).

16. National, Round, 4½″, raised letters "National" at equator (7 colors).

17. Onion, onion shaped (3 colors).

18. Patent '77, marked "Pat'd 77″ (3 sizes, 3 or 4 colors).

19. Patent '78, marked "Pat'd 78″ (3 or 4 colors).

20. Plain, round (4 sizes, 30 colors).

21. Pleat, pointed, vertical pleats (4 sizes, 6 colors).

22. Pleat, round, or Barnett, pleats are rounded (7 colors).

23. Quilt, flat, incised lines form flat diamonds (13 colors).

24. Quilt, raised, incised lines form raised diamonds (8 colors).

25. R. H. F, daisies marked "R," "H," and "F" (6 colors).

26. Ribbed, Grape, equator of grapes, panels (10 colors).

27. Ribbed, Horizontal, or Peewee, stepped concentric rings (8 colors).

28. S Company, "S. Co." in diamond at top (8 colors).

29. Shinn, Belted, embossed "W.C. SHINN MFG CO." (8 colors).

30. Shinn, System, embossed "SHINN SYSTEM" (7 colors).

31. SLR Company, embossed "SLR CO." on equator, no metal caps (6 colors).

32. Staircase, ceramic, staircase, wide-paneled equator.

33. Swirl, raised swirls (9 colors).

34. Thompson, ribbed, "GEO. E. THOMPSON LIGHTNING ROD CO., EST 1910" (5 colors).

Lightning rod pendants hung, usually in sets of four, from cast-iron arms or from wires attached to the lightning rod. They were more susceptible to breakage than balls. They have been categorized into eight patterns and are most common in blue and in white opaque glass.

Windmills

Windmills have harnessed the power of the wind for centuries. In America, they were essential to the success of the settlers of the Great Plains, where rain was scarce and wind to pump water from underground was plentiful. Early wooden windmills provided power for grinding grain and pumping water.

Windmills brought water to farms, businesses, and municipalities all over

America from 1850 until the 1930s, when gas or electric motors powered most pumps. The Halladay Standard Windmill, patented in 1854, was the first self regulating, manufactured windmill. Between 1880 and 1935, 6.5 million windmills were sold in the United States.

Wooden windmills had blades that folded in strong winds to prevent overflowing tanks or destruction of the mechanism. The 10- to 14-foot-diameter wheels were balanced with a vane or a weight.

Windmill weights, cast in iron in figural or functional forms, were made by many manufacturers from 1880 to 1930. Heavy figural weights were mounted at the end of an arm that ran into the hub of the wheel and served to counterbalance the weight of the wheel. Smaller, simpler governor weights regulated the speed of the wheel.

Windmill weights were usually cast in one piece but were sometimes full-bodied to allow insertion of weight. They were shaped like roosters, bulls, horses, moons, stars, eagles, squirrels, buffalos, and letters of the alphabet. Some were mounted on a box so that weight could be added. Most were dipped in paint, usually black. Many were repainted by farmers in later years.

The steel windmill was introduced in the 1880s in America. The smaller, lighter-weight wheel was able to turn to catch the wind as the direction of the current changed.

Whirligigs

Whirligigs are ornamental wind-powered figures. They were mounted on fence posts, porch rails, or on their own stakes. The wind caused the figures to repeat a movement endlessly. Some merely turned their arms or wings, while others, powered by a wheel, performed varied and complicated tasks.

Older whirligigs usually depict a single figure with paddlelike arms. Carved from solid wood and painted, some whirligigs are examples of fine folk art, depending on the originality of design and the skill of the carver.

More modern whirligigs, usually cut from plywood, are still being made. More complicated examples are powered by a wheel at one end. A rod connects the wheel to movable figures. The most common of these whirligigs depict a man sawing, chopping, or milking a cow. Less common are whirligigs with patriotic, occupational, or cartoon themes.

Reproductions

Establishing the age of a weather vane is complicated by the fact that weather vanes have been produced consistently over the last century. New reproductions, especially copper ones, can be aged to look like old vanes. The weathered patina on an old copper vane, though, is green to black and is streaked and mottled by rain and wind. New patina, created with acid, is more evenly colored, is a powdery turquoise blue, and often has drip marks where natural elements wouldn't have left them. Large reproduction copper vanes, available since the 1970s, are available; they have hollow ornaments and copper balls above and below the directionals.

Old reproduction vanes often show enough age to enable them to pass as valuable 19th-century originals. Old rusty sheets of tin can be made into copies of valuable antique weather vanes. Check the cut edges for aging consistent with the surface of the vane. The tube that the vane rotates on should show signs of wear. If a vane is original, its tail and its figure should balance. Traces of gold leaf or zinc parts are often signs that a vane is old. Cast-aluminum weather vanes made in the 1950s are now selling as collectibles, but many are still in production and sell new at lower prices than their older duplicates.

Thompson lightning rod balls are being made in milk glass, amber, cobalt, aqua, and red. Some rare balls are being reproduced from old molds.

Windmill weights are still being produced by a company in Nebraska. These weights are not reproductions but are made as part of a line of replacement parts for windmills. They are cast iron and should be detectable by looking for signs of age. A standing horse with a cut tail is one of this company's weights. The Hummer Rooster #184 with short or long shaft, barnacle-eye chicken, buffalo, squirrel, "BOSS" bull, Fairbanks flat bull, long-tail horse, and chicken with five tail feathers are also still made in pot metal or cast iron with rough, grainy surfaces.

Newsletters

Lightning rod balls: *Crown Point*, 884 Lulu Avenue, Las Vegas, NV 89119

Windmills: *Windmiller's Gazette*, P.O. Box 507, Rio Vista, TX 76093

Recommended Reading

Bruner, Mike, and Rod Krupka, eds, *The Complete Book of Lightning Rod Balls with Prices*. Ortonville, Mich.: Authors, 1982.

Simpson, Milt. *Windmill Weights*. Newark, N.J.: Johnson and Simpson, 1985.

Sites, Donald E., *Windmills and Windmill Weights*. Grinnell, Kans.: Author, 1977.

Lightning rod

copper, plain blue ball, 64" tall **42.00**

copper, "Farm Master," 18" tall on four legs that mount to peak of roof ...**30.00**

copper, plain white ball, circular copper ornament with five spikes at top of 6' rod, vane with 30" iron arrow and hand-made flat tin Holstein cow painted black and white **300.00**

copper, plain white ball, 5' rod has iron tripod base, 20" aluminum arrow with tin tail **68.00**

twisted iron, copper spearhead ornament, plain amethyst ball, 9' high **85.00**

Lightning rod vane, hollow zinc running horse with original gilt finish, horse is 14" × 10", on 32" cast iron arrow, **125.00**

twisted iron with tarnished copper tip, 5½' tall **25.00**

twisted iron with plain blue ball **25.00**

Lightning rod ball

Electra Round, blue opaque **30.00**

Moon and Star, milk glass **30.00**

National, belted, milk glass **45.00**

Plain, amber **45.00**

Plain, blue opaque glass **15.00**

Plain, clear glass, has turned purple **17.50**

Plain, mercury, metal collars, good condition **50.00**

Plain, milk glass **12.50**

Pleat, pointed, metal bands, milk glass **17.50**

Quilt, flat, blue opaque **55.00**

Quilt, flat, dark amber **65.00**

Shinn, belted, copper bands, milk glass **35.00**

Lightning rod pendant

blue milk glass, no metal cap **45.00**

Lightning rod vane

iron arrow, ornate cast iron frame holds red slag glass rectangle **75.00**

iron arrow, missing zinc ornament, "Kretzer" on arrow, circular copper ornament with 5 spikes at top of 6' tall copper rod **47.50**

iron arrow, plain red glass ball, no directionals, on lightning rod, 30" tall **125.00**

rusted cow, 14" × 8" on 32" iron arrow, mounted on 37" copper lightning rod, shorter arrow above has an ornament with "KING" enclosed in a diamond, directionals, cone-shaped ornament at top **1800.00**

sheet metal, flat running horse, 24" long, rusted, on old copper lightning rod, 6' tall, no directionals, probably made recently from old materials **125.00**

zinc cow with bullet hole on iron arrow, "JAMES" on arrow, cone shaped top ornament, 32" × 21" **95.00**

zinc cow, gilded, on cast iron arrow, no directionals or lightning rod **135.00**

zinc pig, on iron arrow, 24", premium from feed company **145.00**

zinc running horse on cast iron 24" arrow,

Whirligig, two flat figures saw log, wooden and metal propeller is 23", green trees are 13" tall, 31" long, 1940s, **120.00**

hollow, premium from feed company, 5′ tall copper lightning rod and white glass ball with embossed moon and star design, no directionals **185.00**

Pinback (campaign-type) button

Challenge Wind Mill and Feed Mill Company, Batavia, Ill., pictures windmill parts **33.00**

Samson Wind Mills, pictures metal windmill **32.00**

Weather vane

aluminum, stamped, black rooster and directionals, 1950s, 24″ high **32.50**

copper, full bodied, draft horse, 13″ horse on a 40″ vane that is a 2″ square rod, rudder below horse **875.00**

sheet metal, cow, c. 1900 ....**325.00**

Whirligig

carved, four small propellers on one large central propeller, green and white, c. 1920 ....**425.00**

carved, sea captain, blue double breasted jacket, white pants, hat, propeller arms **395.00**

flat figures, plywood, one yellow and green man saws log with red bucksaw, missing propeller, 13″ × 10″, c. 1950 ....**65.00**

flat figure, plywood, girl in yellow dress churns, 1940s **75.00**

flat figures, plywood, two American Indians paddle canoe, 20″, 1950s **125.00**

flat figure, woman scrubs over tub, large slatted propeller, 29″ long, early twentieth century **400.00**

flat figures, thin wood, FDR plays tug of war with Hitler, red, white, and blue propeller powers figures, very good condition, faded, 1940s **325.00**

flat figures, thin wood, man sawing log with bucksaw, green, gold, and red paint, propeller missing, 1920s ...**65.00**

Windmill

steel

Aermotor, RA Model, open gear, 12 foot wheel, unrestored, complete except for tail and tail pivot **900.00**

Aermotor, 1897 Model, 8 foot wheel, flat spoke, restored to excellent condition **1600.00**

Aermotor, 1899 Model, 8 foot wheel, unrestored, complete **750.00**

Aermotor, 1903 Model, 8 foot wheel, restored **1000.00**

Aermotor, 1915 Model 502, 8 foot wheel, excellent original condition, made only one year **1600.00**

Challenge "Dandy," 8 foot wheel, single open gear, partially restored **600.00**

Fairbanks Morse, 8 foot wheel, single open gear, unrestored, excellent sheet metal **700.00**

Gem parts, 8 foot wheel, tail, hub, and small parts **120.00**

King parts, 8 foot wheel, complete except for gear box **95.00**

wooden, 10 foot wheel

Baker Monitor Vaneless, football weight style, restored and complete **900.00**

Dempster No. 3 Vaneless, unrestored, all iron including weight box and bobtail horse **700.00**

Eclipse, unrestored, all iron including crescent moon weight **550.00**

Fairbanks Morse Vaneless, unrestored, original restorable wheel, no weight box **600.00**

Original Raymond Vaneless, restored and complete **800.00**

Ozark Vaneless, restored and complete **1000.00**

Ozark Vaneless, iron parts only **650.00**

Pipe Raymond Vaneless, unrestored, all iron including "W" weight ...**550.00**

Windmill, miniature, handmade wooden base painted silver and red, metal wheel, 20″ tall **70.00**

Windmill section, galvanized metal, 4 blades **75.00**

Windmill weight, cast iron

bull, flat, "Fairbury, Nebr." in raised letters, mounted on a wooden base, 24½″ × 1⅛″ × 18¼″ **875.00**

bull, flat, painted to resemble a Hereford, reddish brown and white, 24″ × 18″, 10″ × 18″ metal base **1100.00**

crescent moon, regulator weight, "417," Dempster, 10½″ **85.00**

Windmill weight, rooster, "10 FT NO 2," painted red, 16″ × 14″ including weight box (Hintze Auction, Mazon, IL), 875.00

governor, rectangular, 3″ × 4″ × 6″, weighs about 20 lb **7.00**

horse, short squared tail, old black and white paint, Dempster, mounted on a 6″ wide repainted green weight box lid, "87J" in raised letters on base, 17¼″ × ¾″ × 16⅝″, 13 pounds **325.00**

rooster, full bodied, traces of white paint, elaborately detailed with feathered thighs, detailed comb, and long tail in deep relief, rectangular wooden base, 18″ × 3¼″ × 20″ **1290.00**

rooster, "Hummer E184," Elgin Wind Power and Pump Co., Elgin, Ill., 9⅞″ × 1¾″ × 8⅞″, 9 pounds **375.00**

rooster, four squared off tail feathers, C-shaped open ended base, traces of red and white paint, 18″ × 1¾″ × 19½″ **1275.00**

squirrel, on iron base, white paint, eye hole and hole in front paw, 13½″ × 3″ × 19¼″ **1400.00**

Laundry and Cleaning

The technological revolution of the 20th century had its effect on laundry chores, but many changes came later to rural homes than to city ones. Running water, water heaters, electric irons, washing machines and wringers, manufactured laundry soaps, starches, and bluing and later softeners, automatic washers and dryers, and wrinkle-free synthetic fabrics changed not only the labors of laundry but the standards of cleanliness.

Traditionally, Monday has been known as wash day and Tuesday has been set aside for ironing. Wash day involved soaking, treating for stains, washing, boiling, rinsing, bluing, starching, and drying. Ironing involved not only pressing or ruffling clothes but heating the stove to keep irons hot or building and maintaining a charcoal fire in charcoal irons. Soap was made in quantities that lasted several wash days.

The earliest washing devices were iron pots, which were filled with water and heated. The clothes were agitated with wash sticks and pounders. The wash stick, also called a mangle or battling stick, was a wooden paddle that sometimes had a forklike end. Pounders were wooden or metal plungers on han-

dles that were long enough to keep the launderer away from the heat.

By the 20th century, water could be heated on a cookstove or on special laundry stoves. Laundry stoves are smaller and often plainer than heating stoves. Usually made of cast iron, they are short and often rectangular, with a heating surface designed for an oblong boiler. Copper, tin, or galvanized metal boilers were used to heat water for washing. Boilers had metal or wooden handles and copper or tin lids.

The washing was done in washtubs of staved wood or galvanized metal. Simple wooden benches held the washtubs at scrubbing height. Manufactured plungers agitated the laundry while it soaked in the wash or rinse tub. Plungers were made of tin or steel in single or double sizes. Most had wooden handles.

A washboard was used to rub the fabric clean. The first washboards were handmade from a board that had a corrugated surface and a handle. Later, rollers were fitted into wooden frames to make the ridged surface less likely to wear down quickly. Manufacturers produced washboards with surfaces of wood, brass, earthenware, copper, zinc, tin, glass, graniteware, plastic, and aluminum in standard, lingerie, and children's sizes. During the World Wars, shortages of metal caused manufacturers to turn to wooden and glass surfaces. Victory brand washboards were made during World War I, and some World War II boards were marked with the letter *V*.

Wringers were an improvement over the old method of twisting the water out of a piece of cloth. Wringers were manufactured with wooden frames that attached to a tub, a washbench or washing machine. Their rollers were made of wood or were rubber coated. Folding bench wringers held a tub at each side of a built-in or attached wringer.

Washing machines were depicted as often as laundry tubs in magazine ads by the mid-1920s. Their tubs were made from metal, graniteware, or wood (usually cypress). They stood on their own legs or on separate stands. Manufacturers came up with an abundance of ingenious and not-so-ingenious methods of agitating and wringing laundry. Machines were agitated by paddles, pounders, corrugated rockers, or arms. They were powered by a hand crank, a foot motion, a rocker bar, an up-and-down dasher-type mechanism, or electricity. Their interiors were often corrugated metal. Galvanized metal was a turn-of-the-century improvement that kept the metal parts from rusting.

Soap was made from lye and lard. Lye was obtained by pouring boiling water through a wood funnel filled with wood ashes. The water would be evaporated out and the lye mixed with lard or bacon fat. While the mixture cooked, it might be stirred with a solid or pierced wooden paddle that bleached white from exposure to the lye. The soap might be used in a soft form or it could be cooked until it hardened. Soft soap was kept in stoneware or wooden containers and sometimes was dipped out with a special scoop made of sassafras or another aromatic wood. Hard soap was cut into chunks or bars or could be poured into soap molds.

After the laundry had been wrung dry, it was hung on a clothesline or a drying rack. The clothesline was sometimes handmade from hemp, and sometimes manufactured. It was strung between poles, buildings, or trees. Clothesline winders of wood or metal stored the line while it was not in use. Drying racks were made in many shapes and sizes, from collapsible umbrella-types to folding panels to wall-hung groups of rods. Laundry baskets, handmade or manufactured of splint or wicker, held the laundry as it waited to be dried, ironed, or folded. Laundry carts held baskets at a convenient working height. Clothespins were sometimes hand whittled but were usually manufactured. Bags of clothespins hung from the clothesline by a hook and could be pushed along ahead of the hung clothes. Bags were sometimes made by sewing a small dress together at the hem, and were often a craft item, fashioned especially for their function.

Rugs and pillows were also cleaned by hanging them on the clothesline and beating them with rug beaters. Rug beaters are made of twisted iron, willow, or bent wood in many designs.

Ironing involved not only a variety of irons, but also mangles, ironing boards, fluters, trivets, iron heaters, linen presses, smoothers, and stretchers.

Clothes were smoothed with several tools. Wooden or glass smoothers were not heated, but were repeatedly passed over the cloth as it dried flat. They had flat surfaces and handles, or were mushroom shaped. Long glass canes were sometimes used to smooth bedclothes. Mangles put the wrinkled cloth through rollers or pressed it between heated flat surfaces. Stocking and glove stretchers held stockings and gloves flat while they dried.

Flatirons could be heated on a stove, on a kerosene heater, or over a gas jet. Flatiron heaters held a number of irons over the heat source.

Box irons had an opening that admitted interchangeable slugs, so that a cooled slug could be quickly replaced with a heated one. Flatirons with detachable wooden or metal handles were sold in sets of three, and, like box irons, allowed bases to be heated while another was in use.

Individual flatirons were usually made of cast iron, but were sometimes formed of sheet metal or cast in alloys that contained bronze, copper, nickel, or aluminum. Some of the major foundries that made flatirons were Enterprise, Ober, Geneva, Streeter, and Colebrookdale (which also made Mrs. Potts' irons). Flatirons are sometimes called sadirons. This name is derived from an obsolete meaning of the word *sad*, which was "heavy."

A charcoal iron was heated by an internal fire that had to be tended during its use. Ashes had to be emptied and nuggets of charcoal added to keep the iron at the right temperature. Charcoal irons had a flue to vent the fire and were usually cast iron or brass.

Gas irons made ironing a much more pleasant task in warm weather. More convenient than the charcoal iron, they also didn't require heating a stove and could be used outside. Gas irons were made of polished metal or had enameled finishes. The reservoir that held the gas was sometimes brass. A small pump was required to fill the reservoir.

Electric irons began to replace flatirons after World War I and by 1929, flatirons were no longer being advertised. By 1929, 98% of city dwellers were using electric irons, but it would be two decades later that remote rural households had electricity and could delegate the flatiron to doorstop status. Mrs. Potts' irons were produced until 1952.

Polishing irons with convex bottoms and/or curved edges left a desired sheen on some fabrics. Nickel-plated soles sometimes enhanced the iron's polishing ability and the rounded edges kept the iron from leaving marks.

Goffering irons, ruffling scissors, fluting irons, and plaiters were all used to pleat or ruffle curtains, caps, petticoats, and dresses. Goffering irons were narrow barrels that were heated and then remained stationary on a stand while the fabric was moved around them to create a ruffle. Ruffling scissors had two, three, or five prongs. They were used to pleat curtains or curl hair. Fluting irons were made in many forms, including pairs of ridged rollers or rockers or rollers with matching rectangular, ridged bases.

Special-purpose irons—such as curved collar irons; handled egg or ball irons; miniature irons; and long, tear-shaped irons—were used to smooth puffed or narrow sleeves, bonnets, flounces, fine lace or embroidery, delicate celluloid collars, and silk garments.

Many households had a tailor's iron. Tailors were often itinerants and did not carry their own irons. Tailor's irons were not heated, but smoothed seams with their weight. They usually weigh between 12 and 16 pounds but can weigh as much as 60 pounds. Tailor's irons are cast iron with a handle that is metal, often twisted.

Linen presses held folded linens flat while they were stored. They are made up of two flat surfaces held tightly together by a screw or clamp mechanism. They were sometimes built into a cupboard that was made specifically to store linens.

Any flat surface could be used for an ironing board. Sometimes tables or benches were covered with layers of wool and used as an ironing surface. Ironing boards were handmade or manufactured with wooden surfaces and wooden or metal legs.

Heated irons were kept on iron stands made especially for that purpose. Iron stands are usually called trivets today, although, technically, trivets are three-legged stands. Flatiron trivets were standard laundry equipment from the mid-1800s until World War I. Almost every foundry made them, sometimes as gifts to purchasers of stoves, as advertisements, or to go with a particular flatiron or set of irons. Trivets were made in thousands of designs. Spade-shaped trivets are the oldest type. Wrought-iron trivets were made by amateur and professional blacksmiths and are usually older than cast-iron ones. Twisted wire and cast brass were also used to make trivets.

Tips for collectors

On handleless trivets, look for file marks that might be hiding signs of broken off handles. Wooden handles are desirable. Wrought-iron examples were individually produced and, therefore, are one-of-a-kind items, whereas cast-iron trivets were molded and mass produced.

Miniature irons are considered to be 4½″ or smaller and make up a special collecting category. They are often sold as toys.

Iron bases without handles are not worth much. It can be fun to try to put together a set, but the breakable wooden handles are much harder to find than the bases.

Unusual washboards are more valuable than common ones. Among the most desirable washboards are handmade wooden examples with carved decoration and boards with gray or speckled graniteware surfaces. Solid blue graniteware, although hard to find, is the most common color in graniteware washboards. Clear glass surfaces are common, but green or light blue is very desirable. Small washboards are usually lingerie boards and not the more expensive children's size. Children's boards often have cute names, not just "Junior" or "Midget."

Reproductions

Washboards are still being manufactured for hand washing and for the craft market. They have brass or tin surfaces and carry the brand names "Dubl Handle" and "Maid-Rite." Don't assume that rusty washboards are old.

In the 1980s, many pillow beaters and rug beaters were produced. Pillow beaters and rug beaters in fanciful shapes should be assumed to be new, unless there is strong evidence to prove otherwise. The most telling evidence of reproduction rug beaters is the new look and feel of their wooden handles.

Unusual irons are being recast. Sharp edges, messy joints, and file marks along edges are signs of a newly cast iron. New cast iron is grainy and grayish in color. Paint should be worn in the right places. New rust is orangey red. Old rust is almost black.

Newer miniature irons are sometimes marked with manufacturer's names. The duck or swan iron has been reproduced; the old duck has a bump on its chest; but the new version doesn't. A reproduction of the 4-inch Asbestos Tourist Iron is missing the patent date. Old miniature brass box irons have turned posts, and the new ones have straight posts. Spade-shaped rope-handled miniature irons are new. Massengill irons were given away as advertising premiums in about 1960.

Charcoal irons have been reproduced in ornate styles. Irons with rooster finials and a *K* on the handle are reproductions. The original ones had a *G* on the handle. Old brass charcoal irons and irons with figural finials are imported from Europe.

Trivets for irons have been reproduced for many years. Some of the most desirable trivets were reproduced in the 1960s. By now, these reproductions have reached a respectable age, but they are not the authentic antiques they pretend to be. Some of the reproduced designs are Lincoln Drape, Love Birds, Lantz, Good Luck, Jenny Lind, Ober Leaf, Heart and Urn, Order of Cincinnati, and Grape. The Colt Firearms Company reproduced the Colt trivet recently as an advertising giveaway.

Old trivets were usually cast iron, although some were brass. Some reproductions are aluminum, pot metal, or brass. Check the metal with a magnet. Pot metal, aluminum, brass, or copper won't stick. A cast-iron trivet with depressed numbers or letters is probably not an original. Old castings were more likely to be marked with raised letters. Look for signs of wear on the feet and where the iron might have rested.

Recommended Reading

Hankenson, Dick. *Trivets, Old and Repro.* Des Moines: Wallace-Homestead, 1972.

Glissman, A. H., *The Evolution of the Sad Iron.* Oceanside, Calif.: MB Printing, 1970.

Kelly, Rob Roy, and James Ellwood. *A Collector's Guide to Trivets & Stands.* Lima, Ohio: Golden Era Publications, 1990.

Bench
    folding, wood slats, can hold two laundry tubs, 42″ × 12″, wringer could be attached at center **42.00**

Mangle, two wooden rollers, iron gears and crank, 27″ wide (Illinois Farm Bureau photo/ Country Hearth, Lexington, IL), **40.00**

folding, 48″ × 15″ × 20″, painted white **25.00**

folding, Anchor Brand, with matching rubber wringer, very clear stenciling **155.00**

folding, "Anchor Brand Princess Eclipse Die Hard Folding Bench" **115.00**

folding, wood slats, Horseshoe Brand rubber wringer attached **120.00**

four slats, X-shaped legs fold under, 48″ × 15½″ top **20.00**

mesquite slab, on hand hewn legs that go through top, 80″ × 22″ × 25″ **1200.00**

pine, handmade, 52″ × 20″, old blue paint on legs **120.00**

pine, weathered, 48″ × 16″ **35.00**

wood, hand-hewn, 4′ long, unusually thick top **88.00**

wood, old blue paint, 6″ deep aprons each side, bootjack ends, 34″ × 15″ × 18″ **110.00**

wood, old green paint, bootjack ends, 4′ long **75.00**

Bucket bench, pine, 28″ × 11″ × 18″, shelf 9″ below top, varnished **215.00**

Boilers

chrome plated, no lid **30.00**

chrome plated, with lid, wood handles, excellent condition **60.00**

copper, bent, wood handles, no lid **20.00**

copper, with copper lid, wood handles, polished **115.00**

copper, with copper lid, wood handles, unpolished **75.00**

copper, polished, wood handles, no lid **55.00**

copper, rusted tin lid **37.50**

galvanized metal, red wood handles, lid **35.00**

Boiler lid, tin, wood handle **8.00**

Box

"Kingsford's Silver Gloss Starch - 6 lb- National Starch Co.," wood, dovetailed corners, sliding lid, refinished, 11″ × 7″ × 5½″ **32.00**

Larkin Soap, wood handles, 24″ × 15″, open **25.00**

Cart, wood, holds laundry basket, folds, old red and white paint, wood wheels ..**27.50**

Clothesline reel

metal, red, for use inside the house, enclosed reel with crank holds two lines, 2″ × 3½″ × 4″ **12.00**

painted wood, blue frame, grey and red rods, knob one side, 14″ × 12″ ...**21.00**

"Saturn - Pat. Appld For - United Royalties Corp., N.Y.," two lines, 4″ diameter **27.50**

Soap mold, walnut, hand carved, gouges filled with plaster, 10¼″ × 10¼″ × 2″ (Klein Collection), **95.00**

wood, handmade, H-shaped, 12″ × 8″
....**7.00**
wood, 1½″ diameter rods, refinished
....**15.00**
Clothespin bag
    canvas bag on metal hanger, "Champion Stay Open Clothespin Bag" printed picture of woman hanging checked cloth on line, wire top, originally 49 cents, 14″ × 10″ bag, 1950s **9.00**
    canvas bag on metal hanger, "Genuine Pfister Hybrids," red logo **8.00**
    canvas bag on metal hanger, "Purina Poultry Chows," red and white checkerboard at top and bottom of bag, hens and chick on blue panel at center **22.50**
    child's dress sewn together at bottom, red gingham, hangs on bent wire hanger **7.50**
Crimper, cast iron, clamps down, wood knob, "AMERICAN Pat. Aug. 19, 1879," 8½″ × 6″ × 6″ **115.00**
Drying rack
    folding, wooden, large **32.00**
    folding, wooden, accordion-type ...**30.00**
    hangs on wall, eight bars are hinged to hang or extend, no manufacturer's mark **40.00**
    hangs on wall, "Favorite - L. Hopkins - North Girard, Pa.," eight 28″ flat rods fold down **45.00**
    hangs on wall, "Horse Shoe Brand Clothes Wringer - Empire Clothes Dryer," 10 flat rods hang or extend **135.00**

hangs on wall, iron back, nine poplar arms, dated Mar. 17, 1891, refinished, lock works **125.00**
umbrella type, 55″ tall, 2″ square standard supported by four 13″ metal legs, 17 27″ wood arms hang or extend from iron center embossed "STERLING Pat. 2-2-26," traces of green paint **125.00**
umbrella type, round wood rods, aluminum top **25.00**
umbrella type, sixteen 24″ round wooden dowels hang from ropes through circular metal top, ropes are drawn taut to extend rods, two board stand, four wood feet, 56″ tall **95.00**
Duster, two colored bristles make a 6″ × 12″ cylinder, red turned wood handle, 24″ **15.00**
Dustpan, gray speckled graniteware, worn edges **35.00**
Fluting iron
    Geneva Hand Fluter, rocker type, cast iron, with rectangular base **50.00**
    "Geneva Hand Fluter," "Geneva, Ill." on handle, cast iron rocker, top only **20.00**
    "Geneva Hand Fluter Improved," brass fluting surfaces on base and top, "Geneva, Ill." on handle, "HEATER." in raised letters on tops of two heating slugs, 4″ × 5½″ base **100.00**
    "M. Greenwood Co. - Pat. Nov. 20, 1866," 9″ square base **145.00**
    Shepard Hardware, roller, flat base, 2 heater slugs, and handle for slugs **225.00**

Tailor's iron, pitted cast iron, 20½″ × 2″ × 6″ (Illinois Farm Bureau photo), **25.00**

Gasoline iron, Montgomery Ward, 1930s (Country Hearth, Lexington, IL), **12.50**

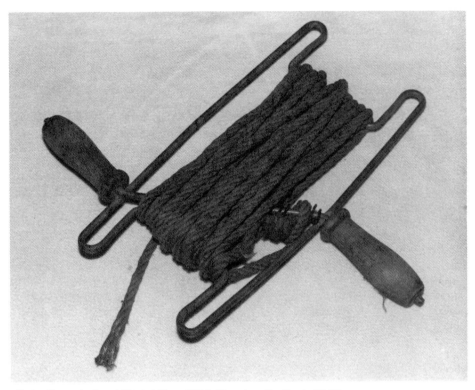

Clothesline winder, 12" × 12", c. 1920 (Busch collection), **12.00**

Iron
　cast iron
　　Enterprise No. 6 ....**14.00**
　　small, Wapak #2, 4⅛" × 2½" **30.00**
　charcoal, cast iron
　　patented 1859 ....**75.00**
　　stenciled "Classen Bros. & Co -Ithaca, NY" on curved metal hand guard under wood handle, front flue ..**135.00**
　　Colebrookdale, with detachable wood handle **18.50**
　gas
　　Coleman, blue enamel iron and reservoir, chrome, excellent condition **60.00**
　　Coleman, blue enameled, brass reservoir **55.00**
　　"The Monitor - Pat. Apr. 14, 1905," gas tank at front **125.00**
　　rusted chrome, triangular reservoir, Wards **20.00**
　　Sensible, wood handle **40.00**

tailor's, "Laclede 14," embossed scallops around base, painted gold, 10½" × 2¾" × 6½" **39.00**
tailor's, raised "20," twisted iron handle, 11" × 2½" × 6" **35.00**
Irons, set of 3 bases and one wood handle, bases are embossed "A.C. Williams - Ravenna, Ohio" and numbered "1," "2," and "3" **50.00**
Ironing board
　all wood, manufactured, green legs, adjustable **15.00**
　all wood, manufacturer's label on top, refinished **22.50**
　handmade, thick wood legs, 65" × 15" **40.00**
Laundry basket
　manufactured, wide splint, wire handles **50.00**
　splint, handmade, two wood handles **135.00**
　wicker **35.00**

Laundry stove, cast iron

"Columbus Iron Works - Columbus, Ga. - 26 Big Box," 13" × 36" × 22" **50.00**

"Eagle" embossed on front, two burners, deep ash lip at front, usable condition, 11½" × 32" × 26" **150.00**

Rockwood Stove Co., No. 1 ....**135.00**

Laundry tub

galvanized metal, round, metal handles **12.00**

galvanized metal, wood handles, red stripe, round **25.00**

Oil can, Maytag, blue, white and orange, squeeze can with tapered nozzle, 2½" × 5" **35.00**

Oil measure, aluminum, embossed "Maytag" on top, two ounce **35.00**

Plaiter, "Young's Improved Plaiter" and instructions on paper label on back, 66 metal bands across 10" × 15½" wood back **55.00**

Pump, for gas iron, Coleman, chromed **6.00**

Rug beater

bentwood, simple loop, wood handle, remnants of paper label on flat handle **45.00**

braided wire loop, wood handle, 28" × 5" **25.00**

fly swatter shape, wire grid, copper and green finial, 34" long **18.00**

simple wire loop, wood handle **12.00**

twisted wire design, wood handle, 21" × 5" **15.00**

twisted wire design, red wood handle **17.50**

Sadiron heater

cast iron, burns coal oil or kerosene, "Brightest & Best," reservoir in base, 11" × 8" × 10" **225.00**

for stovetop, holds three irons, c. 1900 ....**110.00**

Slop pot, ivory granite with green edges, matching lid, bail with green wood handle **28.00**

Soap

lye, creamy yellow-colored chunk **4.00**

Octagon, by Colgate, red striped wrapper **2.00**

Swan's, blue wrapper, bar **4.00**

Washboard, glass scrubbing surface, 24" × 12½" (Sharkey collection), **22.00**

Soap dish, blue enameled, hangs on wall, 5" wide **22.00**

Soap making tub, hand hewn wood, square plug with handle fits into hole in bottom, 26" × 14" × 9" **100.00**

Iron base, Griswold, No. 616, 7" × 3½" × 2½" (Klein collection), **8.00**

111

Soap paddle, all wood, four holes in 7″ × 9″ paddle, bleached white from use, 20″ long **30.00**

Stocking stretcher

maple, embossed "10½," 33″ long, 7 1½″ holes **32.50**

maple, no drying holes, 32″ long **28.00**

maple, 24″ long, adult size **22.50**

Sweeper, "Bissell Century," ball bearing sweeper, wood case and handle **12.00**

Plunger, oak, hand made, rods fit through holes to push plunger up and down, 8″ × 25″ (Ted Diamond photo/Eisele collection), 22.50

Tin

Maytag, one pint, pour spout, color advertising **20.00**

Maytag Motor Oil, one quart, full, very good condition **30.00**

Trivet

brass, "Home Sweet Home," peg feet, c. 1890 ....**75.00**

cast iron

Colebrookdale, crown design **14.00**

"Double Point IWANTU Comfort Iron - Strause Gas Iron Co. Phila. Pa. USA," four feet, 7½″ × 4″ **40.00**

Geneva, W. H. Howell, H-shaped design at center, scalloped lip **8.50**

Geneva, W. H. Howell, "H" shaped design at center, plain lip **14.00**

Geneva, W. H. Howell, intertwined "H" and "Co" at center **20.00**

Griswold, No. 1728 ....**25.00**

Griswold, No. 1902 ....**25.00**

"IWANTU Comfort Iron - Strause Gas Iron Co. - Phila. Pa. USA," 4″ × 6½″ **37.50**

Peerless, pointed oval, old black finish **25.00**

pointed oval, "The W Royal" **32.00**

"Sensible" in cut out letters, 6″ × 3¾″, lid lifter one end, four feet **25.00**

spade shaped, Cleveland Foundry **18.00**

with lid lifter one end, round ornament at center, 3¾″ × 2″ **12.00**

"1884" in horseshoe, three legs, handle, 4″ × 7½″ **75.00**

Wrought iron

elongated heart shape, three short legs, 7″ long, c. 1850 ....**175.00**

triangular, three legs, 3″ wood handle with copper ferrule, 6″ × 6″ × 2″ **45.00**

Vacuum, hand pumped, "National - Harvey Stone Sales Co. - Philadelphia and Chicago - Patented Dec. 26, 1911," 31″ long **75.00**

Wash basin, gray graniteware, 12″ diameter **20.00**

Washboard

aluminum, "Universal Soap Saving Washboard" **12.50**

aluminum surface, "Hand-E" **32.00**

Bear Easy, Columbia Washboard Co., bear
  logo **25.00**
brass scrubbing surface
  "Brass King" on wood frame, refin-
    ished **17.50**
  "Champion" on wood frame **30.00**
  "Shapleigh's" on wood frame **20.00**
  "White Metal No. MM," wood and
    metal frame, polished, 13″ × 26″
    ....**60.00**
glass scrubbing surface, aluminum frame
  is embossed "National Washboard Co.-
  No. 185 - VIM - Patented Sept. 7, 1915,"
  24″ × 12½″ **35.00**
graniteware scrubbing surface, blue,
  "Blue Ribbon" stenciled on wood
  frame, very good condition **75.00**
pine, handmade, hand cut nails, small,
  traces of old white paint **55.00**
stoneware, medium brown, hairline
  crack, rippled surface, wood frame, 23″
  × 12″ **60.00**
tin scrubbing surface, three wood straps
  across top, 14″ × 26″ **65.00**
wood frame is stenciled "National," 24″
  × 12½″ **15.00**
wood frame, lingerie size, "Pearl - Manufactured by Canadian Woodenware
  Co." **24.00**

*Scrub board and scrubber, hand made of
pine, 23″ × 13″ × 7″, 1¼″ thick, scrubber
has a ridge each side for gripping, 10″ ×
3½″ × 1¾″ (Eisele collection),* **150.00**

Iron stand, cast iron, lid lifter at one end, 6″ × 3¾″ (Illinois Farm Bureau photo), **22.50**

wood scrubbing surface
  frame is stenciled "Victory" **45.00**
  lingerie size, frame is stenciled "V"
  ....**25.00**
zinc scrubbing surface
  "Little Monarch" on wood frame, 15″
  × 7″ **30.00**
  wood frame is stenciled "Zinc King,
  Top Notch Sanitary Front Drain"
  ....**12.00**
  zinc, "National" embossed on zinc top,
  Pat'd Dec. 21, 1897, rusted and cracked
  ....**30.00**
Washing machine
  "Adams Washer" on green and red decal,
  galvanized metal tub with green stripes
  on separate metal stand, crank with
  wood knob, wood paddles, Acme 2026
  wringer **120.00**
  "Big 3," galvanized tub on wood legs,
  wood paddles **120.00**
  "Boss Perfection No. 4," wood, rocker-
  type, black stenciling **225.00**
  cypress tub, "Motor High Speed Washing
  Machine made by Michigan Washing
  Machine Co.," handle pulls back and
  forth to turn four-armed wooden agitator, cast iron gears are on top of tub,
  Relief No. 331 wringer **225.00**
  "James Washer - Independence, Kansas,"
  stainless steel tub, arm moves agitator
  with back and forth motion, rubber
  wringer on metal frame, 17″ × 23″ ×
  28″ **75.00**
  "Lovell Mfg. Co. - 22 - Guarantee" on
  white rubber wringer, cypress tub with
  four stave legs, one agitator moves by
  back and forth motion, gears on top,
  lined with corrugated, galvanized metal
  ....**250.00**
  Perfection Interstate Washer Co. No. 2,
  wood tub with red paint, wood rocker
  agitator, open top, galvanized metal interior **250.00**
  "Quick & Easy - New Way Lever Wash-
  ing," wood rocker agitator, 36″ × 20″
  × 23″, lever extends 14″ **185.00**
Washing stick
  carved wood, D-shaped handle, double
  fork, 32″, bleached out from use
  ....**60.00**

poplar, U-shaped stirrer on straight handle, 28″ **20.00**
Wash plunger
  metal, double, "May 27, '64," wood handle **56.00**
  tin, double, "Pat'd Nov. 11, '82," horizontal tin handle **65.00**
  tin, single, metal side handle on wood
  handle **15.00**
  tin, with embossed design, 1890s ...**15.00**
  wood, 8″ circular base holds nine 9″ rods,
  T handle, 35″ long **95.00**
Washtub
  galvanized metal, green stripe, round
  ....**25.00**

*Rug beater, 8″ wooden handle, 34½″ ×
12″ (Ted Diamond photo/Eisele collection), 25.00*

galvanized metal with blue stripes, wood handles, 27″ square with rounded corners, on wood stand 60.00
on metal legs, painted white, embossed "Ideal," spigot 35.00
Wrench, Maytag, (comes in nine sizes) 17.50
Wringer
Anchor Brand, cracked rubber wringers 17.50
Montgomery Ward, rubber wringers, wood frame 30.00

"Pioneer No. 22 - Lovell Mfg. - Erie, Pa." 35.00
small, 8″ wringer, "Wringer Washer" 55.00
stenciled "Horseshoe Brand Wringer," rubber wringers 35.00
three corrugated rollers, 20″ 45.00
white rubber wringers, on folding wooden tub stand 75.00
wood wringers, "LeHigh Washer Co. Pat. Oct. 8, '89″ 75.00
"#2031," 10″ × 1¾″, rubber wringers 17.50

Cooking and Canning

Kitchen tools have evolved along with changes from the hearth to the wood or coal stove to the gas or electric range. The simple, hand wrought iron or wooden kitchen accessories that were necessary for hearth cooking were replaced with cast iron cookware, graniteware, and gadgets of all kinds. During the late 19th century, inventors applied their genius to many kitchen tools, producing a varied and interesting field for collectors.

Most of the preparation of food in a rural household was done by the housewife. Few rural families had easy access to processed foods. Kitchen gadgets, meant to make food preparation easier, were common in farm kitchens. Nutmeg graters, egg and cream beaters, waffle irons, ice cream scoops, kraut cutters, molds, cookie cutters, choppers, grinders, slicers, and mashers are all available in many forms, materials, shapes, and sizes.

Maple was the preferred wood for most uses in the kitchen. White pine or poplar were preferred for stirring hot liquids because they didn't affect the taste or smell of the food. Barrels, kegs, casks, buckets, and tubs were used to store grain, meal, molasses, water, soft soap, rum, cider, and apples and were made of oak, pine, or basswood. Burl was exceptionally durable and was used for bowls, scoops, and ladles.

The introduction of wood-, coal-, and cob-burning cookstoves brought many changes in the tools that were required for cooking. No longer was it necessary to hang kettles over an open fire in the fireplace. The cookstove made it possible for the cook to perform many tasks simultaneously, while providing heat for the rest of the house, whether it was needed or not. Baking temperatures could be controlled by adding fuel or dousing the fire with water. Water could be heated in a special reservoir built into the stove. Warming ovens above the cooking surface were an added feature of some stoves. Cookstoves were made of cast iron or with enameled or graniteware finishes.

With the addition of a cookstove to the kitchen, the cook needed different tools. Graniteware cooking utensils, kettles that fit into stove burners, lid lifters, oven thermometers, open skillets and cast iron ovenware all became part of the kitchen inventory.

By the turn of the century, kerosene-, oil-, and gasoline-burning ranges began to replace the wood burners. Some models offered both wood- and gas-burning capabilities, and the ranges came in many colors and styles, often coordinated with factory built kitchen furniture.

Heavy aluminum cookware came into favor by the 1920s. Guardian Service offered an array of sizes and styles of pots, skillets, roasters, and serving pieces. Recognizable by their embossed glass lids, or scarce metal lids, the durable Guardian Service cookware is still in use in many modern kitchens.

Furniture

Manufactured kitchen cabinets have come to be known as Hoosier cabinets, from the name of one manufacturer, the Hoosier Company. Other major manufacturers were Sellers, MacDougall, Boone, Greencastle, Napanee, and Larkin. All of these except Larkin were located in Indiana. Larkin's cabinets were premiums offered in various plans for selling soap or other products of the Larkin Soap Company of Buffalo, New York.

Manufacturers of kitchen furniture first made dough tables (with or without top sections). The tables had rounded-bottom bin drawers — sometimes called possum bellies, or tilt-out bins — for flour, meal, and sugar. Most were maple with wood work surfaces. Tops had several small drawers for baking soda, salt, spices, and other baking supplies. These cabinets are usually referred to as baker's cupboards.

By 1904, packaged bakery products were becoming more widely available, and flour and meal bins were replaced by manufacturers with metal flour sifters. These cupboards usually had tops and were advertised as convenient work centers where the cook could have all the tools and supplies needed in one place. The cupboards were made of oak, poplar, maple, ash, pine, gumwood, or mixed woods. Wooden work surfaces were now covered with a sheet of zinc-aluminum alloy. Metal-lined drawers with lids were added to keep bread and cakes fresh. Most cupboards offered at least one pull-out cutting board.

Slide-out work surfaces, offering 12 inches of extra work space were introduced by 1906. By the 1920s, drawer sections slid out with the work surface. Metal support brackets that connected the top and bottom appeared after 1910. A rolling curtain replaced swinging doors on some cabinets, increasing work space, in 1915.

Competition inspired many innovations in kitchen cabinets. In 1900, Hoosier offered a galvanized metal drain board under a lid in the work surface. Boone cabinets offered one model with an ironing board that folded under the work surface. They also offered models with clocks, lights, coffee mills, desk sections and swinging stools. Some cabinets had side doors for easy access to storage space. In 1906, a cupboard was advertised with a rolling curtain in its base. Sets of glass canisters and shakers, wire racks, clips, rolling curtains, and slide-out shelves enhanced some models.

After World War I, mixed woods were being used in most cabinets. Thin, glued wooden sections replaced solid wood. White enameled cabinets were more popular than oak (and more expensive) in 1919. Plywood and metal shelves are found in cabinets made in the twenties, as are porcelain work surfaces. During the 1920s, gray, and then other colors (mostly pastels), were offered. Upper frosted or slag glass doors, appeared on Hoosiers in 1925, and rolling curtains were common. During the

1920s, built-in cupboards and the increased availability of bakery goods caused a decline in demand for freestanding cupboards.

Pie safes kept flies, ants, and mice away from pies, several of which were usually baked in one day. Pie safes were manufactured at the turn of the century in Indiana, Michigan, and other midwestern states, and along with "Hoosier cupboards" are most common in the Midwest. Older pie safes, as well as handmade ones, usually had screens instead of pierced tins.

Canning

The produce from the farm's garden and trees was expected to provide the family with fruit, vegetables, and drinks all year long. Preserving fruit and vegetables was done by canning in jars, stoneware, or glass.

Stoneware jars were made in sizes from 1 pint to several gallons. Hand thrown jars might be decorated with slip or left plain. They were sealed with wax. Later, stoneware jars had matching lids that were held in place with wire clamps.

Glass canning jars are usually referred to as fruit jars although they were used to preserve many kinds of foods from meats to vegetables, sauces, and fruits. Jars were sealed with wax and a metal or glass lid until the screw-on zinc lid was patented in 1858. The closure that uses three wires to clamp a glass lid to the jar was patented in 1882. The self-sealing lid was patented in 1903. Before 1900, jars had ground lips and the glass had whittle marks and imperfections such as bubbles and bumps.

Canning kettles, lid wrenches, jar lifters, wax ladles, canning booklets, funnels, tin can sealers, and bottle cappers were also necessary parts of the canning process.

Tips for collectors

Furniture

On Hoosier cupboards, copper work surfaces are replacements. If a wooden work surface is rough or has ½″ grooves, it is missing its zinc top. Watch for warped or wavy wood surfaces, especially on the sides or inside of cabinets. Roll curtains are often missing. Look for tracks where the curtain originally rolled. A working rolling curtain, leaded glass doors, original painted decoration, canister sets, or unusual features can greatly enhance the value of a cabinet.

Replacement hardware is available through publications like *Antique-Week*, *Antique Trader*, or from suppliers listed in David Mahoney's *Antiques & Collectibles Resource Directory*.

Pie safes with many tins are usually more valuable than those with just four or six tins. Unusual pierced designs command premium prices. Old painted finishes can add to the desirability of a pie safe. Patterns that are part of the country look, such as hearts, are popular and are most often found on reproduced tins. Copper "tins" are probably not old.

Fruit Jars

Fruit jars are valued according to rarity, color, size, and type of closure. Most glass fruit jars are aqua or clear. Cobalt blue and black jars are rare. Amber, milk glass, and olive or apple green jars are very desirable. When a jar is dated—1858 or 1908, for example—the date refers to the patent date of the method of closure, and only means that the jar was made after that date.

Zinc lids for standard size openings are easy to find, but lids for wide- or narrow-mouthed jars can account for much of their value. Jars with unusual closures are very collectible, but their lids are especially important.

Miscellaneous

Popular with collectors are unique eggbeaters, combinations gadgets, unusual apple parers, raisin seeders, and salesman samples.

Reproductions

Miniature waffle irons have recently been reproduced. Wapak probably never made a miniature waffle iron. Griswold miniature heart and star waffle irons are new, as are the Griswold "00" skillets with the logo inside. Handles on these fake waffle irons are cigar-shaped. Originals had long, narrow handles. Griswold's tea size #262 cornstick pan is reproduced and is sloppily cast.

Cast-iron reproductions are not as detailed as originals. Castings are grainy, and if rusty, the rust is orangish and even. Old cooking utensils show signs of wear. Built up grease and rust and worn, polished surfaces should signal age.

Glass fruit jars in cobalt should always be suspected of being reproductions. Mason's pint jars have been reproduced in many colors. New Globe Lightning jars in amber are flooding the market.

Canning

Canning booklet
Ball Blue Book, 1944, very good condition **3.00**
Home Packing Preserving - The Red Wing Way, 6″ × 9″ **12.50**
Mrs. Kerr's Modern Homemaker, 1947, 8″ × 11″ **5.00**
Red Seal Lycons... The Farmer's Friend, 48 pages, 1940 ....**2.00**
Canning funnel
glass, 4″ top, throat fits into glass jar ..**3.50**

graniteware, gray, strap handle, slightly rusted **15.00**
Canning kettle
cream enamel with green trim, 1940s **55.00**
gray granite, good condition **35.00**
Colander
aluminum, cone-shaped on metal legs, wood masher **7.50**
tin, cone-shaped on metal legs, green handle, wood masher **15.00**
tin, cone-shaped, tin strap handle, wood masher **12.50**
Fruit jar, glass
Ball, aqua, glass lid (also aqua), Pat. 1908, pint or quart **4.00**
Ball, clear, glass lid
half pint **10.00**
pint or quart **2.50**
Ball, Perfect Mason, aqua, zinc lid
pint or quart **2.00**
two quart **3.50**
Dandy, "Trade Mark - The Dandy," aqua, quart, clamp on glass lid, "Gilberd's IL" on bottom **35.00**
Globe, two quart, amber, glass lid and wire clamp **90.00**
Lightning, amber, quart, wire clamp and glass lid **45.00**
Putnam Lightning, aqua, one pint, glass lid **12.50**
The Leader, one quart, amber **165.00**
"The Wears Jar" in circle, quart, aqua, glass clamp on lid **9.00**

Pantry box, wood, dark varnish, 10½″ diameter, 7″ tall, bail with wood handle, **95.00**

Jar lifter

lifts jar by lip at lid, wire with two wood handles **3.00**

wire, oblong grippers hold jar by sides, scissors-type, loop handles, 14½″ × 4″ **10.00**

wire, holds entire jar while heating, bail handle **12.00**

Jar, stoneware, *see "Stoneware" below*

Lid for glass fruit jar, zinc, with glass liner, embossed "Ball," standard size **0.35**

small size, 2⅜″ opening **8.00**

Cookbooks

Balanced Recipes by Pillsbury, spiral bound, in aluminum book shaped box, silver and black deco design, 1933 ..**45.00**

Betty Crocker's Picture Cook Book, 1950, General Mills, 483 pages, very good condition **26.50**

Choice Recipes & How to Operate a Fireless Stove, 1920, Toledo Cooker Co., 53 pages, soiled cover **8.00**

Congress Cook Book, Congress Yeast Co., 3rd edition, 1896, 72 pages, very good condition **15.00**

Cow Brand Soda: Cook Book & Facts Worth Knowing, color cover, 1900, 32 pages, ...**15.00**

The Dairy Cook Book, by Ruth Berolzheimer, 1941 ....**5.00**

Farm Journal's Country Cookbook, 1959, 400+ pages **7.00**

Good Housekeeping's Book of Menus, Recipes & Household Discoveries, 1922 ....**10.00**

Good Things to Eat Made with Bread, Fleischmann Yeast Co., 1916, 32 pages, very good condition **8.00**

Guardian Service Tested Recipes, 72 pages **12.50**

Home Comfort Cook Book, Wrought Iron Range Co., 1905, 219 pages, fair condition **10.00**

Housekeeper's Companion, 1894, by Heffernan, 40 pages **15.00**

Housekeeping in the Bluegrass, Ladies of the Presbyterian Church, 1875, poor condition **50.00**

The Ideal Receipt Book: A Manual for Busy Housekeepers, Harriet McMurphy, 1898, color lithographed cover, 64 pages, Ideal Food Cutter & New Triumph Meat Cutter Recipes **25.00**

My Better Homes and Gardens Lifetime Cook Book, 1934, cover yellowed ..**35.00**

New Delineator Recipes, 1929 ....**9.00**

The New Hydropathic Cook Book, with Recipes for Cooking on Hygienic Principles, 1865, engravings, 226 pages, slightly foxed ....,.........................**35.00**

Pillsbury Grand National Recipe and Baking Contest—100 Prize Winning Recipes, 1950, 96 pages **25.00**

Pillsbury's 100 Prize Winning Recipes, 2nd Bake Off, very good condition, 1951 ....**15.00**

Pillsbury's 100 Prize Winning Recipes, 4th Bake Off, very good condition, 1953 ....**10.00**

Pillsbury 7th Grand National Cook Book - 100 Prize Winning Recipes, 1956, very good condition **10.00**

Wooden bowl, 26″ × 12″ × 4″ (Country Hearth, Lexington, IL), **120.00**

Pillsbury 18th Annual Bake Off, 1967, very good condition **5.00**

Port Huron Cook Book, Port Huron, Mich., 1889, First Baptist Church, 53 pages, ads, very good condition **15.00**

Ransom's Family Receipt Book, 1887, 32 pages, very good condition **14.00**

Rumford Cookbook, fair condition **5.00**

Cookware

Aluminum, Guardian Service
    canner, with cookbook **150.00**
    chicken fryer, with glass lid **65.00**
    cleaner
        blue cardboard and tin shaker, full, helmet logo in yellow, red, black and white, elves around bottom, 5½" **12.00**
        silver colored cardboard and tin shaker, full, helmet logo in red, black, white, and silver, 6" tall **12.00**
    coffeepot, complete **25.00**
    double boiler, with glass lid **55.00**
    double boiler, no lid **40.00**
    gravy boat **35.00**
    ice bucket **75.00**

    kettle **150.00**
meat tray, drain design, 12" × 8" **12.00**
omelet pan, oblong, with hinged lid, black handle **37.50**
roaster, 15" × 10", glass lid **85.00**
sauce pan
    1 quart, glass lid **25.00**
    2 quart, glass lid **45.00**
    2 quart, metal lid **35.00**
    10½", glass lid **45.00**
serving tray, eight sided **25.00**
triangular pans, with lids, set of three **60.00**
triangular pan, with lid **20.00**
Cast iron
    "Biscuit Iron," Barker **28.00**
    boiler, cast iron, oval, tab handles, rack in bottom **30.00**
    breadstick pan, "Griswold 11-950 - Erie" **65.00**
    cake mold
        lamb, "No. 866" (made by Griswold, but unmarked) **120.00**
        rabbit **300.00**
        Santa, with recipe book, "Hello Kiddies" embossed on front of sack, Griswold **345.00**

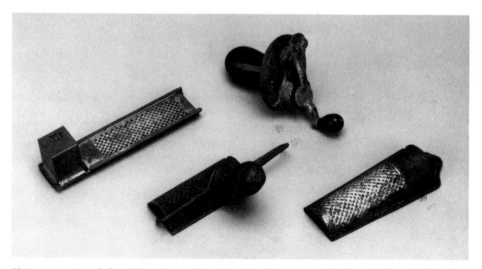

Nutmeg graters: left, *sliding box with spring-loaded prongs, 5¾" × 1¼" × 1½",* **75.00;** center top, *"Gem," two black wood handles, 3¾" × 3½",* **125.00;** center bottom, *"The Edgar - Pat. Aug. 18, 1891, No. 7" wooden knob on top of spring-loaded tin cylinder, 5½" × 4", c. 1890, missing wooden handle at center of grater,* **75.00;** right, *tin, hinged lid over grater, 5¼" × 2", (Illinois Farm Bureau photo/Eisele collection),* **10.00**

corn stick pan

Griswold

"Corn Bread Pan - Erie, Penn. USA -
954A," 15" × 8" **45.00**
#273, Crispy Corn Stick Pan, 13"
....................................**35.00**
chromed, #273 ....**25.00**
red and beige enamel, #273, excellent condition **165.00**
unmarked, seven ears facing alternate
directions **12.50**
Wagner, Junior Krusty Korn Cobs
....**22.00**
dutch oven, Griswold No. 12, with lid
....**85.00**

kettle

rounded bottom, three applied feet, 20"
diameter, 10" high, bail handle
....**140.00**
three feet, one tab handle, lid is
embossed "Greer & Co. Small 7
Inch," 8" diameter, 11" tall **45.00**

muffin pan

"Muffin Pan No. 8," makes eight 3"
muffins, 12¾" × 7" × 1" **24.50**
"R & E Mfg. Co. - Patent April 1859,"
makes twelve 2" × 3" muffins, 13" ×
7½" **38.00**
unmarked, makes 9 muffins, two handles **30.00**

skillet

Griswold

square, "Bacon and Egg Breakfast
Skillet" **27.00**
square, yellow and white enameled
"Bacon and Egg Breakfast Skillet"
....**50.00**
#0, no lid, 4⅛" **12.00**
#0, enameled red and beige, no lid
....................................**27.50**
#3 with lid **50.00**
#3, no lid **12.00**
#3, yellow and white enameled,
good condition **22.50**
#6, small logo, no lid **10.00**
#6, chrome, no lid, dirty **15.00**
#8, no lid **7.50**
#8, enameled red and beige, no lid
....**30.00**
#9, large logo, no lid **25.00**
"Martin Stove & Range Co. - Florence,
Ala." on bottom, "3" on handle, 6½"
diameter **35.00**

Wagner

#3, no lid **9.00**
marked "Sidney 10" **22.50**

Wapak, No. 9 ....**22.50**

Flour bins, tin: left, black with ivory and gold stenciled decoration, 14" × 22", **35.00;** *right, white with brown stenciled decoration, 17" × 28", worn paint on lid,* **35.00**

Measure, brown fiber, galvanized metal handle, aluminum tag reads "C & H - N.Y.- Sole Agents - 1 Qt. Liq.," base is embossed "United Indurated Fibre Co.," 4½" × 6" (Ted Diamond photo/Eisele collection), **22.00**

waffle iron

"Farner Mfg. - Cleveland - No. 8," spring handles, no base, 8″ **12.00**

Griswold

"American #8, Pat'd July 11, 1922″ on base **44.00**

high base, spring handle **30.00**

hearts and stars, low base, #19 ....**135.00**

Wagner, embossed "Wagner Mfg. Co. - Sidney, Ohio - Patented July 26, 1892," wooden handle, 7″ square pans, wire bail, base is 4″ high **125.00**

Coffee boiler

cream enamel with green trim, bail with wood handle **45.00**

grey graniteware, tin lid, excellent condition **45.00**

tin with copper bottom, wood handle **35.00**

white enamel with navy blue trim, wood handle **17.50**

white enamel with red trim, wood handle **25.00**

Coffeepot

enameled, white decorated with hummingbirds **65.00**

graniteware, blue and white swirl, gooseneck spout, one quart **350.00**

graniteware, blue and white swirl, triangular spout, one quart **150.00**

Double boiler, graniteware

gray mottled, granite lid, two quart base, small chips **25.00**

green and cream, two quart base **17.50**

light green with medium green edges, one quart base, chipped lid **10.50**

Kettle

enameled cast iron, blue with white speckles, one gallon, bail handle, chips around edges **30.00**

gray graniteware, lid with granite knob, bail with wood handle, three gallon **40.00**

Pie pan

blue and white marbleized graniteware **30.00**

graniteware, dark green and white swirl **25.00**

Popcorn popper, 10″ × 7″ metal pan on 27″ wood handle **12.00**

Potato boiler, heavy wire basket, rounded bottom, coiled metal handle, 13″ diameter, 17″ high **145.00**

Roaster, graniteware, blue and white swirl, slightly chipped base, 20″ × 12″ **95.00**

Roasting pan, aqua and white marbleized graniteware, 27″ × 18″, good condition **65.00**

Furniture

Baker's cabinet

base only, pine, zinc top, 18″ one board sides, wainscoting front is a bin door, divided interior, gallery at back, 40″ × 20″ × 36″ **625.00**

maple, table-type base with two bin-type drawers and dough boards, top has six small drawers, base and top were not originally together **500.00**

Kraut cutter, walnut, 42″ × 15″ × 3½″, 14″ × 12″ box slides in track, **85.00**

maple, base has a divided flour bin and two dough boards, top has spice drawers, excellent condition **895.00**

mixed woods, upper glass doors and three drawers, base with wood work surface has two drawers over two bins, turned legs, refinished **795.00**

oak, base has a bin drawer at left, large drawer at right, top section has four small drawers below two doors and one long door at left side, refinished, 45″ × 29″ × 72″ **750.00**

Bin, meal, pine, two doors over a drop front over two drawers **1495.00**

Clock, oak, Ansonia alarm, pressed design in wood, reverse painted glass door, label on back reads "Dove," c. 1900 ....**225.00**

Popcorn popper, "Mazola Corn Popper," metal with red wooden handle, 28″ × 7½″ (Ted Diamond photo/Danenberger collection), **60.00**

Dough box

grain painted, on separate base with straight legs, box is 42″ × 20″ × 18″, hand dovetailed, lift top, divided interior **600.00**

poplar, turned legs, 40″ × 24″ top, made in Pennsylvania **400.00**

poplar, red paint striped with yellow and white, with lid, handmade, nineteenth century **575.00**

Dry sink

one drawer near top, two doors, grain painted, 52″ wide **900.00**

pine, washbench sides, raised panel doors, beaded frame, one drawer beneath well, refinished **875.00**

pine, work surface at left over one paneled door, sink is at right side and 10″ lower than work surface, one drawer and one paneled door below sink wood knob, cast iron latches, refinished, 38″ × 20″ × 40″ **595.00**

wainscoting, one door, 3″ depression for sink is 24″ wide at left, old spring latch, 36″ × 24″ × 34″ **400.00**

wainscoting, two doors, set in cast iron sink is 36″ × 20″ × 5″, pump with brass stem at one end, painted white, 47½″ × 22″ × 28″ **295.00**

Icebox

ash, three door front, original latches, needs major restoration **210.00**

metal, green and cream, one door at left, two at right, "Sanitary" decal at center top, 34″ × 20″ × 48″ **245.00**

metal, "Zero" on brass tag, three doors, Deco style hardware, repainted black, 32″ × 14″ × 42″ **300.00**

oak, three door front, porcelain lined at right, galvanized lined at left, 35″ × 20″ × 48″, brass hardware, refinished **695.00**

oak, four door front, paneled sides, brass hardware, original interior, missing panel at base, 36″ × 24″ × 12½″ **600.00**

oak, lift top, "Alaska - Muskegon, Mich. - A Life Preserver for Foods," one door at front, 25″ × 17″ × 42″ **595.00**

oak, lift top, "Alaska," pressed panels and trim, ornate hardware, 24½″ × 20″ × 51″ **800.00**

oak, lift top, pressed design on three front panels, flap door at bottom, White Mountain label 700.00

oak, lift top, paneled top, sides and doors, one front door, flap door at bottom, "Reliable" label, nickel-plated hardware, original interior, refinished, 26″ × 17½″ × 40″ 550.00

Ice chest, pine, White Mountain, lift top, paneled 295.00

Jelly cupboard

mixed woods, two hand dovetailed drawers over two paneled doors, shaped crest, refinished, traces of grain painting 600.00

pine, original red paint and hardware, two doors under two hand-dovetailed drawers 695.00

walnut, two drawers over two doors, 40″ × 16″ × 62″, refinished 475.00

walnut, gallery top, two hand dovetailed drawers with fruit pulls over two doors, 45″ × 15″ × 45″, refinished 485.00

Can, cardboard, Guardian Service Cleaner, silver-colored, 12.50

Kitchen cabinet

mixed woods, originally white finish, Napanee, top has a two rolling doors flanking stack of four metal drawers, porcelain work surface, 36″ × 22″ × 63″, refinished, c. 1930 ....275.00

oak, dry sink in work surface, three doors and three drawers in base, top has two glass doors flanking narrow center door and three small drawers, refinished, glass knobs 1700.00

oak, McDougall, Frankfort, Ind., caramel slag glass at top of doors, rolling curtain opens to flour sifter, white porcelain top, refinished 800.00

oak, McDougall, slag glass door tops decorated with enameled teapots, rolling curtain, flour sifter, porcelain slide-out work surface, cardboard inserts, original finish in fair condition 750.00

oak, painted bright blue, wood work surface, base has four drawers at center, door and drawer at left, and bin door at right, iron bin pulls, paneled sides, open work area below top, top has two glass doors flanking center stack of 3 drawers below a blind door, wood knobs, molded cornice 575.00

oak, left side of zinc top extends for work surface, drawer and two legs pull out to support it, bin at right, top has three glass doors over three drawers, partially refinished 950.00

painted white with red and black Deco designs on doors, roll down front, white porcelain work surface with black edge, original metal and plastic hardware, missing side of bread drawer, fair condition 150.00

white finish, Hoosier, sifters and sugar bin, cutting board, white porcelain top with blue edges, shakers 225.00

Pie safe

ash, paneled blind doors, two doors over two drawers over two doors, oval screened hole each side, shaped crest and apron, cast iron bin pulls, refinished, 76″ tall 285.00

corner cupboard, screens at top, thick poplar, pegged, refinished 975.00

screens in two doors, pink paint, hand made 200.00

screens in two doors under long drawer 260.00

6 tins pierced with an unusual geometric pattern, old green paint, high legs, shaped apron, excellent condition 450.00

6 tins, tall, gumwood, two doors, each with three tins pierced in a geometric design, over two drawers over two blind doors, straight legs, refinished 500.00

8 tins pierced in a star pattern, two drawers at top, 66″ tall 350.00

8 tins, two piece, pie safe on a stand, pine, green paint over brown, tins are punched with a diamond design with tulips and stars, from N. Carolina 1540.00

12 tins, cherry, hand dovetailed drawer at bottom, from Pennsylvania, c. 1865 ....1600.00

12 tins, drawer at bottom, several coats of paint 450.00

12 tins pierced in a butterfly pattern, green paint 575.00

12 tins, poplar, drawer at bottom, refinished 600.00

12 tins, poplar, tins are pierced with baskets of flowers flanked by blue jays, two drawers over doors, shaped apron, from New Bremen, Ohio, dark cherry finish 1250.00

16 tins, gumwood, on legs 625.00

Table

painted turned legs, 42″ × 34″ scrub top, drawer 155.00

porcelain top is green with red floral design, wood base painted green, plain legs, 42″ × 20″ top 85.00

work, primitive, drawer, 60″ × 48″ top 95.00

Spice cabinet, new mustard paint, five drawers each side of a long center door and a drawer, 17″ × 22″ × 6″ 145.00

Spoon, graniteware, gray, slightly rusted, 15″ 7.00

Steamer

tin, dome-shaped lid with wooden knob, "Connolly Mfg. Co.," 9½″, slotted metal base 18.50

white enamel with red trim, two 9″ pans, inner one has a pierced bottom ..22.50

Ranges

Gas

Chambers, red enamel and chrome, four burners, griddle at left, 27″ × 37″, 1950s, very good working condition 3500.00

Chambers, yellow enamel and chrome, 1940s, very good working condition 2100.00

Detroit Star, cream and green enamel, four burners, oven and two drawers, 44″ × 21″ × 32″ 250.00

green and ivory with black trim, four burners with enameled lids on left, oven, broiler, and warmer have drop handles, work surface over oven, bottom of oven is rusted out, 36″ wide 100.00

Magic Chef, dark green with light green marbling, cream trim 275.00

table top model, two gas burners, cast iron, Griswold No. 502, on four short legs, porcelain handles, 24″ × 12″ × 6″ 55.00

Ward, three burners, ivory with black trim, working condition 250.00

White Star, white porcelain with nickeled trim, four burners, two ovens, open shelf under burner unit 300.00

Gas and wood, Superior, four gas burners, two wood burners, light blue, 30″ × 24″ × 56″ 300.00

Kerosene

"Acme - Newark Stove Works - Chicago," three burners, two burner ovens, two kerosene tanks mounted on right side, black with nickel trim, ornate brackets and corner trim 625.00

New Perfection, three burners, two ovens, 44″ × 48″ 225.00

Wood burning

Famous brand NO-02-18, white porcelain, warming oven at top 425.00

Home Comfort, gray granite 425.00

Jungers, green and cream enamel finish, "Model E No. 2 - Jungers Stove & Range Co. - Grafton, Wis.," warming oven over top, water reservoir in base, excellent condition, 45″ × 60″ 550.00

Majestic, cream and mauve enamel, copper water reservoir 550.00

"Majestic Mfg. Co. - St. Louis," burns wood or coal, "Majestic Malleable Iron and Steel Stove," black with nickel trim, six burners, warming shelf one side and two drop down shelves below two warming ovens, 34" × 29" × 29" to work surface, 24" upper warming oven section, working condition, 1901 ....**895.00**

"Prince - A. Kalamazoo - Direct to You - Kalamazoo, Michigan," cream and white porcelain, water reservoir, 29" wide warming oven above, shelf at right side, 42" × 54" **700.00**

"Walker's Culinet - Patented October 18, 1895 - Walker & Pratt Manufacturing Company - Boston, Massachusetts," ornate embossing, warming oven, brass trim and drying racks, cast iron, excellent condition **2000.00**

Windsor, blue and white with nickel trim, six burners, two warming ovens, water reservoir, 48" × 25" × 30" to work surface, 27" upper warming oven section, excellent working condition **2200.00**

Cooler, stoneware, "Western Stoneware - 2" on reverse, nickel-plated brass spigot, two gallon (Hintze Auction, Mazon, IL), **165.00**

Stoneware

Beater jar, blue banded stoneware, "You can't beat our butter but you can whip our cream - A.H. Eddy - Soo, Mich." **170.00**

Bread canister, stoneware, marked Uhl, blue stripes, badly damaged lid **1200.00**

Bowl

  mixing

    blue bands on white, 4" **60.00**

    blue and white, embossed Greek Key design, 15" **80.00**

    blue, Ruckels Stoneware, Sawtooth pattern **50.00**

    blue, unmarked Uhl, 10" **60.00**

    white, Ruckels Stoneware, Sawtooth pattern, large **20.00**

  salt glazed, Hamilton and Jones, Greensboro, Pa., 1½ gallon **150.00**

Canning jar

  "A. Conrad - New Geneva," quart **150.00**

  "Jas. Hamilton & Co. - Greensboro, Pa.," one gallon, salt glazed with blue stenciling **225.00**

  Harrington Burger, Rochester, N.Y., salt glazed, double flower in cobalt slip on salt glazed jar, three gallon, with lid **522.50**

  "Macomb Pottery - Pat. Appl. For" embossed in base, screw on zinc lid, quart **35.00**

  "Macomb" on base, screw top, half gallon **20.00**

  "Maysville, Kentucky," quart **200.00**

  Peoria Pottery, paneled, medium brown, chipped around rim, two quart ...**15.00**

  Peoria Pottery, paneled, dark brown, two quart **22.50**

  Red Wing, one half gallon **225.00**

  unmarked

    Albany glaze, two gallon, slanted shoulders, with lid **22.00**

    brown and white, five gallon, bail handle, with wire clamp and stoneware lid **150.00**

    salt glazed, line of blue commas in descending sizes, quart **130.00**

    salt glazed, three blue stripes, quart **85.00**

    salt glazed, wax sealer, 8" **15.00**

Western Stoneware
  one quart, with lid, embossing worn and illegible 22.50
  one gallon, white, No. 5, clamp on embossed lid 65.00
Williams & Reppert, Greensboro, Pa., one gallon, salt glazed, smeared stenciling 95.00

Crock, (or jar)
"Alexis Pottery," eight gallon 47.50
"Bayless McCarthy & Co. - Louisville, Ky." stenciled in blue, salt glazed, one gallon 225.00
"Blue Band"
  one gallon, Bristol glaze, blue stripe 45.00
  six gallon, Bristol glaze, blue stripe 65.00
"Blue Ribbon," blue ribbon logo
  six gallon 40.00
  eight gallon, tiny hairline 45.00
  thirty gallon 120.00
blue, unmarked, made by Uhl, small 35.00
"Burger Bros., & Co., Rochester, N.Y.," two gallon, salt glazed, cobalt daisy 365.00
"Donaghho, Parkersburg, W. Va.," salt-glazed, one gallon, chipped 80.00
"ES&B, New Brighton, Pa.," one gallon, stenciled 55.00
"Galesburg Pottery," one half gallon 40.00
"Greensboro, Pa.," one gallon, salt glazed, faded stenciling 80.00
"Hamilton and Jones, Pennsylvania," salt glazed, one gallon, stenciled shield, hairline in base 85.00
"James Benjamin - Stoneware Depot - 14 Water St - Cincinnati, O." stenciled in blue, one gallon 150.00
"Lowell Stoneware, Tonica, Il.," five gallon, leaf logo 45.00
"Macomb" in circle, Bristol glaze, ten gallon 50.00
"Monmouth Pottery Co., Monmouth, Ill." in leaf logo, ear handles, eight gallon, crack in bottom 60.00
"Peoria Pottery," four gallon, molded, Albany glaze, ear handles 40.00
"Red Wing"
  two gallon 45.00

three gallon, blue and red wing logo 50.00
four gallon 55.00
ten gallon, wire and wood handles, blue and red wing logo 185.00
twelve gallon 80.00
salt glazed
  2 gallon, "S. O. Mills, Colchester, Ill." 55.00
  4 gallon, tan, ear handles, blue "4" in diamond 75.00
  6 gallon, "bee sting" cobalt decoration, ear handles 90.00
  12 gallon, bee sting cobalt decoration, ear handles 265.00
undecorated, no manufacturer's name, molded
  one gallon, Bristol glaze 11.00
  three gallon, Bristol glaze, stenciled "3" 25.00
  three gallon, Bristol glaze, ear handles 35.00
  six gallon, Bristol glaze, stenciled blue "6" 30.00
  eight gallon, Albany glaze, mismatched lid 30.00
  ten gallon, ear handles, Bristol glaze, small crack 70.00
  twenty gallon, Bristol glaze, stenciled "20," ear handles 65.00
"Uhl Pottery," Evansville and Huntingburg, Indiana
  two gallon 30.00
  three gallon 65.00
"Western Stoneware, Macomb, Illinois"
  one gallon, cornflower design 32.50
  two gallon, maple leaf logo 37.50
  two gallon, cornflower design 32.50
  three gallon, cornflower design ..50.00
  three gallon, maple leaf logo in black 40.00
  six gallon, with handles, maple leaf logo 80.00
  six gallon, fruit logo 50.00
  ten gallon, maple leaf logo 50.00
  ten gallon, maple leaf logo, wire and wood handles 75.00
  fifteen gallon, maple leaf logo 55.00
  twenty gallon, maple leaf logo, two wood handles 130.00
  twenty-five gallon, maple leaf logo 120.00

Canning jar, stoneware, salt glazed, cobalt decoration, 7" × 9½" (Eisele collection), **220.00**

"A. White & Son, Utica, N.Y.," salt glazed, two gallon, deep cobalt leaf decoration **335.00**
"White Hall Stoneware, White Hall, Illinois"
  two gallon, state of Illinois logo ..**20.00**
  two gallon, marked 1870, Ruckels Pottery **75.00**
  four gallon, state of Illinois logo ..**35.00**
"Williams and Reppert, Greensboro, Pa.," one gallon, stenciled blue on gray, slatglazed, chipped, hairline **65.00**
Mug
  blue, embossed warriors' heads, white interiors **40.00**
  blue, embossed grapes on waffle background, unmarked Uhl, 3½" × 5" **135.00**
  blue and white, embossed bluebird design **85.00**

Pitcher
  barrel design, light blue glossy glaze, half gallon **22.50**
  blue bands, four gallon **80.00**
  bluebirds in flight, embossed, brown glaze **190.00**
  cattail, unmarked Uhl Pottery, nick on base **500.00**
  grape design, embossed, brown glaze, two quart **65.00**
  grape design with waffle background, embossed, unmarked Uhl Pottery, blue, 9½" high **400.00**
  Indian, blue and white, rim repair **150.00**
  Lincoln bust, half pint, blue, unmarked Uhl Pottery **275.00**
  peacock and urn, embossed, McCoy Nurock **65.00**
  sawtooth pattern, unmarked Ruckels Stoneware, blue, base chips **110.00**
  sawtooth pattern, unmarked Ruckels Stoneware, brown, squat **50.00**
  tulip decorated, unmarked Roseville Pottery, hand painted in green, rust and ivory, heavily crazed **85.00**
Salt jar, blue, dragonfly pattern, chipped lid **150.00**
Water cooler
  "Red Wing"
    two gallon, "Union Stoneware," with lid **2000.00**
    four gallon, with lid **400.00**
  Western, five gallon **150.00**
  White Hall, three gallon **150.00**

Utensils and Gadgets

Apple-related, *see Bees and Trees chapter*
Bean slicer, "Spong's No. 633, British Made," green **36.00**
Bottle capper, on wood base, 18" tall, c. 1920 ....**10.00**
Bottle corker, traces of original paint ..**25.00**
Bread maker, metal bucket with embossed lettering on lid, crank fits through lid, Universal **45.00**
Bread peel
  wood, 8' long **65.00**
  wood, 8" × 10" end, 30" long, refinished **35.00**

129

wrought iron, pitted, 4″ end on 20″ handle **32.00**

Butter mold (*For more listings, see Dairy chapter*)

maple, rectangular, dovetailed corners, no design **20.00**

maple, round, star design, warped ..**50.00**

stoneware, round, wood plunger with pineapple design **210.00**

Cherry pitters, *see Bees and Trees chapter*

Chopper

hand made, 7″ wood handle, 8″ deep wrought iron blade **50.00**

three intersecting blades on a cast iron handle, "Pat'd May 2, 1893 - No. 60″ **22.00**

vegetable, wood handle, single curved blade, 5½″ w. **10.00**

vegetable, wood handle, single heart-shaped blade is pitted, 7½″ × 5½″ **16.00**

Coffee grinder

cast iron front, wall mounted, "The Telephone Mill - The Arcade Mfg Co. - Freeport, Ill.," crank at front, missing box to catch ground coffee **85.00**

lap, embossed cast iron body mounted on a new wood base, drawer with brass knob, wood knob on crank, 5″ × 5″ × 8″ **85.00**

Egg beater, cast iron wheel embossed "Pat. June 29 '80," wooden knob (Hintze Auction, Mazon, IL), **40.00**

lap, maple, dovetailed corners, drawer, embossed cast iron top and crank with wood knob **75.00**

lap, maple, paper label, "Colonial" **60.00**

wall, "Crystal" embossed on glass jar, cast iron grinder, rectangular glass jar to catch ground coffee **95.00**

wall, pottery coffee container with blue Dutch scene **125.00**

Cookie cutter, tin, one cutter cuts a pig, bird, dog, fish, frog, and goat, 6½″ diameter **68.00**

Corn creamer, board with slot across center, ear of corn is pushed across eight small spikes in front of slot, two washboard-type legs, 11½″ × 4½″ × 3¼″ **17.00**

Cream extractor, "Economy," siphon, in box **12.00**

Cream whip

Fries, tin, no lid **30.00**

Fries, tin, black handle, 6½″ × 5½″ × 10″ **62.00**

Hodges, one gallon, tin **65.00**

Dipper

enameled cream with green trim **15.00**

enameled white with red trim **12.50**

gray graniteware, one quart, 15″, slightly rusted **22.00**

Dough pan, tin, with pierced lid, 22″ diameter **22.00**

Egg coddler, F.A. Walker, 1870s **55.00**

Flour bin and sifter, "Cream City Flour Bin and Sifter - Pat. Apr. 26 92 - Nov. 21 95 - Pat. Pending," crank at base, two metal handles, lid, black with gold and gray stenciled design and lettering, 13″ × 27″ **150.00**

Food chopper, *see grinder or chopper*

French fry cutter, Bloomfield Mfg. Co. **25.00**

Fruit crusher, wooden, metal gears and wood handle **75.00**

Fruit dryer, tin, "The Lady Friend Fruit Dryer - D. Stutzman - Ligonier, Indiana - Dryers & Evaporators - Six Sizes," screens inside, handle at top, door one end, 22″ × 12″ × 24″ **65.00**

"Fruit press, Enterprise Mfg. Co. - Philadelphia, Pat.' Sep. 30, '79, No. 1″, clamps to table, hopper is 6″ diameter at top, wood handle, 13″ high **75.00**

Griswold, cast iron with red and cream enamel: left, *corn stick pan, No. 273,* **150.00;** center, *No. 0 skillet,* **35.00;** right, *No. 8 skillet (Illinois Farm Bureau photo),* **25.00**

Funnel

    copper, 8″ at top to¾″ at bottom, polished **17.50**

    glass, 9″ at top **12.00**

    gray granite, 5½″ at top, chipped **10.00**

    gray granite, 5½″ at top, very good condition, loop handle **25.00**

    wood, 6″ diameter at top, 7″ high ...**25.00**

Grape crusher, wood hopper, 16″ × 12½″, is stenciled "Junior Grape Crusher," two ridged iron rollers at base, crank handle, sits over a crock **100.00**

Grater-slicer

    "Climax - USA - Pat. Pend. - Hamilton, Ohio," green cast iron side and crank with wood handle, interchangeable slicing and grating cylinders fit into tin body, clamps to table, 5″ × 10″ ..**35.00**

    maple with metal slicing blade one side, grater on reverse, 5″ × 19″, carved knob-like handle at one end **75.00**

Grinder

    Enterprise No. 2½ **525.00**

    Griswold, No 111 ....**35.00**

    Keen Kutter, KK11 ....**10.00**

    Keen Kutter, KK21 ....**15.00**

    Keen Kutter, KK23 ....**15.00**

    "Keen Kutter, K110, Pat. Jan. 5, 1909, Feb. 21 11. Jan. 5 15," 10″ × 12″ **36.00**

    Larkin **24.00**

    "O.V.B., Food Chopper No. 70 - Hibbard Spencer Bartlett & Co. Chicago - Pat. May 17 '04," with three blades including nut butter grinder, 11″ **10.00**

    Rollman, No. 11, 7″ **36.00**

    Rollman, No. 15 ....**15.00**

    Universal, No. 1 ....**3.50**

    Universal, No. 1, in box **7.50**

    Winchester **25.00**

Ice cream freezer, "White Mountain Freezer - Pat'd June 12, 1923 - 6xG," green wood bucket **55.00**

Ice sign, cardboard, for window, rotates to show different weights when turned, red with white numbers, 18″ × 18″ **25.00**

Ice shaver, "Grey Iron Casting Co.- Mt. Joy, Pa.USA, Arctic No. 25," 6½″ **12.50**

Kerosene bottle, glass, with metal band, lid and bail, one gallon **14.00**

Kraut cutter

    "Indianapolis Kraut Cutter - Pat. Apr. 18, 1905 - T & D Mfg. Co.," box and pusher, 27″ × 9″ **45.00**

"Indianapolis Kraut Cutter - Pat. Apr. 18, 1905 - T & D Mfg. Co.," with box, 30" × 11" **40.00**

Keen Kutter, Pat. Oct. 1904, with box **65.00**

no manufacturer's name, no box, 15" **7.50**

no manufacturer's name, box, 30" ..**25.00**

no manufacturer's name, no box, 30" **15.00**

no manufacturer's name, no box, 41" × 15" **55.00**

no manufacturer's name, 15" × 36", 12" × 12" × 9" hand dovetailed box with lid, cast iron handle on lid **95.00**

"Queen - Patented Oct. 18, 1904 - Indianapolis" embossed on hardware each side of blades, with box, 9" × 26½" **35.00**

"T & D Mfg. Co." over a swan trademark, maple, three adjustable blades, 10½" × 8½" sliding box, 30" × 11" × 3" **40.00**

Ladle, one cup copper bowl, 14" iron handle **12.00**

Lid lifter for wood burning cook stove, handle embossed "Peninsular," 9" **9.00**

Masher, maple, turned from one piece of wood, 10" **9.00**

Measure, composition, brown, 12" diameter **42.50**

Pie bird, black chef, yellow **90.00**

Pie cooling rack, wire, holds six pies ..**48.00**

Pie lifter
  wire, 12" long **9.50**
  wire, 19" long **40.00**

Potato grater, wood, hinged lid, grater wheel, mustard paint, 9" × 6" × 15", two mouseholes in base **150.00**

Pump, pitcher
  brass and iron, "Wistrand Mfg. Co. - Galva, Ill.," iron is newly painted red **40.00**
  copper and iron, "Peter's Pump Co. Kewanee, Ill. E28", polished and painted **56.00**
  Demco, red paint **35.00**
  "Hazen Mfg. Co.," 10" × 19" **45.00**
  "McDonald Mfg. Dubuque, Iowa," new black paint **34.00**

Raisin seeder, cast iron, "No. 36 - Enterprise - Pat. Apr. 2 Aug. 20 '95 Oct. 5 '97 - Wet the Raisins," wood knob, clamps to surface, 12" **60.00**

Rolling pin, yellowware, wood handles **350.00**

Scale
  Chattillons Spring Balance, New York, round face on square brass front with scallops top and bottom, weighs to 10 lbs., 5½" × 4½" face, 9½" long ...**55.00**
  "Maid of Honor," red and white **10.00**
  OVB, marble or glass top **35.00**

Pie lifter, wood and wire, 21" × 7½" (Busch collection), **35.00**

red cattail decal on white, scratched
....**10.00**
Sieve
gray graniteware, two handles **20.00**
tin, two handles, 11″ diameter **7.50**
tin, two handles, 21″ diameter **35.00**
Slicer
paddle shaped, maple with metal slicing
blade, hole for hanging, 5″ × 12″
....**25.00**
"Universal Vegetable Slicer - Pat. Apld.
For - Made by Landers, Frary & Clark
New Britain, Conn. U.S.A - Pat'd Nov.
13, 1900 - CRGM No. 145343 - Other
Patents Pend'g," cast iron, hinged plate
with wooden knob pushes vegetables
into 5″ round slicing blade which is
turned with a wooden handled crank,
clamps to table top, 11″ × 14½″
....**35.00**
Spatula
gray granite, granite handle, pierced spatula **25.00**
wrought iron, signed Kime, c.1815
....**65.00**
Toaster, stovetop, clips hold four slices over
stove burner **8.00**
Trivet, wrought iron, heart-shaped, three 8″
tall legs, 22″ × 10″ **140.00**

Miscellaneous

Bowl
burl, 9″ diameter, excellent condition
....**425.00**

wood, 14″ diameter, machine made,
slightly out of round **50.00**
wood, 18″ diameter, worn red, white and
blue sponged paint **160.00**
yellowware, mixing, two blue stripes, 7″
....**25.00**
Firkin (sugar bucket)
traces of red paint, wood straps and handle, 12″ diameter at base, lid **85.00**
yellow paint in good condition, 12″ diameter at base, lid **135.00**
Lard can, "Wabash Brand Pure Lard - Home
Packing and Ice Co. Terre Haute," one
gallon **15.00**
Lunch bucket, tin
cup acts as lid, bail with wood handle
....**35.00**
"Cream City" embossed on lid, painted,
bail with wood handle **42.50**
graniteware, dark blue and white mottled,
rectangular, wire bail **135.00**
Plate, 9″, cream and green enamelware
....**6.00**
Spice box, tin, rectangular, holds six covered stenciled tins, nutmeg grater in the
lid, black, simple tole painted decoration,
c. 1890 ....**135.00**
Sugar bucket (*see firkin*)

Needlework

Works of art created by the needles of Victorian crafters are not likely to be found in rural America. Farm families did not have the leisure time necessary to produce textiles that were not functional. Even in cities, the motivation to produce outstanding examples of needlework diminished as women began to learn skills other than domestic ones. Self-expression was no longer limited to needlework, and extraordinary examples of quilting or embroidery were rarely produced after the turn of the century. As factory-made goods became more readily available, needlework became more functional and was more likely to be produced and used in the rural home than in the urban home.

Quilts and rugs were produced to recycle fabric into useful bedding and floor coverings. Quilts made from remnants of fabric or usable scraps of worn clothing were usually pieced in geometric designs or appliquéd to make bedcovers.

Crazy Quilts and Log Cabin patterns, often worked on a foundation of cotton sacking or paper, were especially popular from 1880 to 1920. Silks were more often used in these quilts in the late 19th century. They were treated with metallic salts to give them more body, and many have deteriorated badly. The 20th-century Crazy Quilts and Log Cabin quilts were more likely to be made with wool and cotton and tended to be darker in color. Tied comforters were very popular from 1900 to 1925.

With the colonial revival of the 1920s, modern women updated old quilt patterns, creating old standards in new pastel color schemes. Many of the quilts that were made during the Depression were popular, not so much because they were affordable, but because they were made fashionable by the colonial revival. Dresden Plate, Double Wedding Ring, Grandmother's Flower Garden, appliquéd Sunbonnet Sue's and butterflies, and outline-embroidered quilts were popular in the 1920s and 1930s. Magazines and newspapers sold patterns and templates that reached readers all over the country, minimizing regional differences.

Hooked rugs were made from yarn or from fabric strips, hooked through a burlap backing. Like quilts, hooked rugs were standardized with the popularity of published patterns. The earliest hooked rugs were made with backings of recycled burlap grain or sugar sacks. The size of the bag dictated the size of the rug. Hearth and welcome mats, made in geometric or floral designs, were most common. The earliest rugs were usually geometrics or florals. In the 1870s, E. Frost & Company began to market patterns for hooked rugs printed on burlap. By the 20th century, catalogs for hooked rug patterns were in circulation. A revival of the rug-hooking craft in the 1920s and 1930s resulted in new designs with Art Deco elements and with reworked patriotic and floral patterns.

Practical rag carpets were in such demand that, in the late 19th century, there was one rag carpet weaver for every 2000 people. Families cut rags, remnants, and scraps into strips and wound them into balls. The balls were taken to the area carpet weaver who made the rag strips into runners, rugs, and stair cloths. Rag carpets were made on single-harness looms in widths up to 36 inches. Runners were sewn together to cover large areas.

The sewing machine was patented in 1846 and was commonplace in homes by the 1870s. The earliest machines were operated by a hand-cranked wheel or a treadle. (If a machine can stand up on its own and has no groove for a belt on its flywheel, it was originally a hand-cranked model.) Portable, hand-cranked models sometimes came in a wooden case. Treadle machines often had ornate iron bases and a wooden surface that held the machine. Some models had boxlike covers that could be lifted off or folded down to create a work surface. Some had a flat, hinged lid that opened to one side. Others were enclosed in cabinets with a door to conceal the treadle. Drawers held supplies and attachments, sometimes in hinged wooden boxes that folded flat.

Cotton bags that originally held feed, seed, flour, sugar, or meal were used by rural needleworkers to produce clothing, curtains, quilts, dishcloths, and doilies. Colorful feed sacks in stripes, florals, geometrics, and prints were very popular in the 1940s and 1950s. Labels were often printed in ink that washed out and the cotton bag could be reused as fabric.

Homes were decorated with examples of embroidery and crocheted, knitted, tatted, and bobbin lace. Runners, chair sets, dresser sets, doilies, tablecloths, and bed linens were likely to display decorative needlework. Framed mottoes, worked on punched paper or cloth, decorated the walls. Aprons sometimes were embellished with embroidery, cross-stitch, and crocheted edging.

In addition to mending clothes, farm families repaired their own shoes and boots. Most families had a set of iron shoe lasts and some cobbler's tools. The same skills and tools that were needed to maintain horse harnesses were used to keep the family footwear in good condition.

Tips for Collectors
Quilts

Quilts, like any other needlework, should be judged on the quality of workmanship. Age, condition, provenance, color, and pattern are all important considerations, but if it isn't well made, unless it has sentimental value, it is a poor investment.

The aesthetic value of a quilt is in the eye of the beholder. Its technical merits should not be ignored in making a decision about value. Look at the closeness of quilting lines, the size and regularity of the stitching, and the complexity of the design. A pieced quilt should meet smoothly at the centers of the designs. Appliquéd elements should lie flat. About 10 to 12 stitches per inch on the top of the quilt is considered to be excellent needlework; 7 to 8 stitches per inch is average work.

Machine piecing has been done since the mid-19th century. Dating a quilt can often be done by learning about fabrics, dyes, patterns, and techniques that were popular during different periods in quilt-making history. Zigzag stitching was done commercially as early as the 1870s but was not available on domestic machines until about 1950. Barbara Brackman's *Clues in the Calico* (see below) is an excellent reference.

Crazy Quilts and Log Cabin patterns in dark colors were popular from 1880 to 1920. Pastels were popular in the 1920s and 1930s in old patterns reworked for the colonial revival. Between 1925 and 1950, cotton sateen was used in quilts, and appliquéd designs were often outlined with a black buttonhole stitch. Synthetic fabrics were developed in the 1940s and began to be used in quilts in the 1950s.

Polyester batting was also introduced in the 1950s. Polyester batting is fluffier than cotton or wool batting. It feels slippery when the quilt is rubbed between the finger and thumb. Less quilting is necessary with polyester batting. Sometimes there are as many as 3 to 5 inches between the lines of stitching. Polyester batting is used by many quilters with old quilt tops, so polyester batting may date just the quilting. Wool batting shrinks when washed, causing the quilt to be puckered and misshapen. Specks in the batting are not an indication of age but of cheap batting.

Needlework is especially prone to family stories concerning the age of a piece. Remember that Great-Grandma, who died 20 years ago, when she was 91, may have made that quilt 21 years ago. Too often, families date needlework by the year of the maker's birth. Learn to let the quilt tell you how old it is.

Sewing Machines

Singer Featherweights (Model #221) are popular among quilters. They are reliable, portable machines, and quilters will usually value them more than collectors.

Treadle machines were saved by many families. They can usually be returned to working condition with the replacement of a belt. Unless a machine is a rare or early model, its value is probably in the cabinet. Fancy oak cabinets, with decorated drawers and veneer in good condition are popular for decorating, but a machine in a plain or peeling cabinet won't be worth much. Closed front cabinets are often converted for use as liquor cabinets or other purposes.

Rugs

To most collectors of hooked rugs, aesthetics and condition are more important than age. Rugs designed by their makers are the most desirable. Animals, people, birds, buildings, and patriotic designs are popular subjects. Naive or whimsical subjects command the best prices. Dates or signatures add to the appeal of a rug. Minor fading doesn't hurt a rug badly. Worn edges and cracked backings seriously detract from the desirability of a rug. Look for rugs marked with the names of early pattern makers, such as "E. Frost & Co., Biddeford, Maine" or for labels of workshops from the 1920s, such as "Abanakee "CR," and "Ouia."

Reproductions

New quilts shouldn't really cause a problem if quality is the first consideration. New handmade quilts of good quality are expensive. The new, imported, hand-stitched quilts finding their way into the antiques market today are poor-quality quilts, often with less than five stitches to the inch. New or old, poor-quality quilts shouldn't be expensive or desirable to collectors.

Rag rugs wider than 72″ are probably imported from China or Japan.

Recommended Reading
Brackman, Barbara. *Clues in the Calico: A Guide to Identifying and Dating Antique Quilts*, McLean, Va.: EPM Publications, 1989.

Apron, blue and white gingham, fine cross-stitched snowflakes, 38″ long, ties at waist **20.00**
Attachment box, "Wheeler & Wilson - W & W - Sewing Machines" pressed in on top of dovetailed birch box, full of attachments **18.00**
Bedspread
    crocheted, bull's eye and popcorn pattern, double bed size, ecru, c. 1940 ....**95.00**
    pieced from dark velvets, Starburst design, c. 1900 ....**130.00**

Book
    American Quilts, by E. W. Robertson, 1948, 152 pages **57.50**
    Collecting Hooked Rugs, by Elizabeth Waugh and Edith Foley, 1927, first edition, 140 pages, 41 photos, dust jacket **45.00**
    The Dreams Beneath Designs: History and Background of Hooked Rugs, Pearl McGown and Bruce Humphries, 1939, 63 black and white illustrations, 96 pages, 5½″ × 8″, dust jacket ..**14.00**
    Historic Quilts, by Florence Peto, 1939, first edition, 62 black and white plates, 6½″ × 9¼″, dust jacket damaged, otherwise very good condition **14.50**
    Machine Sewing, Singer Sewing Machine Co., 1925, 159 pages, several photos, care and use of sewing machine ..**25.00**
    Progressive Lessons in Needlework, 1895, second edition, 120 pages **12.50**
    Quilts, Their Story and How to Make Them, Webster, 1943, 178 pages, ex-library **22.50**
    The Romance of the Patchwork Quilt in America, by Hall & Kretsinger, 299 pages, 1935, dust jacket **25.00**
Bookmark, embroidered on punched paper, "Simply Cling to Thy [cross symbol]," 8″ × 2½″, broken edges **15.00**

*Motto "Kind words can never die" embroidered on punched paper, framed in a 14″ × 26″ walnut criss-cross frame, c. 1900, tattered edges, **85.00***

Quilt, appliquéd stylized poppies in pastel green and pink, on white background, fine quilting, 1920s, very good condition, 84" × 78", 475.00

Darning egg, glass, cobalt blue, blown into a mold, turned wood handle, 7" **200.00**

Dress, crocheted, child's size, fine thread, white, c. 1900, excellent condition **185.00**

Dress form, adjustable cloth covered body, cast iron feet **30.00**

Iron, tailor's , embossed "22," 9" × 3" × 7" **25.00**

Motto, cross stitched
alphabet, stagecoach and horse, floral border, line of birds, red and black on ecru, "Mother to David 1935" embroidered at lower center, framed 14" × 20" **39.00**

"Home is Where the Heart is," man and woman in wing chairs in front of fireplace, multicolor, framed, 14" × 20", 1920s **85.00**

Pattern catalog, *R.W. Burnham's Patterns on Burlap for Making Hooked Rugs Catalogue*, 1928, 42 pages, illustrated cover, worn **15.00**

Pillow, hooked fabric strips, geometric design, multicolor, 27" × 18" **65.00**

Pillow cover, outline embroidery, turkey red on white, crocheted edge, "Sweet Dreams," flowers and leaves, c. 1900 ....**30.00**

Pillow covers, pair, outline embroidery, turkey red on white, reclining woman on chaise, fans, lilies of the valley, bobbin lace edges **65.00**

Pincushion, pot metal, wart hog **90.00**

Plaiting loom, label reads "H.A.R. Wyckoff - Peoria," wood, 12" × 15" **15.00**

Quilts, (double bed size unless noted)
Amish, red and gray stripes, c. 1900 ....**990.00**

appliquéd birds, black embroidery outlined, calicoes and light blue, fine quilting, c. 1925 ....**220.00**

Bear Paw, multicolor, c. 1900, worn **150.00**

Birds in the Air variation, multicolor prints on pink, marked on the back "1886 J. Wesley Taylor - This was peaced [*sic*] by Great Grandma Taylor, and Mother finished it 1932," quilted 10 stitches to the inch, worn **195.00**

Bow Tie, red and white, with some prints, 1930s, very good condition **275.00**

Broken Star

red, white, and blue; much fine quilting, c. 1920 ....**400.00**

tied instead of quilted **27.50**

Butterflies, appliqúed, embroidered outlining, coverlet size, rose and white, 1940s **135.00**

Carpenter's Wheel, red, white, and blue, c. 1870, fine quilting, very good condition **745.00**

Double Irish Chain, solid pink and blue on white, quilted in 1932, 12 stitches to the inch **260.00**

Double Wedding Ring

multicolor pastel prints on white background, 1925–50, magenta backing, quilted six stitches to the inch **150.00**

fine stitching (ten stitches to the inch) **300.00**

Dresden Plate

plain lavender squares alternate with appliqúed squares, 1930s, worn **110.00**

yellowed, multicolor calicos, good quilting **250.00**

Quilt, Lone Star pieced in pink and white cotton sateen, fine quilting, 86″ × 78″, 1940s, very good condition, 350.00

Drunkard's Path, blue and white, c. 1890, excellent quilting, very good condition **850.00**

Dutchman's Puzzle, blue and white, scalloped edge, c. 1890, 78″ square, excellent condition **640.00**

Fan, multicolor prints on white, quilted in 1932, 10 stitches to the inch **250.00**

Quilt, appliqúed Double Tulip in red and green calicos on white, hand quilted, strong colors, stains in white background, 90″ × 74″, c. 1900, 450.00

Motto; cross-stitched in blue, red, and black on beige background; 14" × 20", 1940s, **25.00**

Feathered Star, red and white cotton **275.00**

Flower Garden, calicos and pastels on blue, 1930s, ten stitches to the inch quilting, excellent condition **375.00**

Log Cabin

    Split Rail variation, dark colors ..**380.00**

    crib-size, c. 1910 ....**95.00**

Lone Star, c. 1900 ....**231.00**

Maple Leaf, appliquéd, red and white, 1930s **225.00**

Martha's Choice, blue and white, fine quilting, excellent condition, c. 1920 ....**450.00**

Nine Patch, pink ground, 1930s ...**175.00**

Postage Stamp, c. 1890, slightly worn and faded **385.00**

Poppy, appliqued, scalloped edges, 1940s **175.00**

Potted Tree (Fruit Basket) pattern, navy blue and white, very good condition, c. 1900 ....**360.00**

Rose Wreath, appliquéd, red and green on white cotton, fine quilting **550.00**

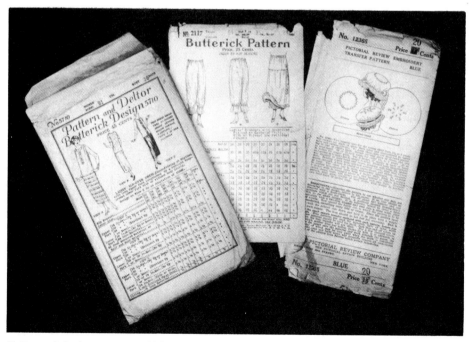

Patterns: left, *dress pattern, 1920s,* **3.00;** center, *bloomers, 1910s,* **3.00;** right, *child's hat and embroidery transfer (Illinois Farm Bureau photo),* **2.00**

140

Star, scalloped edge, double bed coverlet size; blue, red and green **400.00**

Stars

    5 ten-pointed stars in calico on white, c. 1900 ....**325.00**

    4 six-pointed stars, signed and dated 1938 ....**250.00**

Sunbonnet Sue with balloons, 63″ × 74″, 1930s **375.00**

Thousand Pyramids, over 1200 pieces of calico, herringbone quilting, c. 1860, 64″ × 82″ **575.00**

Three Windmills, slightly frayed edges, average quilting **150.00**

Tulip Cross, pink and green on white, pale yellow flowers, dated 1851, initials embroidered, 81″ × 106″ **3000.00**

Turkey Track, c. 1900, very worn, blue and white **110.00**

YoYo, twin size, multicolor prints on pink background with skirt **120.00**

Quilt top

    Bow tie, hand pieced, greens, dark reds, paisleys, 54″ × 74″, c. 1900 ....**65.00**

    Mohawk Trail, cotton, multicolor prints **70.00**

Tin, Huberd's Shoe Oil, blue and white, ¹/₁₆ gallon, 4¼″ high (Antique Mall of Chenoa, IL), **12.00**

Hooked rug, yarn, purple grapes outlined in black, green leaves; yellow, green and black in borders; 34″ × 20″, c. 1940, **35.00**

Hooked rug, yarn and strips of fabric; beige, black, red and green; worn edges are turned under, 44" × 28" (Eisele collection), 425.00

Trivets, crocheted cotton over bottle caps, grapes are shades of purple with green leaves, 13½" × 8" pair, 12.00; star is multicolored, 22" diameter (Ted Diamond photo/Eisele collection) , 17.50

Rug, hooked
> fabric strips, gray donkey, 36" × 24", excellent condition **230.00**
> fabric strips, two horses, a collie, tulips, and birds carrying cherries, dated March 1925 in pattern, 45" × 30" **700.00**
> fabric strips, multicolor peacock, black and gray background with pink and purple flowers, faded, but otherwise in very good condition, 42" × 28" **145.00**
> yarn, eight sections with beige backgrounds, separated by black borders, with alternating star and floral patterns, 42" × 24" **38.00**

Ruler, wood, "Churngold - Ohio Butterine Co. - For the Ladie's Workbasket," 6" **15.00**

Scissors, "Faith," steel, decorative brass pin, 6" blades, c. 1890 ....**27.50**

Scrapbook, hundreds of newspaper clippings with patterns for lace, knitting, crochet, 1884, 111 pages **30.00**

Sewing basket, manufactured, cylindrical with round lid, two wood handles, 12" tall, 16" diameter **70.00**

Sewing box, handmade, upper drawer holds spools on pegs, minarets, original gold paint, c. 1900 ....**185.00**

Sewing chest, ash, three drawers in front, two side compartments with lift tops, refinished, c.1910 ....**235.00**

Sewing kit, "Gulf" logo, "Wilson's Cabin Camp - Route 31 - Eighty four, Pa.," pat. no. 2084780, orange and blue, contains thread, needles, thimble closure **8.50**

Sewing machine

Domestic, treadle, walnut hinged box top folds out to flat surface, last patent 1871, worn gold decoration, refinished **125.00**

The Free, oak case with six curved front drawers, needs refinishing **95.00**

Kenwood, oak case, treadle **170.00**

Minnesota Model H, treadle, oak case with door at front, drawers inside cabinet, painted white, applied ornament at front, $17\frac{1}{2}'' \times 22'' \times 28''$ **50.00**

Singer, treadle, walnut case, box lid folds flat with several hinges, machine has mother-of-pearl inlay, last patent date 1855, refinished case **175.00**

Singer Featherweight No. 221, with case, electric, in excellent working condition **275.00**

Singer Lite, No. 221-1, in black case, electric, in excellent working condition **275.00**

White Rotary, patented Nov. 1927, black machine with embossed scroll design, mahogany case with door at front, top is hinged at left, short turned legs **75.00**

Willcox & Gibbs, gilded stenciling, last patent 1883, hand wheel operated, 10″ × 4½″ × 11″ **68.00**

Sewing table

ash, folding, with printed yardstick along one side, refinished **65.00**

folding, painted white **20.00**

Simplicity, folding, 36 inch guide, 1884 ....**70.00**

Shoe lasts and stand, cast iron

"Jersey," stand and four lasts **27.00**

stand with three sizes of lasts, 27″ high **20.00**

Shoe polish, Brown's Liquid Dressing, full bottle in like new condition box, $2\frac{1}{4}'' \times 2\frac{1}{4}'' \times 5\frac{1}{2}''$, c. 1905 ....**18.00**

Shoe shine stand, cast iron, camel with shoe holder on back, traces of blue and black paint, $7'' \times 3'' \times 7''$ **65.00**

Shoes, women's, black, pointed toes, high button, worn **40.00**

Skirt hem marker, "Boco Skirt Marker," patents 2202659 and 2202680, squirts chalk on hem line, iron base, glass jar, rubber bulb, wood ruler, 30″ **25.00**

Skirt hemmer, "Dritz," 1930s **20.00**

Sock darner egg shaped on turned handle, painted black **10.00**

Tape measure

celluloid pig **35.00**

Lewis Lye **25.00**

Thimble

brass, embossed geometric border, c. 1920 ....**2.50**

nickel plated brass, "The Prudential Life Insurance" **2.50**

Towel, huck weave on damask, scalloped edges, c.1890 ....**22.00**

Yarn reel

maple, four arms, skein counter inside stand **160.00**

primitive, two horizontal arms cross on center pole, 4″ tall rods at each end of arms hold yarn **85.00**

Pillow cover, embroidered with turkey red on white, knit lace edge, 24″ square (Illinois Farm Bureau photo), 30.00

Lighting and Heating

Many rural homes did not have electricity until the 1940s. This meant that farm families had to depend on wood, coal, or gas for heat and cooking, and kerosene or lamp oil for light, well into this century.

Wood-burning stoves for the parlor were often made in ornate styles, with nickel-plated ornaments and embossed decoration. Some had isinglass windows, through which the fire could be viewed. Some stoves burned coal. These were equipped with coal baskets inside the burning chamber.

Coal hods and bins held coal near the fireplace or stove. They were made in brass, copper, japanned tin, galvanized metal, and wood lined with metal.

Stoves were often taken out of the house in the spring and returned in the fall. The flue was covered with a decorative cover, which was often a print that was mounted under glass, framed, and hung from a brass chain or ring. Some flue covers are metal, shaped like paper plates, with a picture glued to the center. Flue covers are usually round, but can be found in rectangular, square, oval, and diamond shapes. Some advertise local businesses. Some were sold in sets of two or three so that they could

be arranged together to conceal the flue better.

Lamps that burned kerosene, oil, or gas were used as fixtures or could be moved from room to room. Lanterns in specialized shapes and sizes were used outdoors to light the barn or yard or for night driving. Outdoor lighting had to be resistant to drafts and very durable. After electricity came to rural areas, these lamps and lanterns were kept by families for use during frequent power failures.

Tips for collectors

Old coal hods and bins were sometimes tole decorated, but a painted hod should be carefully evaluated before assuming its decoration is original. The recent popularity of tole painting wasn't its first revival. Decorators were encouraged to paint hods with occupational scenes and other themes in a 1954 edition of *Hobbies*. Such paintings are now 40 years old and have developed a patina.

Reproductions

Brass and copper coal hods in a helmet or pitcher shape with blue-and-white ceramic handles and lion's head ornaments on the handles are available new and have been for many years. Brass, galvanized metal, and black metal coal buckets are still available new, as are coal shovels.

Reproduction flue covers are on the market. They have fresh prints and shiny brass chains. Pie plate-type covers are still sold at stores that sell wood heaters.

Aladdin's Lincoln Drape lamps have been reproduced. The short lamps were made by Aladdin and are dated in the mold at the base. The reproductions of the tall Lincoln Drapes were not made by Aladdin. They were made in two parts and glued at the joint between stem and font. They are 9⅞ inches tall, while originals are 10⅛ inches. Many new lamps have hollow stems. Amber tall Lincoln Drapes were made only after 1977.

Recommended Reading

Hobson, Anthony. *Lanterns That Lit Our World*. Spencertown, N.Y.: Golden Hill Press, 1991.

Box, pine, stenciled "Dietz Lanterns," 36" × 24", open **40.00**
Can, coal oil, wood over metal, two gallon, bail handle with wood handle, fair condition **17.50**
Coal bucket and shovel **10.00**
Coal or cob bin
    pine, mustard paint, lift top, extended base is open at front, 15" × 17" × 26", metal lined, crudely made **165.00**
    pine, worn red paint, twentieth century, slant lid, 24" × 22" × 36" **225.00**
Coal hod, metal, painted black with hand painted floral design, metal liner, ornate rack at back for tools, coal tongs, and shovel **125.00**
Cob scoop, open wire scoop with D-shaped wood handle **17.50**
Flashlight, Winchester, brass **30.00**

Hanging kerosene lamp, electrified, tin shade, font marked "T.F. Hammer - Pat. Mar. 1, 1890," **175.00**

Flue cover, glass over colored paper print, brass chain border, 9½" × 7½" (Country Hearth, Lexington, IL), **35.00**

Dash lantern, "OVB No. 2," reflector at back, bull's-eye lens at front, 15" high (Eisele collection), 35.00

pink roses, 10" round, chain rim
....**27.50**

windmill scene, gold band around print, solid metal edge, hangs by chain, 9½" diameter **45.00**

tin "pie plate," painted beige, paper scene at center, 9", wires clip into 6" flue **12.50**

Foot warmer

copper and brass reservoir, 12½" × 7½" × 3", stopper in center of top, polished
....**65.00**

copper hot water reservoir, oval, stopper in center of top screws in, 14" × 8" × 3" **47.50**

pierced tin panels in wood frame, tray for embers, metal handle, very good condition **295.00**

Cob scoop, 13½" × 16" scoop, 26" handle, 17.50

Floor register

cast iron, ornate design, 9" × 11", with louvers **17.50**

cast iron, ornate, 10" × 12" **12.00**

cast iron and steel, 15½" diameter, embossed ring opens and closes vents, embossed "Manufactured by the Adams Company, Dubuque, Iowa - Design Pat. Aug. 31, 1897" **30.00**

stamped metal, simple grid, with louvers, 10" × 14" **7.00**

Flue cover

glass over color picture, round

"Angelus," couple praying over basket of potatoes, gold-colored rim, metal edge, 8½" diameter **50.00**

girl with puppies, 9" round **75.00**

pasture scene, 9" round **25.00**

stainless steel, "Landers Frary & Clark - Universal," 1923, 9" round × 1½" stoneware, blue and white, Sta Hot **350.00**

Kerosene can

black, ½ gallon, long spout, cap near back of top **11.00**

cylinder tank, metal, glass gauge one end, 14" long, 5" diameter **5.00**

jug shaped, wood over tin, one gallon, red wood bands **40.00**

reticulated tin holder, glass bottle, tin spout, holds about a gallon, embossed "Daisy - Pat'd Apr. 26, 1881" **55.00**

Kerosene container, wooden, stenciled "Kerosene Oil," metal bands around top, bottom and waist, metal spigot, three gallon, very good condition **80.00**

Kerosene heater

black, rusted **10.00**

blue, trim repainted silver, Perfection Oil Heater, wire handle, 25" high **35.00**

blue with chrome trim **60.00**

Lamp, kerosene or oil

Aladdin,

Beehive, clear **55.00**

Beehive, green **95.00**

Colonial, clear **70.00**

Corinthian, amber **75.00**

Corinthian, green, Model B **100.00**

floor lamp, Model 12, nickel-plated, hand painted shade **160.00**

Lincoln Drape, alacite, tall **120.00**

Washington Drape, amber **90.00**

Washington Drape, clear **50.00**

Naugatuck, nickel plated brass, "Sept. 90 Apr. 93" on burner, 12" high, no chimney **38.50**

Quartered Block **95.00**

Poppy, glass, 8" high, embossed poppies all over, 1880s **90.00**

Rayo

brass, ornate hand painted pink floral shade **180.00**

brass, electrified, original milk glass shade **195.00**

Two handled standard sewing lamp by U.S. Glass, chip under base **100.00**

Lantern

"Blue Grass Air Pilot - Belknap Hdw. & Mfg. Co. - Louisville, Ky." **20.00**

Coal scoop, 14" × 9" wire scoop, 36" wooden handle, paper label reads "Champion Coal Savers" (Illinois Farm Bureau photo/Busch collection), **15.00**

"C.T. Ham Manufacturer," 13" **55.00**

Dietz,

#2 lantern with Dietz D-Lite globe, 13½", crank inside side tube ...**30.00**

Berger, "Patented," painted silver **22.00**

Junior, with red reflector in rear shield, 11¾", 1914-45 ....**35.00**

"Little Giant - 70 Hour Fount Capacity," red Dietz globe, 11½" **45.00**

Monarch, red globe, blue finish, 1938–60s **35.00**
with OVB #2 globe **22.00**
Wizard, painted dark blue, large font, soldered crack in font **65.00**
"Embury Mfg. Co. - Warsaw, N.Y. USA - No. 2 Air Pilot," Dietz globe with tiny hole, 13½" **20.00**
"Embury Mfg. Co. - Warsaw, N.Y. USA - Supreme Pat. Jan. 8, 1924," 8" high, electrified **20.00**
"Feuerhand No. 260, Made in Germany," embossed logo of hand holding fire **20.00**
"Paull's No. 0," last patent June 30, 1903, repainted orange, 14" tall **39.00**
Stonebridge folding lantern, Pat'd Nov. 20, 1906, June 9, 1908, 11" tall ...**52.00**

Matchbox holder
tin, red and ivory with decal of rose on front, embossed "Matches" **12.00**
tin, black, "Winged Horse Flour," flying horse logo in silver **22.50**
wood, painted blue **5.00**

wood, painted cat **22.50**
Match holder, cast iron, hangs on wall
double, dated 1869 ....**60.00**
embossed "MATCHES," looks like an ink-well **40.00**
ornate, hangs on wall **40.00**
two trays, "Matches are cheaper than gas," six-sided **55.00**
Skater's lantern, Dietz, 1914, good condition **65.00**
Stove, cooking, *see cooking and canning chapter*
Stove, laundry, *see laundry chapter*
Stove, parlor
cast iron
"Air Blast Universal - No. 221," restored, 4' tall, nickel trim **695.00**
Art Laurel, No. 14, nickel-plated, embossed with scrolls and lion heads, isinglass, very ornate, excellent condition **1700.00**
"Charter Oak, No. 15," ornate casting, plinth base, urn finial, needs restoration **245.00**

Lantern, galvanized metal, remnants of paper label, blue stripes at top and bottom, one-gallon can (Ted Diamond photo/Danenberger collection), **35.00**

"The Estate Stove of Hamilton, Ohio - Model 15," enameled, isinglass windows **1200.00**

embossed "German Heater 1914," painted black and silver, isinglass window, finial, 5″ tall, not safe to burn **175.00**

"Peoria Oak - 414 - Culter & Proctor Stove Co.," 10″ nickel plated urn finial, ornate embossing, 40″ **320.00**

"Revere Air Tight - Design Secur'd," cathedral design, damper on lip, crack in front, 25″ × 22″ × 28″ **175.00**

"Round Oak - Estate of P.D. Beckwith - Dowagiac, Michigan - MJ6," sound but needs restoration, 42″ high **225.00**

steel, King Oak **25.00**

Trim collar, ornate cast iron, fits around 8″ diameter stove pipe **15.00**

Tripod, curved cast iron legs with holes, holds kettle over fire, 14″ high **32.00**

Wick trimmer, wide blades **25.00**

Farm Toys

Farm children enjoyed playing with toys that represented the life they saw around them. Pretending to do the jobs they saw their parents doing, children played with miniature tractors and toy horses or worked with small tool sets or laundry equipment. Miniature tractors were sometimes given as a premium to the children of farm families who purchased the real thing.

Farm toys include horse-drawn equipment; animals; buildings; tractors and implements; wagons; tools; pedal toys; and lead, rubber, or plastic farm sets complete with families, animals, vehicles, and pets.

Cast-iron horse-drawn vehicles of many types have delighted children since the late 19th century. The first toy tractors were cast iron and were manufactured by Arcade, Vindex, and Hubley in the 1920s. They had smooth or lugged steel wheels. Arcade catalogs from the 1920s offered McCormick Deering and Fordson models. By 1927, Arcade offered these tractors with rubber tires on iron wheels. Implements made by Arcade in 1927 included the McCormick Deering plows, Oliver plows, and McCormick Deering threshers with steel wheels. In the late 1930s, ½s scale

tractors and implements were offered with rubber wheels. Hubley still offered cast iron Fordson, Avery, and Monarch tractors with steel wheels in 1933.

Early Ertl tractors used Arcade wheels in the 1940s. The first Ertl tires were all rubber. These were replaced with rubber tires with rims that changed from stamped steel to die cast to plastic.

After World War II, many companies began to produce die-cast miniature farm toys, mostly in ¹⁄₁₆ scale. Ertl, Slik, TruScale, and others marketed tractors and implements bearing the John Deere, International Harvester, McCormick, Farmall, Case, Ford, Massey Ferguson, Oliver, Minneapolis, Allis Chalmers, and other labels. Foreign manufacturers, notably Dinky, joined the market.

Tips for Collectors

Condition and rarity are very important factors in evaluating miniature farm machinery. White rubber tires tend to deteriorate badly. Restoration of miniature farm machinery and pedal toys is common. Excellent original condition is, of course, more desirable than excellent restored condition, but a toy that has been professionally restored is not devalued the way many antiques are.

Recommended Reading

Farm Toy Price Guide: The Blue Book of the Hobby. Paradise, Pa.: Nolt Enterprises, 1993.

Miniature Farm Machinery (¹⁄₁₆ scale unless noted)

Auger, TruScale, red **45.00**
Baler
  John Deere, plastic teeth, metal rims, 1950s **65.00**
  Tru Scale **40.00**
Blade, John Deere **55.00**
Combine
  Allis Chalmers, with bagger, orange, made by Ev Weber **410.00**
  Allis Chalmers Gleaner by Ertl **45.00**
  International Harvester 915, plastic reel, 1970 ....**50.00**
  International Hydrostatic 915, metal reel, 1960 ....**135.00**
  John Deere, 6600, with some plastic parts **90.00**
  John Deere pull behind, cloth belt, 1950s **110.00**

Marx, tin **25.00**
Massey Ferguson 760, some plastic parts **80.00**
Massey Harris Clipper, orange and yellow **505.00**
"Massey Harris Self-Propelled Harvest Brigade," wood blades at front, with driver, red and yellow **325.00**
New Holland, plastic parts, red and yellow **80.00**
TruScale, pull behind, 1950s, cloth belt, red, played with condition **65.00**
TruScale, pull behind, 1950s, cloth belt, new in box **200.00**
Corn picker
  International Harvester **35.00**
  made by Arcade, red, cast iron, ¹⁄₂₅ scale **85.00**
  New Idea, gray and green, with elevator **110.00**
  Oliver, two row, green and silver with white wheels, made by Ev Weber **385.00**
  TruScale, red, two row, fits an M ..**100.00**
Corn planter, made by Arcade, green, cast iron, ¹⁄₂₅ scale **85.00**
Crawler, John Deere, 1950s, missing steering wheel and treads **125.00**
Cream separator, International Harvester, made by Arcade, with plated bucket, c. 1930 ....**325.00**

Combine, Dinky Toys, red and yellow, black plastic tires, ¹⁄₄₃ scale, 1950s, worn (Ted Diamond photo/Danenberger collection), **120.00**

Tractor and wagon, Dinky Toys, red and yellow with gray tires, $\frac{1}{43}$ *scale, 7³/₄″* × *2¹/₄″* × *8¹/₄″, 1950s (Ted Diamond photo/Danenberger collection),* **130.00**

Disc
  Dinky, 1951, ¹/₄₃ scale 30.00
  John Deere 65.00
  International, plastic rims 35.00
  International McCormick 60.00
  McCormick Deering Disk Harrow, by
    Eska, in box, red 50.00
  TruScale, red, 1950s 30.00
Elevator
  John Deere 85.00
  McCormick 75.00
  TruScale, red, 1950s 35.00
Engine, Arcade, Fairbanks Morse Z, cast
  iron, red and green paint 4″ × 2″ × 2³/₄″
    ....125.00
Gleaner, Allis Chalmers, plastic wheels,
  worn 25.00
Grain drill, TruScale, red, 1950s 40.00
Harrow, Arcade, ½₅ scale 65.00
Hay loader, made by Vindex, cast iron, John
  Deere, red with yellow wheels, 1930s
    ....1750.00
Hay rack, International 32.00
Hay rake, cast iron, made by Arcade, red
  frame and seat, nickeled wheels, rakes
  and hook, ½₅ scale 195.00
Loader
  International, white 40.00
  McCormick, red, 1950s 35.00
  TruScale, fits an M 45.00
Manure spreader
  Case, plastic 300.00
  Dinky, 1950s, ¹/₄₃ scale 65.00
  John Deere, long lever 85.00

John Deere, 1950s 75.00
McCormick Deering Tractor Spreader,
  red, heavy 20.00
  rubber 10.00
pot metal, worn red paint, 5″ 5.00
TruScale, red and white 40.00
Mower
  Arcade, cast iron, rubber wheels, steel
    hook, hinged cutter bar, cast iron seat,
    ½₅ scale 60.00
  green and orange, cast metal 40.00
  John Deere, plastic wheels 45.00
  Oliver, red with silver blade, "Oliver" in
    yellow 25.00
  TruScale, worn 10.00
Plow
  Arcade, two bottom, cast iron, ½₅ scale
    ....45.00
  Case
    two bottom, chartreuse wheels, 1950s,
      original, mint condition 175.00
    two bottom 75.00
  David Bradley, rubber 12.00
  Ertl, orange, four bottom 50.00
  John Deere, four bottom 40.00
  Oliver, two bottom, plastic wheels
    ....12.00
  pot metal, two bottom, red, black rubber
    wheels, 4½″ 15.00
  International, rubber tail wheel 75.00
  TruScale, two bottom, red, 1950s ...40.00
Threshing machine
  Arcade, McCormick Deering, cast iron,
    gray and red, 10″ 325.00

Arcade, McCormick Deering, very good
paint, missing straw stacker **225.00**

Tractor

Allis Chalmers

Arcade, cast iron, with attached driver,
1930s, 3″ long **130.00**

Arcade, cast iron, white rubber tires are
marked "Arcade Balloon" **195.00**

190, bar grille, plastic rear wheels, 1960
.....................................**120.00**

190, console control, slightly worn
.....................................**100.00**

7060, maroon belly, no air cleaner,
1970 ....**85.00**

Auburn Rubber, orange and silver, with
driver **20.00**

Case

930 Comfort King, round fenders, original, very good condition, 1960
.....................................**200.00**

930 Comfort King, round fenders, restored **125.00**

1370, Agri-King, with cab, 1970
.....................................**135.00**

2590, silver muffler, 1980 ....**50.00**

Dinky, 1930s, ⅟₄₃ scale **400.00**

Farmall

plastic, (with box) 1947, with wagon
.....................................**165.00**

M, Arcade, 1940s, rubber tires, restored, 5½″ **135.00**

404, narrow front, white plastic rims,
1960s **75.00**

450, excellent condition, 1950
.....................................**750.00**

560, dual rear wheels, 1967 .....**135.00**

560, with corn picker **325.00**

806, round fenders, 1965 ....**200.00**

1206, white seat and rims, mint condition, 1965 ....**550.00**

Ford

961, 1960, three point hitch, wide
front, with original box, ⅟₁₂ scale
.....................................**90.00**

8000, 1970s, ⅟₁₂ scale **15.00**

Fordson

Arcade, cast iron, gray and red, with
driver **335.00**

cast iron, red and green, with driver
.....................................**325.00**

John Deere

"A," aluminum **35.00**

"A," attached driver, open flywheel,
worn paint, 1945 ....**150.00**

"A," closed flywheel, attached driver,
1947 ....**125.00**

"Field of Dreams," mint in box ...**27.00**

60, cast stack and square seat,
steerable, with loader **400.00**

110 lawn tractor, with wagon, 1965
.....................................**60.00**

140 lawn tractor, red, yellow, or orange
and white, 1960s, excellent condition **110.00**

140 lawn tractor, blue and white
.....................................**75.00**

430 with three point hitch, repainted,
1962 ....**475.00**

440 with three point hitch, yellow repaint, 1965 ....**395.00**

620, no three point hitch, worn, 1956
.....................................**90.00**

620, with three point hitch **200.00**

630, red, 1959 ....**700.00**

4010, three point hitch **175.00**

5010 I, 1963, yellow, mint in box
.....................................**40.00**

5020, wide front, fenders, plastic air
cleaner and seat, 1969 ....**75.00**

7520 with a gang disk, mint in box
.....................................**650.00**

7520, one-hole, excellent original paint
.....................................**410.00**

Hubley

Jr., red, played with condition **7.50**

red, worn paint, no steering wheel, ⅟₁₂
scale **17.50**

International

460, 1958, repainted **90.00**

966, wide front, white front rims, 1971
.....................................**110.00**

1256, duals, wide front, cab **150.00**

1456 Farmall Turbo **165.00**

1466 with metal cab, 1974 ....**110.00**

1466 with plastic cab **50.00**

5288, duals, 1985 ....**20.00**

Super M by Freheit, 1980 ....**335.00**

Leyland, Dinky, c. 1970, ⅟₄₃ scale ...**40.00**

Massey Ferguson, Dinky, 1959-64, dark
blue, ⅟₄₃ scale **35.00**

Massey Harris

Dinky, red and yellow, c.1950, ⅟₄₃ scale
....**75.00**

Dinky, with hay rake, 1953, ⅟₄₃ scale
....**100.00**

44, pot metal, silver driver, no muffler
....**30.00**

McCormick Deering, cast iron, Arcade, 7″
....**425.00**

Minneapolis Moline

four star, wide front, 1960, played with
....**35.00**

G1000, wide front, white rims, excellent condition, 1972 ....**140.00**

G1355, 1974 ....**145.00**

New Holland, red and yellow **120.00**

Oliver

cast iron, by Arcade, with three implements, ½₅ scale **400.00**

Row Crop, by Slik, worn paint **65.00**

70, cast iron, narrow front, red
....**135.00**

77, with driver **350.00**

880, 1950s **145.00**

1850, wide front, excellent original condition **120.00**

1850, no fenders, 1968 ....**85.00**

tin wind-up, green, 10″ **60.00**

Tru-Scale

M, beige or yellow rims, 1950 ....**70.00**

M, red repaint **50.00**

890, green, 1970 ....**80.00**

red, with loader, 1950s **135.00**

red, with rubber stack, 1950s **50.00**

red, with metal stack, 1950s **60.00**

White, silver muffler, c. 1980, in box
....**30.00**

Trailer, Tru-Scale, tilts, rope winch **30.00**

Truck, Dinky, covered farm truck, Studebaker, Ford, or Dodge, 1950s, ⅟₄₃ scale **85.00**

Wagon

cast iron, red, no tongue, tin wheels, 3½″ × 2″ × 2¼″ **75.00**

Allis Chalmers, plastic, 1950s **50.00**

John Deere

112, chuck wagon, worn **12.00**

large rubber wheels, worn **35.00**

tin rims, worn paint **15.00**

tin rims, good condition **35.00**

International, plastic rims, bent shaft
....**12.00**

McCormick, plastic, 1950s, red **50.00**

McCormick Deering, cast iron, high wheels, worn red and green paint, horses missing, not ⅟₁₆ scale **225.00**

TruScale, red, 1950s **25.00**

TruScale, red, 1950s, with hay rack top
....**35.00**

Pedal Toys, Tractors

AMF Ranch Trac, chain drive, yellow, plastic tank **85.00**

BMC, knee action tractor with cart ...**520.00**

Case

400, wood seat, John Deere decals, 1955
....**450.00**

1070, orange and white, very good condition **150.00**

Flying Dutchman, needs restoration
....**750.00**

Hamilton Heavy Duty, rusty red and white, 1950s **95.00**

International

Farmall 400, 1950s, decals worn ..**350.00**

Farmall 400, repainted **290.00**

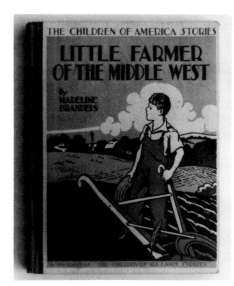

Book, Little Farmer of the Middle West, 7″ × 8¾″, colorful cover, 1937, 143 pages, **12.00**

Farmall 856, very good original condition, 1967 ....**250.00**

560, shift lever, 38", professionally restored **250.00**

repainted red and white, plastic front wheels, metal back wheels, 1960s **200.00**

wagon, pulls behind tractor, rectangular, sharp corners, red **60.00**

wagon, pulls behind tractor, IH decal on back, beige rims, rounded corners **50.00**

John Deere

620, original, excellent condition, 1956 ....**475.00**

630, stripe along hood, 38", 1958 ....**325.00**

4430 ....**100.00**

Minneapolis Moline

Power Trac, red, chain drive **115.00**

Tot Tractor **200.00**

Oliver

88 Row Crop, open grille, restored, 1940s **1200.00**

1850, excellent original condition, 1960s **575.00**

Western Flyer, chain drive, with matching trailer, yellow and black, plastic steering wheel **185.00**

Other Farm Toys

Animals

die cast metal, set of six, (two horses, two cows, pig, sheep), by Dinky, in box, 1932-40, 1946-53 ....**75.00**

papier mâché, six **70.00**

Bank, cast iron, standing horse, gilded, 4" long **65.00**

Barn

handmade, plywood, red and silver, gabled roof, two doors, four windows, 24" × 18", 1950s **30.00**

handmade, wood, white with red roof and shutters, doors open, 24" × 14" **35.00**

Book

Corn Farm Boy, by Lois Lenski, 1954, with dust jacket **9.00**

Dynamo Farm, by Adam Allen, 1942 ....**4.50**

Farm Friends, linen, cover pictures girl, boy, and rabbits, Whitman Publishing #1014, 1945, 10" × 14" **12.50**

Feet and Wings, of the Four Footed Friends Series published by McLoughlin Bros., color cover pictures cows, 6 color pages, back is missing, 8½" × 11" **16.50**

From Farm to Fortune, Horatio Alger, Stitt, 1905 ....**8.00**

John Deere: Blacksmith Boy, by Margaret Bare, 1964 ....**9.00**

See How We Work, by Sophie Lilienthal, courtesy of J. I. Case, 1940 ....**12.00**

BB gun, Daisy, Buffalo Bill, in box **85.00**

Bucksaw and sawbuck, red paint, usable, child's size **65.00**

Windmill, miniature, handmade of galvanized metal, red circles at center of 5" wheel, 5½" square, 17" high, 1960s (Johnson collection), 35.00

Game, The County Fair, by Milton Bradley, 1937, board, dice, spinner, five counters, cardboard coins, broken multicolor cover (Illinois Farm Bureau photo/Eisele collection), **45.00**

Pull toy, "The Cackling Hen" by Fisher Price, wooden wheels, played with condition, 1950s (Sharkey collection), **90.00**

Cow, "Milka Moo," by Ideal, 1950s **40.00**

Crawler, Marx, tin, wind up, silver with red wheels, treads, no driver, c. 1920 ....**160.00**

Doll buggy, resembles a miniature covered horse-drawn buggy, wood body painted black with striping, door each side, folding hood, wire wheels **850.00**

Dollhouse, handmade, dated 1863, hinged interior opens to letter reading, "This cottage to us erected in the year 1863 expresly a memento for Elizabeth Lewes by Grandpa Russell . . . ," picket fence, arch and stepped cornice over door, center chimney, working shutters, paned windows **2600.00**

Farm set

rubber, 35 pieces, figures of tractor, truck, car, cattle, horses, sheep, pigs, ducks, chickens, dogs, people with Asian hats, painted in primary colors, 1930s **50.00**

wood, handmade, includes water tower, steam engine, tractor, 1930s **185.00**

Figurine, Breyer, plastic

Appaloosa **20.00**
Charolais bull **25.00**
Deer, 6" high **12.00**
Draft horse **24.00**
Hereford bull **40.00**
Holstein bull, 5½", and calf **25.00**
Paint colt **12.00**
Quarter horse **18.00**

Figurines, set of 3, cow, bull, and calf, Hereford, painted, hollow pot metal, 2" tall **20.00**

Game

"Farmer Jones' Pigs," McLoughlin Brothers, cover shows man with hoe and dog chasing pigs through broken fence, chromolithographed box and board, 6 wooden counters, spinner, 8½" × 14½", c. 1885 ....**125.00**

"Game of the Stubborn Pig," Milton Bradley, spinner and 4 wooden counters, chromolithographed box and board, man and pig on box, board shows pigs at market and has numbered squares around edge, 15" × 9", c. 1910 ...**45.00**

"Honey Bee Game," Milton Bradley, box is chromolithographed scene of boy and dog running from hive of swarming bees, 24 metal discs, revolving metal disk at center of floral board, and magnet, 12¼" × 12¼", c. 1913 ....**65.00**

"Scratch," 10" square metal spinner with hen and eggs at center, color, time tables printed on spinner, "Educating Games Co." and instructions on box **45.00**

Goat cart, "Dreadnaught Farm Wagon" stenciled each side, 17" × 36" × 7" box, seat, chassis and two shafts, old green paint with yellow and black, 14" front wheels, 20" back wheels, very good original condition **1200.00**

Horse

rocking, wood platform base with curved supports, painted red with yellow striping, horse has old dapple gray paint, shaggy horse hair tail and mane, wood and leather saddle, c. 1920 ....**775.00**

wind-up, cloth body, wood feet **80.00**

Ice skates

Klipper Klub, clamp on, 1921, in original box **55.00**

Winchester, clamp on, slightly rusted **25.00**

Jack, Simplex Screw Jack, "Jack in the Box," 1920, 3½" tall, original box **40.00**

Toy iron and trivet, "The Pearl," wooden handle, polished surface, 3¾" × 2" × 2", cast iron trivet has three feet, fits iron (Illinois Farm Bureau photo/Eisele collection), **95.00**

Lawn mower, miniature, Dinky, 140 mm, 1950s, green and red **50.00**

Milk van and horse, tin wind-up, Marx Toylands Farms Products, 10″, excellent condition **375.00**

Puzzle

"Farm Friends," by ZigZag Puzzles, 200 cut plywood pieces, 12″ × 10″, in cardboard box, 1933 ....**22.50**

"Old Dobbin Scroll Puzzle," by Milton Bradley, two puzzles in one box, each has 15 die cut cardboard pieces and is 7½″ × 10¼″, 1920s **15.00**

Sewing machine, Singer, side wheel, in original box **90.00**

Sled

Dan Patch, red **500.00**

red with daisies, c. 1900 ....**395.00**

"Scout," green paint, wood runners with metal reinforcements are 6″ high **175.00**

wood painted yellow, sides with red striping and metal reinforced runners, two oval hand holes each side, wood rod across front, 39″ × 15″ × 6″, c. 1910, replaced center support **145.00**

Soap, "Farmyard by Wrisley," four animal-shaped soaps in cardboard display box **10.00**

Stove, parlor, Little Fanny, made by "Adams Peckover and Co. Cin. O.," complete **225.00**

Tractor, Marx, tin, blue and orange, 12″ **100.00**

Tractor and wagon, wooden, red tractor and green buckboard wagon, red tires, "Farm Toy" "Dee Bros.," approx. 2′ long **250.00**

Tractor and implements

Ford 4000 Industrial, tin, battery operated, backhoe and scoop, made in Japan, red, ivory and black, red tin hubs **235.00**

Marx, red and yellow, with three bottom plow, blade, rake, and blue mower, 1950s, tractor is about 14″ long **325.00**

Truck

Arcade, cast iron

ice truck with an ice block, red, slight damage **240.00**

International Harvester, paper labels, driver, excellent condition, c. 1930 ....**1050.00**

International Harvester, pickup, 10″ **600.00**

Mack, stake truck, 11½″, "Mack" in raised script on door, white iron spoke wheels **2700.00**

"Buddy L Cattle Transport," red and white, black stock rack **225.00**

Chevrolet, tin, made by Asihitoy, in Japan, canvas cover over bed is stenciled "Farm Products," green and orange, 1950s **30.00**

Ertl Livestock Van **25.00**

Fisher-Price, all wood, pull toy **55.00**

International, plastic, 1948, with box **225.00**

"Structo Cattle Farms, Inc. - Load Limit 48,000 lbs." on green and orange truck **50.00**

Structo truck, horse trailer, and wagon, Angus and horse decals, aqua and white, white wall tires **65.00**

Tonka Farms, pickup truck and trailer, Angus decal, green and white, 1960s, with two horses **160.00**

Wagon

farm, Studebaker, wooden, 36″ × 16″ × 8″ body, removable seat, refinished **425.00**

farm, cast iron, horse-drawn, 2″ × 5¼″, red **75.00**

wood, Dan Patch, metal disc wheels **425.00**

Washboard

glass scrubbing surface, "Midget Washboard" **22.50**

wood and tin, 11″ × 5″ **15.00**

Wheelbarrow

miniature, 82 mm, Dinky **25.00**

wood, usable size, metal front wheel, c. 1930, painted green **110.00**

Catalogs and Farm Literature

Catalog shopping was especially important to people in rural areas. An array of factory goods was available through the mail. Many general catalogs, like Montgomery Ward and Sears Roebuck, catered to farm customers with agricultural products. Catalogs sold everything from baby chicks to houses, buggies, wagons, automobiles, and tombstones.

Montgomery Ward of Chicago, Illinois, began their mail-order business in 1872. Sears Roebuck followed in 1886. The Rural Free Delivery, begun in 1896, made merchandise available to the most remote of homes. Sears published their first "big book" in 1896. Ward printed their first Christmas edition in 1932, and Sears followed in 1933. During the war years of 1942 and 1943, Sears' Christmas catalogs were produced in digest size. Sears discontinued their "big book" in 1993.

The Larkin Soap Company was one of many companies that printed catalogs that offered premiums for labels from their products. The Larkin Soap Company's catalogs offered such a range of premiums that, in 1901, the Larkin Pavilion at the Pan-American Exposition featured a library, reception room, parlor, dining area, music room,

and bedroom, entirely furnished with Larkin premiums.

The Larkin Company, of Buffalo, New York, was founded in 1875 by John Larkin and his enterprising brother-in-law, Elbert Hubbard. Their first effort at premium merchandising was to include a picture of a president in each bar of soap. Soon they were offering "silver" spoons, collar buttons, and other prizes.

By 1888, the company was advertising the "Club Plan." If a group made an order of 100 bars of family soap and 44 bars of complexion or household soap, they would also receive their choice of a piano lamp, an oak bookcase desk, an oil heater, or a recliner rocker. Soon the company offered a variety of club plans, including door-to-door plans for children and church aid plans.

By 1893, the Larkin Company was doing so much business that they began to publish a catalog and opened their own branch post office. Premiums were being manufactured in their furniture factory. By 1901, they opened the Buffalo Pottery to supply their own china premiums. Buffalo's Deldareware was offered as a premium in the fall 1922 catalog only. Noritake's Azalea pattern was offered in Larkin catalogs between 1925 and 1937.

Elbert Hubbard, aspiring to be a writer, sold out his share in the Larkin Company in 1893, explaining, "He who would excel in the realm of thought must not tarry in the domain of dollars." In 1895, inspired by William Morris's Kelmscott Press, he established the Roycroft Press in nearby East Aurora, New York. Roycroft was soon producing Arts and Crafts furniture, leather goods, and metalwork along with its books, pamphlets, and magazines.

Almanacs provided information about planting and harvesting, weather, phases of the moon, railroad rates, weights and measures, postal information, recipes, anecdotes, and medical information. Most were paperback. Many were given away as advertising premiums.

The Old Farmer's Almanac has been issued annually since 1793. Ben Franklin's *Poor Richard's Almanac* was issued for 25 years in the 18th century. Advertising almanacs often offered little more than ads and recipes between attractive and interesting covers.

Plat books, atlases, and directories are collectible regionally. They are valuable tools to genealogists and historians, detailing property ownership, businesses, farmers, and property lines. Local advertising is also of interest to those who are investigating local history. Sometimes these books include biographies and pictures of farmsteads, homes, or people for those who paid a fee to be included. Often pages with township maps are cut out and sold separately.

Tips for Collectors

Catalogs are valued by many as research tools as well as for their own collectibility. Condition is much more important to a collector than to a researcher, except in the case of missing pages. Pages are sometimes torn out and framed. Missing pages seriously detract from the value of a catalog. Toy collectors are especially interested in Christmas catalogs. Reprints of some early catalogs, such as Ward's and Sears', are available.

Almanacs from the early 20th century were given away by the millions by drugstores, feed stores, and mercantiles. They were often saved, making them quite common. Collections might be made with many themes. They might be of a series of almanacs offered by one company, with local advertising, or with interesting illustrations. Because of their availability, they should not command top prices unless they are in excellent condition. Exceptions include the English Kate Greenaway Almanacks and almanacs that predate the Civil War.

See the machinery chapter for more literature pertaining to farm machinery.

Catalogs

Farm buildings
> *Farm Buildings*, Carter & Foster, 1941, 404 pages, photos, plans, drawings **35.00**
> *Our Latest Book of Practical Farm Buildings*, 1930, farm scenes in color on cover, paperback, 96 pages, 9″ × 12″ **15.00**

Farm equipment
> Agricultural Implement Supplies, printed 1932, Peoria, Il. 500+ pages, illustrated in color and black and white, very good condition **65.00**
> Avery Tractors, Trucks, Motor Cultivators, Threshers, Plows, etc., 1922 ......**15.00**
> Barnard Saddlery, 1935, Shoe Findings and Auto Accessories, Rome, N.Y., green and black cover, 8″ × 11″, 223 pages **55.00**

The Beery Runabout, Jesse Beery, Pleasant Hill, Ohio, engravings of buggies and parts, 15 pages, c. 1911 ....**15.00**

Buckle Harness Catalog, Walsh, 1934 ....**25.00**

Case, J. I., Threshing Co., Racine, Wis., Special Supply Catalog, 1902, 36 pages, soiled **25.00**

Cleave Carriage and Wagon Hardware, 1911, 974 pages, 8½", illustrated, slightly worn **25.00**

Diesel Engine Catalog, #16, 1951, 410 pages **35.00**

Eagle Carriage Co., Cincinnati, 1912, carriages, harness, etc., 56 pages, 6" × 8½" **65.00**

Elgin Windmills, 1920, windmill weights **65.00**

Excelsior Wire & Poultry Supply Co., 1901, loose front cover, 128 pages, illustrations, prices **12.00**

Eureka Mower Co., Utica, N.Y., 1918, potato planters, 16 pages, 6" × 9" **20.00**

"The Famous Old Trusty Incubator and Brooder," 1917, 106 pages, color cover, 6" × 11" **19.00**

Frick Company, Waynesboro, Pa., 1906, gilt decoration, 56 pages, engines, threshers, sawmills, fair condition **55.00**

Great Western Endless Apron Manure Spreader, color cover pictures man on spreader driving two horses, 15" × 12", excellent condition **115.00**

John M Brant Co., Bushnell, Illinois, 1928, red cover with farm scene, 7"x 10", 74 pages, torn cover **5.00**

John Deere 420 Tractors, 1955, 30 pages, soiled **5.00**

John Deere Plow Works, Moline, Ill., 1930, power lift disc tiller and power lift, 8" × 9", 12 pages **12.00**

Jim Brown's Bargain Book, Brown Fence and Wire, Spring and Summer, 1936, colorful cover shows many uses of fencing, 57 pages **12.00**

Leader Incubator and Brooder Co., Descriptive Catalog and Price List, Quincy, Ill., no date, c. 1895, 32 pages, engravings, paper cover **25.00**

Louden Machinery, Iowa, 1916, 224 pages, hay tools, dairy and stable equipment, fully illustrated, 3 missing pages **22.00**

Moline Farmer's Catalog, 1922, man with blade, orange and brown, 6" × 9", 32 pages **25.00**

Moline Plow Co., 1879, pocket size catalogue **24.00**

Myers, F.E., & Bros., catalog #16, hay unloading tools, pumps, 1929, good condition **15.00**

Myers Spray Pumps, Ashland, Ohio, 1925, 88 pages, color cover is dirty, otherwise very good condition **8.00**

Parlin and Orendorff Plows, catalog #67, 1909, 370 pages, illustrated each page, soiled **55.00**

Phillips and Garcia, Cheyenne, Wyoming, saddles, rare **1800.00**

The Plano Manufacturing Co., 17th Annual, 1899 ....**40.00**

R. Herschel Manufacturing Co., Minneapolis, Minn., 1925-26, No. 78, red, black, and gray cover, 350 pages, 6½" × 9½" **43.00**

R. Hershel Manufacturing Co., Makers of Agricultural Equipment, Minneapolis, Minn., 1932, 448 pages **27.00**

Trade card, Larkin Soap Co., color lithography, 6" × 7½", back is stamped "Val Nafziger - Danvers, Ill," c. 1890, **17.50**

Red "E" Tractor Catalog, 1949, 31 pages and price list **10.00**

Reliable Gasoline Stove Catalog, 1895, manufactured by Schneider's & Trenkamp Co., Cleveland and Chicago, 72 pages, illustrations, 4½″ × 7″ **15.00**

Rumsey, L. M., St. Louis, Mo., 1884, 511 pages, wide range of farm implements, illustrated, 6″ × 9″ **85.00**

Savage Factories Catalog, buggies, Dan Patch items, 1913, 560 pages, 9″ × 11″, good condition **32.50**

Vermont Farm Machine Co. Bellow Farms, Vt., 1883, dairy and maple syrup supplies, 22 pages, 6″ × 9″ **42.00**

W.A. Patterson, horse-drawn carriages, 1903 ....**55.00**

Weir Plow Co. Catalogue, Monmouth, Ill., 1880, 3½″ × 6″, very good condition **55.00**

General

Baltimore Bargain House Wholesale, 1906, 28 pages, soiled covers **20.00**

Charles Williams Stores, fall and winter 1926-7, "Your Bargain Book," 338 pages, 8½″ × 11½″, clothing and shoes **32.00**

George Worthington Co., 1925, hardware, stoves, tools, guns, clocks, 1447 pages **150.00**

Henry Field's Merchandise Catalog, 1928 ....**7.50**

L.L. Bean Catalog, Fall 1935 ....**15.00**

National Cloak and Suit Co., 1918, July-August sale, 100 pages, color inserts, missing some back pages **20.00**

Real estate catalog, descriptions and photos of farmsteads in Ohio, Indiana, Michigan, Minnesota, etc., 1926, 8″ × 11″, 142 pages **12.00**

Sears

1902, reprinted 1969, good condition **19.00**

1903, hardback **150.00**

1905, #114, worn **60.00**

1908, reprinted 1969, very good condition **18.00**

1913, #126, inserts, envelope, order forms, shelf worn, otherwise very good **45.00**

1913, spring and summer, inserts **35.00**

1915, 7th annual July-August Sale, 116 pages, inserts **30.00**

1927, reprinted in 1970, good condition **19.00**

1931, spring and summer **45.00**

1934, spring and summer, soiled cover **20.00**

1945, spring and summer, 1002 pages, soiled cover, good condition ...**16.50**

1946, Christmas, very good condition **15.00**

1947, spring and summer, soiled cover, good condition **16.50**

Christmas, 1950 ....**15.00**

Christmas, 1964, 214 pages **45.00**

Spiegel, fall and winter, 1944, 9″ × 13″, fashions, toys **35.00**

Montgomery Ward

1918, No. 88, yellowed pages, very good condition **65.00**

1923-1924, fall and winter **65.00**

1931-1932, fall and winter, Book of Golden Opportunities, soiled and torn cover **45.00**

1964, fall and winter, worn cover **5.00**

1975, Christmas **18.00**

Groceries, Montgomery Ward, Jan. 1901 ....**22.00**

Hardware, tools

Brown & Sharpe Small Tools, No. 34, 1941, 512 pages **9.50**

Hardware Supply Company/Los Angeles, 1947, large, leatherette covers, approximately 1000 pages of tools and prices, very good condition **65.00**

Hynson Tool & Supply Co., annual catalog, 1903, St. Louis, 80 pages, coopers' tools, very good condition **70.00**

Keen Kutter, E. C. Simmons, 1930, paper cover, used but complete **525.00**

Keen Kutter, E. C. Simmons, 1935 ....**350.00**

Keen Kutter, in black binder with red lettering, Simmons Hardware, St. Louis, 1939, 5″ thick **450.00**

Keen Kutter, Shapleigh, 1942 ......**170.00**

Keen Kutter, Shapleigh, 1957, leather bound **300.00**

Starrett Tools, catalog #18, 1900, 232
pages, fully illustrated, soiled cover
....**12.00**
Starrett Tools, catalog #26, 1938, tapes,
saws, etc., 282 pages, illustrated, prices
....**10.00**
Winchester, No. 78, 1913, New Haven,
212 pages, slightly soiled **75.00**
Winchester Simmons, 1924 ....**450.00**
Winchester Simmons, 1927 ....**390.00**
Premiums
American Tobacco Co. Descriptive List of
Presents Offered by Premium Dept.
For Tobacco Tags, Coupons, Etc., 1906,
32 pages, 3½″ × 6″, good condition
....**20.00**
Ladies' Home Journal Premium Catalog
and Premium List, 1891, large format,
fair condition **12.00**
Larkin, 1930, 224 pages, 8″ × 11″ ..**37.00**
Larkin, 1934-1935, fall and winter
....**35.00**
Standard Soap Works Catalogue, Boston,
no date, c. 1900, 64 pages, 6″ × 9″,
with envelope **20.00**
Stoves, Kalamazoo Stove Company, 1912,
96 pages, order blanks, illustrated, color
covers **25.00**
Toys, Arcade Mfg. Co., Freeport, Il., 1932
....**120.00**

Catalog-related Items

Catalog holder
"Catalogues from Montgomery Ward &
Co." fiber cylinder with lid, yellow and
black, 15″ long, leather strap **28.00**
Sears Roebuck, tin, hangs on wall, brown
and black, excellent condition ...**50.00**
Larkin collectibles
Box, "Larkin Soap Co." stenciled in black
each side, pine with wood handles, 24″,
no lid **25.00**
Library table, Larkin paper label, quarter-
sawn oak, Mission style, center drawer
flanked by bookcases each side, front
lift-up doors open to bookshelf, wood
knobs, square legs, lower shelf
....**360.00**
Medicine cabinet, oak, Larkin paper label
on back **165.00**

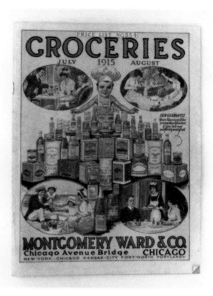

*Catalog, Montgomery Ward Groceries, July
August 1915, No. 554, 8½″ × 11″, 65 pages
of all types of merchandise, multicolor
cover, good condition (Antique Mall of
Chenoa, IL),* **35.00**

*Catalog, A.J. Child & Sons, 1924, variety of
merchandise, multicolor cover, 8″ × 11″,
84 pages,* **7.00**

Kitchen scales: left, *Sears, Roebuck & Co., coral and white, 6½" × 8" × 8¼",* **14.00;** right, *Montgomery Ward Family Scale, dark green with gold face, 5½" × 5¾" × 9¼" (Eisele collection),* **12.00**

Tin, Larkin Oiled Mop, tan and brown, rusty spots, 7″ diameter **7.50**

General Farming Literature

Almanac

Agricultural Almanac, 114th volume, 1939 ....**9.00**

American Agriculturalist Yearbook and Almanac

1899, 512 pages, cover illustration of men plowing **35.00**

1907, fair condition **14.50**

Dr. Miles, 1938, 9½″ × 6¼″ **3.00**

Leavitt's Farmer's Almanac, Concord, N.H., 1893 ....**25.00**

Rush's Semi-Annual Guide of Health Almanac, Rush's Bitters, color pictures of leaves and fruit on cover, 52 pages, 6″ × 8½″ **22.50**

Atlas

Atlas of Hardin County, Ohio: From Records & Original Surveys, 1879, folio, 131 pages, good condition **133.00**

Atlas of Madison County, Ohio, J. A. Caldwell, 1875, spine worn, otherwise very good **90.00**

Atlas of Morrow County, Ohio, 1901 ....**75.00**

Combination Atlas Map of Trumbell County, Ohio, 1874, folio size, 122 pages, some torn, 30 undamaged maps **65.00**

Historical Atlas of Tuscarawas County, Ohio, 1875, some replaced pages of text, professionally restored, original covers **95.00**

Book

Breeding, Training, Management & Diseases of Horses and Other Domestic Animals, Heard, 1893, first edition 224 pages, 95 engravings, 16 pages of ads, cover with gold decoration **50.00**

A Dictionary of Every-Day Wants Containing 20,000 Receipts in Nearly Every Department of Human Effort, Youman, 1872, first edition, leather binding, 529 pages, ads, carpentry, cooking animals, hunting, medical, good condition **27.50**

Farm Ballads by Will Carleton, 1873, worn condition **15.00**

Farm Ballads, 1873, very good condition **40.00**

The Farmer's and Mechanic's Manual, W.S. Courtney, 1869, 506 pages, 200 illustrations, gilt decorated, very good condition **20.00**

The Farmer's Barn Book, Clater, 1851, leather binding, heavy foxing, hand colored plates **50.00**

The Farmer's Complete Encyclopedia, Mercantile Publishing, 1891, 778 pages, good condition **22.00**

Farming, by Munkittrick, 1892, 150 illustrations, approximately 100 pages **25.00**

Farms and Farmers: The Story of American Agriculture, William Clark, 1945, ex-library, 3546 pages **12.00**

Harvest, An Anthology of Farm Writing, edited by Wheeler McMillen, 1964, first edition, dust jacket, 424 pages **10.00**

The Home and Farm Manual, by Jonathan Periam, 1884 edition reprinted in 1984, 1056 pages **15.00**

How the Farm Pays, 1884, first edition, gilt decorated, 400 pages, engravings of livestock, fruit, machinery, vegetable, buildings **37.50**

Practical Home Veterinarian, R. David Roberts, Waukesha, Wis., self-published, 1911, 183 pages, photos, ads, soiled **18.00**

Calculator booklet, *The World's Ready Reckoner and Rapid Calculator*, 1890 ....**4.00**

Directory

Directory of Kent County, Michigan, Grand Rapids, 1870, county atlas, rebound **125.00**

Prairie Farmer's Directory of farmers and breeders

Brown and Schuyler Counties, Ill., 1918, worn **15.00**

Carroll County, Ill., 1918, very good condition **35.00**

Bureau County, Illinois, 1921 .....**36.00**

Hendricks County, Indiana, 1920, 231 pages, good condition **25.00**

Journal, or record book

Bickmore's Farm Account Book, brown with black lettering, 64 unused pages, 5″ × 8¼″ **12.00**

Cost system book, Nash advertising on cover, 1921, yellow with black printing **2.00**

"Farm Record Book - 1948 - In Appreciation from Coast-to-Coast Store - Oakes, North Dakota," blank, paper cover, 12½″ × 9¾″ **3.00**

personal financial journal and diary, 1861–84, 56+ pages of records, farm and weather information, Geneva, NY **40.00**

"The Sterling Simplified Cost System for Farmers," 1924, 48 blank pages for record keeping, ads from Galesburg, Ill., 7″ × 10″, paper cover **5.00**

Magazines

Country Gentleman, cover illustration by Hintermeister, June, 1937 ....**5.00**

Country Home, January 1936 ....**2.50**

E.H. Howe's Monthly: A Farmer's Magazine for Town People, Potato Hill Farm, Kansas, 24 issues bound in two volumes **100.00**

Catalog, McCormick Works and Twine Mills, no date, 6″ × 9″, 56 pages (Antique Mall of Chenoa, IL), 48.00

Farm and Fireside, January 1926, color cover pictures man singing by radio **4.50**

Farm Journal, October 1929 ....**2.50**

Indiana Farmer's Guide, 1927 ....**5.00**

National Farm Journal, June 1930 ..**3.00**

Utah Farmer, 1914 ....**3.00**

Plat book

Atlas and Plat Book, Elkhart County, Indiana, 1929 ....**45.00**

Calhoun County, Michigan, 1873 ....**110.00**

Kalamazoo County, Michigan, 1910 ....**75.00**

Official Farm Plat Book and Directory, Wood County, Ohio, c. 1958, 56 pages **12.00**

Pocket Companion, "Empire Farmer's Pocket Companion," Sieberling & Co., Akron, Ohio, 1892, 3½″ × 6¼″ **30.00**

State report

Indiana State Board of Agriculture Twelfth Annual Report, 1870, Professor E. T. Cox, 430 illustrations, plows, reapers, stoves, sewing machines, advertising **37.50**

Kansas, *Biennial Report of the State Board of Agriculture, Kansas, Vol. XVI*, eleventh annual, 1899, 840 pages **9.00**

Maine, *Agriculture of Maine*, 40th Annual Report, 1897 ....**10.00**

New York, *Annual Report of the Dept. of Agriculture for the Year 1911*, color map, farms for sale **14.00**

Ohio, *Forty-Fifth Annual Report of the Ohio State Board of Agriculture*, 1890, 600+ pages **7.00**

Pennsylvania, *Report of the State Board of Agriculture, Pennsylvania, 1887*, 654 pages, color plates of fruit, engravings of horses, cattle, etc. **10.00**

Pennsylvania, *Third Annual Report of the Pennsylvania Dept. of Agriculture*, 1897, 897 pages **12.00**

U.S. Reports

Department of Agriculture Special Report on the Beet Sugar Industry in the U.S., 1897, slightly soiled **12.00**

Report of the Commissioner of Agriculture

1862, illustrated, good condition **35.00**

1878, soiled **10.00**

1885, 640 pages, color plates **12.50**

1887, 723 pages, stained cover ...**10.00**

Report of the Commissioner of Patents

1852, Part II, Agriculture, 1853, 448 pages, water damage **20.00**

1858, Agriculture, 552 pages, spine worn, foxing **15.00**

1861, 656 pages, worn **10.00**

1868, four volumes, two text and two with 1611 pages of illustrations, good to very good condition **110.00**

Yearbook

Department of Agriculture Yearbook, 1868, very good condition **13.00**

U.S. Yearbook of Agriculture

1903, soiled **13.00**

1916, meat inspection, turkey raising, potash **14.00**

1927, GPO, 1234 pages, octavo ... **9.00**

1939, 1165 pages, large octavo ...**10.00**

1952, 780 pages, 72 color plates ...**8.00**

1959, health and fitness, recipes ...**8.00**

Yearbook of the USDA for 1900, 888 pages, maps and charts, very good condition **13.00**

18 *County Fairs and Farm Organizations*

County fairs combined entertainment and education. They stressed quality and strove for improvement of agricultural production by promoting competition through the exhibition of livestock, crops, needlework, canning, and cooking. They were a social occasion for farm families and were a modern version of the ancient celebration of the harvest, with carnival, dances, singing, races, and games.

Farm organizations have served rural families since the 19th century. The Populists spawned Farmer's Alliances to work for the political interests of farmers. The Grange, or Patrons of Husbandry, was both a social and a political force at the turn of the century. Grange halls still dot the countryside in some parts of rural America. Farm bureaus and home extension units help rural families with advice and education. Children are served by the 4-H and Future Farmers of America (FFA) chapters. Protective associations and cooperatives have aided farmers to help each other for many years.

County and State Fairs

Booklet, Sandusky County Fair, Centennial 1852–1952, 88 pages, advertising **9.00**

Calendar, Indiana State Fair, 1935, girl with puppy **8.00**

Jug, stoneware, miniature, Uhl Pottery Co., "Kentucky State Fair" in script, peach color **140.00**

Pin, brass, Delaware State Horse Show, c. 1940 ....**20.00**

Pinback button, "Attendant - International Livestock Exposition - 1941," red and white, 1¾" **10.00**

Plaque, brass, shield-shaped, hangs on chain, embossed with eagle, "AMO Rabbit Club - Illinois Trophy -Peoria - Second Annual Show - Best Display - 1935," 7" × 9" **42.50**

Pinback button, green and white, St. Louis Button Co., ⅞" (Ted Diamond photo/Van Dolah collection), **7.50**

167

Postcard, color, Grundy County Agricultural Fair, Mazon, IL, 1909, Talbott-Eno Co., Des Moines (Johnson collection), **12.00**

Premium List, Fairbury (Ill.) Fair, 1954, lists premiums, programs and rules, 216 pages, plastic ring binding, 7"x 5", heavy green paper cover **7.50**

Quilt top, made from fair ribbons from the 1940s and 1950s, mostly blue, red, white, yellow, and purple, 52" × 72" **225.00**

Ribbon

"First Prize - Fifth Annual Show - Boyertown Poultry and Pigeon Association - December 25-29, 1917," 8" blue ribbon **10.00**

Great Reading Fair, first place, blue satin, 1956 ....**2.50**

"Morton Horse Show - 1950 - Fifth Prize," button at top is decorated with printed gold horse head and ruffled edge, faded pink satin, 17" **2.50**

"Special Prize" on 1¾" blue, gold and white pinback, "Ninth Annual Exhibition - Lancaster County Poultry, Pigeon and Pet Stock Association - Lititz, Pa., 1913," 8" purple satin ribbon, Keystone badge **14.00**

"Third Prize Nineteenth Annual Exhibition - The Ever Greater Lebanon Fair" on gold ribbon, celluloid covered 1¾" pinback is white with blue, reads "Ever Greater Lebanon Fair - Aug. 17-20, 1915," 9" long, made by Edward H. Schlechter, Allentown **15.00**

Table, child's, birch, "Illinois State Fair - 1953," capitol dome and Abe Lincoln in blue, 20" × 16" × 16" **58.00**

Organizations

Badge, "Twenty Second Annual Convention - Illinois Brotherhood of Threshermen - Peoria, Ill. - March 1-2-3, 1932," green satin ribbon is 5" × 1½", pin is a stamped brass figural ear of corn embossed "Peoria" with an empty holder for name tag **27.00**

Book

The 4-H Story: A History of 4-H Club Work, by Franklin M. Reck, 1951, ex-library **17.50**

Farmer's Alliance History and Agricultural Digest, 1891, gilt trim, 742 pages **40.00**

Johnny of the 4-H Club, by Alice Lide, 1941 ....**6.50**

The Grange—Friend of the Farmer 1867-1947, C. Gardner, 1949, 531 pages, first edition, dust jacket in fair condition **20.00**

Transactions of the New York State Agricultural Society, 1895, Wynkoop, Hallenbeck, Crawford, 831 pages, illustrated, report on gardens, livestock, dairies, farms, members, weak binding, good pages **6.00**

Booklet, *Program of Work,* Future Farmers of America, Chenoa Chapter, Illinois, 1945-46 ....**5.00**

Medal, brass, Hawthorne Club Horseshoe Pitching, 1930 ....**30.00**

Pencil, mechanical, wood, Sangamon County Farm Bureau **2.50**

Pencil holder, figural ear of corn, "Bloomington, Ill. PTA" on shield **15.00**

Pinback button

"Pony Club Member - The Farmer's Wife - St. Paul, Minn.," boy and girl on ponies **33.00**

"The Needlework Guild of America - Service," yellow **13.00**

"United Farm Workers - Affiliated with CIO," green and black, 1″ **10.00**

Pocket mirror, Indiana Farm Bureau Service and Producers Co-Operative Live Stock Sales," red with black, 3″ × 2″ **12.00**

notary, Farmer's Society, black with painted gold scrolls c. 1900 ....**45.00**

Sign

"Kankakee County 4-H Clubs Welcome You - Cabery Gay Girls," 4-H clover logo, green on white, enameled metal, 36″ × 24″ **50.00**

"Member Farm Bureau," porcelain over metal **15.00**

"Member Wallace's Farmer Service Bureau," yellow with black and red, 10″ × 7″ **12.00**

"Member Wallace's Farmer Service Bureau," red, white, and blue, fair condition **7.50**

Badge and ribbon, "Grange Social No. 1308, Whitehall, Ill." in silver on blue ribbon with silver fringe on one side; black ribbon reading "Memoriam" in gold on other side; celluloid covered pin at top reads either "Pomona P of H" or "Patrons of Husbandry," (two versions exist), with original envelope from Whitehead & Hoag Co. (Illinois Antique Center, Peoria, IL), ***10.00***

"Member Wayne County Farm Bureau," metal, blue with white lettering, white space for name of member, 12″ × 8½″, bent **10.00**

"No Trespassing - Member Prairie Farmer Protective Union," yellow and black **20.00**

"Protected by Wallace's Farmer and Iowa Homestead Service Bureau," blue, orange, and textured silver tin, 8″ × 12″ **25.00**

"This Farm Protected by Wallace's Farmers Protective Service - $50 Reward," yellow, red, and black tin, 8″ × 12″ **25.00**

Song book

National Grange Choir, Grange Publications, 1888, 127 pages, staple holes, fair condition **7.50**

National 4-H Club Song Book, 1954, 62 pages, 6″ × 8½″ **4.50**

Sticker, "Safe Operator - 1954 Corn Picker Safety Campaign - Illinois FFA," unused, 4″ × 5″ **1.00**

Thermometer, "Join Your Farm Bureau - It's Doing the Job - Illinois Farm Bureaus - IAA Service," metal, yellow with red and black, working thermometer at left of logo, 9″ diameter **48.00**

Watch fob

American Aberdeen Angus Breeders, Compliments of, embossed steer's head **38.00**

Future Farmers of America, brass ...**35.00**

Hoard's Dairyman Jr. Club, embossed bust **25.00**

Iowa Dairy Association, pictures cow and tub of butter, 1911, on leather strap **45.00**

Sign, porcelain; red, black and yellow; 14″ × 9″ (Fireside Creations/Lexington, IL), ***22.50***

Farm-related Advertising

Rural consumers were a vital market at the turn of the century. In 1900, two-thirds of Americans lived in rural areas or towns with populations under 8000. Large-scale farming on the prairies or the Great Plains required different implements from the tools that eastern farmers used. As land was settled in the west, new implements were constantly developed and marketed across the country.

Competition between turn-of-the-century farm-equipment manufacturers led many to offer a wide range of premiums, signs, and printed advertising. De Laval and Sharples offered tip trays, pinback buttons, match holders, pot scrapers, watch fobs, signs, calendars, thermometers, and song books. The big farm machinery companies also competed for new customers through advertising and giveaways. John Deere, Case, McCormick, Deering, Allis Chalmers, Oliver, Avery, Ford, and International Harvester offered an abundance of material to encourage farmers to buy their products. Loyalty to these companies was strong. Many of the items offered by these companies also advertised local dealers. Many bore logos that changed over time. Some companies' items can be dated because they went out of business during the early 20th

century. Other companies joined together, as in the case of International Harvester, which was formed through the merger of McCormick of Chicago; Deering of Plano, Illinois; P & O Plows of Canton, Illinois; and Chattanooga Plows of Chattanooga, Tennessee. Recently, Case has joined International Harvester.

Many manufacturers of farm machinery gave signs to buyers of their products. Farms displayed signs announcing that they were using a De Laval, Sharples, or McCormick Deering cream separator; Near's Products; or a Massey Harris tractor. Many farmers were seed corn dealers, and advertising signs for many brands of seed corn were displayed along rural roads.

Also collectible are items related to employment at any of the manufactories of farm machinery. Manufacturers awarded their workers with service pins and other awards. Badges were issued to security workers or served as a means of identification.

Tips for Collectors

Values for advertising collectibles are determined by their rarity, condition, design, age, and the collectibility of the company represented. Rarity can be determined by experience in the collectibles field or by research. A rusted, faded, or bent sign, match holder, or pinback button is worth much less than one in pristine condition. Items with designs that incorporate company logos, especially logos that can be used to date an item, or colorful, attractive designs are more desirable than simple, functional objects. Age is often a factor in assessing an item's rarity. It is sometimes hard to determine, but investigation into company history or magazine advertising may turn up clues. The collectibility of a company's advertising might be influenced by the availability of a wide range of items, such as those offered by De Laval cream separators. Interest is also generated by collector's groups. International Harvester, Case, and John Deere each has its own collectors' club. Advertising for regional companies that have closed or become part of larger companies is very collectible.

Reproductions

On printed paper items, such as posters or labels, look for evidence that an old example has been photographed and reproduced. Often original tears and stains are printed on the new copy.

New metal signs advertise many farm-related products. These are commonly found in gift shops and at flea markets. Examine them where they are sold as new so you can recognize them when they are misrepresented. They are usually smaller than 14 by 20 inches and are brightly colored.

The John Deere match holder in cast iron (10 by 16½ inches) is a reproduction.

Almanac (*see also catalogs chapter*)
　Barker's Illustrated Almanac, "from Barker's Horse, Cattle & Poultry Powder," 1893, color cover, 6″ × 8½″ **16.00**
International Harvester Co., almanac and encyclopedia, 1911 ....**15.00**

Anvil, miniature
　"Detroit Stove Works," 4″ × 2″ × 3″ **35.00**
　John Deere, green **25.00**
Ashtray
　"Co-op Agri-Power," tractor tire, 7″, glass insert with fired on logo **12.00**
　Firestone lugged tractor tire, clear glass insert embossed "All Traction Champion," 6″ **25.00**
Award, three-dimensional copper horse's head stands out 3″, brass plaque reads "Fox Valley Agriculture Service, Inc. Trophy - Roosevelt Aurora Post #84 - American Legion Horse Show 1947 - Stock Horse Stake," framed, 15″ × 19″ **50.00**
Badge
　brass, "IH Plant Protection - Lieutenant," enameled logo at center **190.00**
　brass, "IH Plant Protection - Guard," enameled logo at center **175.00**
　embossed "Oliver Chilled Plow Works - Plowmakers for the World - South Bend, Ind.," #1654 shows through plastic rectangle on front **29.00**
Bag, brown paper
　"Garrard Cracked Corn - Lancaster, Ky. - 25 lbs. Net," rooster picture, red and blue print **3.00**
　"Geo. Agle & Sons, Inc. Feed Store - Bloomington, Ill.," red and blue print, 15″ × 24″ **2.50**

Thermometer, convex glass over metal; red, yellow, black and white; 15″ (Country Hearth, Lexington, IL), **35.00**

171

Sign, enameled metal, "McCormick-Deering Farm Machines - Geo. A. Slagel & Co. - Flanagan, Ill.," black and gold, 27½" × 9¾" (Antique Mall of Chenoa, IL), 65.00

Bank

Allis Chalmers, quart oil can with slot in top **6.00**

Case, airplane, in box **20.00**

Bolt measurer, metal, "A Full Measure Every Time - From T.M. Livingston - Grain, Seeds and Supplies - Minonk, Illinois - Phone No. 4," stepped left side, 8″ ruler right side, yellow and black, 8″ × 6″, excellent condition **8.00**

Fan, paper, printed each side, Caterpillar Tractors, yellow and black, 10½″ × 9″ (Antique Mall of Chenoa, IL), 22.00

Booklet

Uncle Sam's Poultry Book, Sure Hatch Incubator Co., Fremont, Nebr., red, white, and blue cover, 62 pages, c. 1915 ....**12.50**

White Gold in the Swine Kingdom, Morton Salt Co., 15 pages **2.00**

Bowl

stoneware, beige glaze, ribbed, "Grettenberg Grain Co. - Coon Rapids - Thank You," 8″ diameter **20.00**

yellowware, "Wyoming HDW Co. - Appliances, Farm Supplies - Wyoming, Ill.," 10″ diameter **30.00**

Box

Dixie Distemper Remedy, orange and black, heavy paper, Dixie Stock Medicine, Marianna, Ark., 3¼″ × 2″ × 6½″ **10.00**

ISF Distemper Cure, red, paper **20.00**

Brochure, Keystone Hay Loader, Sterling, Ill., 1888, 6″ × 8″ trifold, yellow and black **12.50**

Broom hanger

Denehy's, tin back with printed advertising, loop for broom, 3½″ **6.50**

"Compliments of The Forest Dale Hatchery - Phone 29W - New Concord, Ohio," light and dark green, 3½″ × 6″ **35.00**

Brush, wood painted red, natural bristles, "McKee Feed and Grain Co. Muscatine, Iowa," 3″ × 7″ **5.00**

Cabinet

"Corona Wool Fat for Horses and Cows," oak case **150.00**

"Corona Wool Fat," burned into front of oak case, glass front door, three shelves, brass escutcheon, working lock, refinished, 14″ × 9″ × 23″ **250.00**

"De Laval Cream Separators - The World's Standard" on embossed tin front with color picture of separator, oak cabinet, 18″ × 11″ × 24″, slightly rusted front **275.00**

"Dr. Daniels' Veterinary Medicines - Home Treatment for Horses and Cattle," oak cabinet, color lithographed tin front shows Dr. Daniels and several products, red lettering on green background, 21½″ × 8″ × 28½″ ...**1400.00**

"Humphrey's Veterinary Specifics for Horses, Cattle, Sheep, Dogs, Hogs, Poultry," several animals pictured in color on tin front, list of cures, four shelves, oak cabinet **1150.00**

Pratt's Veterinary Remedies, slightly rusted lithographed blue tin door front, oak cabinet, 17″ × 7″ × 33″ **675.00**

"Syramed Co. Liniment" in red on wood case, glass front door, three shelves, 12″ × 7″ × 15″ **215.00**

Calculator

card with spinning metal arrow, "Acme Breeding Calculator - Acme Feeds - Forest Park, Ill.," orange and black, 3½″ × 5½″ **8.00**

metal dial, Streator, Ill. advertising ..**17.50**

metal dial, Vernon, "Critic Quality Feeds," red center, blue arrows all around, 1948, 12″ **25.00**

Calendar

"Clay Robinson & Co. Livestock Commission," heavy paper, color hunting scenes, 1919, 36″ × 15″ **95.00**

"Foreman and Smith - Dealers in Farm Implements - Centre Hall, Pa.," color print of "The Bride" by James Arthur, 1905, missing calendar pad at bottom, 8½″ × 14½″, excellent condition **23.00**

"M. D. King Milling, Pittsfield, Ill.," cardboard, 1934 ....**18.00**

Minneapolis Harvester Works, Minneapolis, Minn., color lithograph of two men harvesting with grain cradles, 1885 calendar on back, 6″ × 9″ **18.00**

Calendar, "The Bride" by James Arthur, 1905 calendar pad missing, color lithography, very good condition, 8½″ × 14½″ (Antique Mall of Chenoa, IL), 23.00

Calendar, "C.W. Zehren - Harness and Horse Furnishing Goods - Flanagan, Ill. - Phone 71," 1912, 10¾″ × 13¾″, excellent condition (Antique Mall of Chenoa, IL), 50.00

"S.F. Scattergood & Co. - Grain and Feed House - The Bourse - Philadelphia, Penn.," metal back has gold finish with blue lettering, flip number pad, movable month and day of week, 10½" × 15" **75.00**

Sharples cream separator, Harry Roseland print of mammy and child, 1914 ....**225.00**

Calf feeder, "Purina Nursing Chow" embossed on black metal bracket, holds aluminum bucket, 8" × 5½" **15.00**

Can, Plow Boy Tobacco, cardboard, faded **60.00**

Cap, polyester
Cargill Seeds **4.00**
"We Support Agricultural Strike" **5.00**

Children's book
Corny Corn Picker Finds a Home, John Deere, 1988 ....**4.00**
Johnny Tractor and his Pals, John Deere, grinning tractor on color cover, 7" × 8" **40.00**

Clock
Burpee Seeds, "Time to Plant," color picture, square wood grain case, electric, 1970s **50.00**
"Farnam - Nation's Leader in Horse Health Products," 25" × 12", lighted, blue and white, five horses, c. 1960 ....**35.00**
Illinois Valley Milk - Grade A, electric, 14" diameter **25.00**
Keen Kutter, square, lighted, electric **875.00**
Pioneer Brand Seeds, electric, 12" diameter, green logo **45.00**
"Purina Chows - Sanitation Products," electric, 16" diameter, red and white checkerboard border, 1950s **75.00**
"Quality Buckeye Feeds," red, white and blue, 14" round, electric **65.00**

Coffee mug, "Go with the Green - John Deere Service," green traffic light, Model D on reverse **5.00**

Cream pitcher
stoneware glazed white, pint, "For the Land's Sake - Use Phosphate - Millway Phosphate Co." **32.00**
brown and green mottled stoneware, ribbed, "Marple's Rendering Works, Monterey" **35.00**

Watt Pottery, Starflower, "Davenport Elevator Company" **95.00**
Crock, McCormick Deering Lye Solution **85.00**
Cup, tin, bottom embossed "Moor-Man's Cow Mintrate," red and yellow striped paper label, 3½" × 2½" **7.50**

Display
egg, milk glass, in metal holder, "Williams Poultry Food - 25 Cents," red hen and lettering, 5" **195.00**
figure, chalkware, full bodied horse, "Columbia Gall Salve Healing Powder," 16" × 14" **395.00**
rack, for John Deere implement, red wood frame with "Deere 99" stenciled in yellow, bolted together, 57" × 22" × 16" **50.00**

Drawer tag, brass, oval, "Allis-Chalmers Co. Tool No. _____ - Springfield Works," from tool drawer at plant, 2½" × 1¾" **4.00**

Dustpan, metal, swivels on long wire handle "DeVries Livestock - Austinville, Iowa," black on green **32.50**
"Federal Iowa Grain Co.," black on yellow, 34" × 13" **25.00**

Shaker, transparent amber plastic, 2½" × ⅞" × 3¼" (Illinois Farm Bureau photo), **7.00**

Folder, cloth with black binding, "David Bradley Mfg. Co. - Plows, Cultivators, Sulky Hay Rakes, Disk Cultivators, Disk Harrows - Chicago, Il., 6" × 3" folded **22.00**

Key chain

Allis Chalmers, brass **12.00**

"*Farm Journal*, Washington Square," metal, oval, space for phone number for key return **6.00**

Massey Ferguson, red plastic **12.00**

Lapel button, "John Deere Bicycles" deer logo, white with brown, ¾" **50.00**

Level, red, "Porch Grain Co., Toluca, Ill., Phone 7," 10" **7.50**

License plate tag, "DeKalb" figural winged ear of corn, metal, red, yellow, green and black, 9" × 4½", "J.V. Patten Company - Sycamore, Ill." **35.00**

Matchbox holder, tin, 3" × 4½"

"American Steel Fence - Made in All Heights," green and red lithography, match striker base **120.00**

"Washington Co-Operative Farmer's Grain Co. - Coal and Feed - Phone 44 - Washington, Ill.," green with black lettering **30.00**

"W.C. Trecker - McCormick Deering Machinery - Odell" in black on yellow **30.00**

Match holder, tin

De Laval Separators, hanging, die cut figural separator and three dimensional pail, original paint in very good condition **175.00**

Sign, canvas, green with white, 18" × 15" (Country Hearth, Lexington, IL), **15.00**

De Laval, same as above in fair condition **125.00**

De Laval, figural cream separator, repainted black and silver, 3½" × 7" **15.00**

"Economy Stove Co. - Cleveland, O. - The Original Elevated Oven and Broiler" in raised letters on 4½" square base, cast iron, copper finish, figural stove holds matches in top oven, 5" tall **135.00**

Keen Kutter, cast iron, emblem embossed on back reads "E. C. Simmons Cutlery and Tools," painted red, tray at bottom holds matches, 4½" × 2" × 7" ..**160.00**

Sharples Tubular Cream Separator, "The Pet of the Dairy" lithographed dairy scene, excellent color **225.00**

Universal Stoves, tin, lithographed, 3½" × 5" **75.00**

Vulcan Plows, die cut top, bearded blacksmith at anvil, lithographed on tin, excellent color **525.00**

Memo book

"Canton Plows and Agricultural Implements," 1895, 48 pages with ads, 6" × 3½", very good condition **60.00**

"Hefner Commission Co. - Union Stockyards, Chicago," 1939 calendar inside back cover, red and black, 2½" × 5½" **4.00**

Moor Man's Mineral Mixture **1.00**

Pilgrim's Binder Twine, red with black, 2¾" × 5½" **4.00**

Swift's Red Steer Fertilizers, red, white and blue, 1945 ....**1.00**

Mug, Round Oak Stoves, standing Indian, Doe Wah Jack **120.00**

Newspaper ad

"The Rock Island Hay Loader, The Loader that Never Comes Back," Rock Island Plow Co., 1902, 3½" × 14" **2.00**

Waterloo Boy, with illustration, 1919, 5" × 7" **6.00**

Opener, chromed metal, "Drott Tractor Co, Inc. - 1949," 5" × 10" **25.00**

Pancake turner, green handle with black lettering "A Thank You from Pat Kirk - Cash for Poultry and Eggs" **22.00**

Paper clip, celluloid pin at center of round clip, "Rockford & Huffman Co. Macedonia, N.Y.," picture of dump rake **45.00**

Paperweight

blue on brass, "Jno. H. Miller's Sons - Shippers of Grain, Feeds, Hay & Straw - Tyrone, Pa.," brass knob at center top, 3″ diameter **24.**00

bronze, "Caterpillar Tractor - 1904–1954," 3″ diameter **40.**00

Pencil

bullet

"Armour Fertilizer Works," celluloid center **10.**00

"Crow's Hybrid Corn - Milford, Ill.," plastic center **3.**00

John Deere, four legged deer logo in green on yellow plastic, "Brinkman Implement Co. - Colfax, Ill.," 4″ **15.**00

"Roy Webb - Custom Grinding," ear of corn printed design, picture of truck with burr mill mounted behind, c. 1940 ....**15.**00

mechanical, J.I. Case, plastic, orange with gold lettering **12.**00

string attached to brass end, "John Deere - L.E. Eagan Implements," never sharpened, c. 1950, green on white **12.**00

Picnic basket, wood lid is stenciled in blue and red "Feed Corno Feed," splint, two wood handles, 14″ square **50.**00

Pie pan, "Compliments of Farmer's Co-Op Elevator Co. - Fercus Falls, Minn.," yellowware with green stripe, Even Bake Oven Ware **45.**00

Pin

"Billings Farm Jerseys" and head of Jersey cow on pin, hanging miniature cow bell on striped ribbon **25.**00

Ford Farming, Dearborn Farm Equipment, red, white, black, and yellow, 1½″ **8.**00

Globe Scratch Feed, egg-shaped, celluloid over tin, rooster, globe, hen on nest **33.**00

John Deere, employee anniversary award, 10 K gold top, ½″

oval, embossed bust of John Deere **25.**00

with one red or green stone **35.**00

with two red or green stones **40.**00

with three red or green stones **45.**00

John Deere, employee anniversary award, 14 K two-tone gold

top, embossed bust of John Deere **40.**00

with three green or red stones **45.**00

The National Cream Separator, "Meets Every Demand," flag shaped, celluloid over lithographed tin; red, white and blue **26.**00

Pinback (campaign-type) button

"Ask for Vitality Feeds," rooster, green and red, 1½″ **9.**00

"The Badger Farmer's Friend Gasoline Engines - Milwaukee, Wis.," picture of gas engine **39.**00

"The Bucher & Bibbs Plow Co. The Imperial is the Best Plow in the World," two men and plow, color, 1″ **49.**00

Challenge Wind Mill & Feed Mill Company, Batavia, Ill., pictures windmill parts **33.**00

"Crown Mfg. Co. Phelps, N.Y.," picture of dump rake **27.**00

"Dietz 'D-Lite' The Latest Lantern Triumph," pictures a hand lighting a lantern **24.**00

"John Deere - Inventor of the Steel Plow," bust of John Deere **95.**00

LCS Poultry Feeds, 1″ **4.**00

"Lentz, C.E. - Rabbit Breeder - Des Moines, Iowa - Our Prices are Low," pictures rabbit **28.**00

"Maplecrest Farms Extra Fancy Turkeys," turkey on maple leaf, 1¼″ **32.**00

Moline Plow Co., winged man with corn, 2″ **87.**00

Moline Plow Co., 1½″ **45.**00

Night Commander Lighting Co. - Quincy, Illinois," black and white, 1¾″, with red, white and blue ribbon **28.**00

"Old Trusty Incubator - M.M. Johnson, Clay Center, Neb," picture of dog, color **40.**00

Oliver Chilled Plow, green with red rim, 1″ **15.**00

P & O Canton Plows **19.**00

Patrick, "A Genuine Patrick Product," picture of sheep **5.**00

"Saginaw Silo - The Modern Way of Saving Money on the Farm," black and white **20.**00

Samson Wind Mills, picture of metal wind mill **32.00**

"Seeds That Grow! The Nebraska Seed Co.," children on seesaw, color, 1⅛" **240.00**

Sharples Cream Separators, "Different from the Others, The Tubular Cream Separator," two girls at separator, color, 1" **20.00**

Sharples Cream Separators, "Different from the Others, The Tubular Cream Separator," woman at separator, gold edge, red and blue, 1" **40.00**

"Wapsie Valley Superior Pen Fattened Turkeys," blue and white shield on white background **2.00**

"Waterloo Boy," picture of boy in straw hat above Waterloo Boy tractor, 1" **80.00**

Plaque, wood base with standing plow share marked "Turning the Earth With IH Plows - Canton Plant" **75.00**

Plate, "For Good Results Feed Moor Man's - Quincy, Ill." in red, black and yellow center logo, "Buy Only the Feeds You Need but Cannot Raise or Process on Your Own Farm" around edge, beige background, made in 1962 by Vernon Kilns, 11" **25.00**

Pocketknife, "Purina" checkerboard, red and white handle **15.00**

Pocket mirror

"Garland Stoves," 1½" × 3" oval, color, celluloid over metal, very good condition **75.00**

"Indiana Farm Bureau Service and Producers Co-Operative Live Stock Sales" red with black lettering, 3" × 2" **12.00**

"New Hampshires - Eureka Hatchery - Eureka, Illinois," pictures birth stones, 3½" × 2" **9.00**

"Rock Island Stove Co., Rock Island, Kansas City - Riverside's," black and white celluloid covered metal top, 1¾" **22.50**

Sears Roebuck, printed guarantee, 2" round, made by Parisian Novelty Co., Chicago **45.00**

Sharples Cream Separator, oval **85.00**

"Updike Grain Corporation - Omaha - Use Updike Service - Consignment," oval, stained edges **7.50**

"Vulcan Best Chilled Plows - Vulcan Plow Co. - Evansville, Ind.," celluloid over metal, black on ivory, Vulcan statue logo at center, 2" round **65.00**

*Memo book, tan with brown printing, 2" × 4½", 1911, **4.00***

*Sign, cardboard; red, black, and white; 12" × 12" (Country Hearth/Lexington, IL), **12.00***

Postcard, International Harvester, 1909, one of 12, 5½″ × 3½″ (Illinois Farm Bureau photo), **5.00**

Postcard

Allis Chalmers Manufacturing **2.50**

Buckbee Seeds, pictures of women with fruit, vegetables, and flowers **7.50**

"De Laval Separator Co. - De Laval - The World's Standard," picture of separator against wood grained background **7.50**

"Duel Stable Blanket - 5A Bouncer - Low priced, strong and durable," man and dog with horse wearing blanket ..**10.00**

"Hinman Milking Machine Co. - Oneida, N.Y.," two cows being milked by machine **7.00**

International Harvester, "Harvest Scenes Around the World," show reapers, binders in use in foreign countries, copyright 1909, set of twelve **60.00**

J.I. Case Threshing Machine Co., Racine, Wis., 10 ton road roller illustrated **9.50**

Keen Kutter, E. C. Simmons, children and ax **100.00**

Premiums, De Laval Cream Separators, die cut lithographed tin

Guernsey, 5½″ × 3″ cow and 2½″ × 1¾″ calf, printed advertising on back, "De Laval" on front of cow, calf reads "Skim Milk for Me," with printed envelope **175.00**

Holstein cow and calf, with printed envelope **125.00**

Holstein cow **77.50**

Jersey cow and calf, no envelope ..**100.00**

Print

"Cooksville Grain Co. - Grain, Coal, Feeds - Cooksville, Il.," deco border, picture of elevator, 8″ × 10″ **12.00**

"Doe Wah Jack," Round Oak Stoves, Dowagiac, Mich., framed **175.00**

"Plant Ferry Seeds," woman in checked jumper holding hat and ears of corn, faded and scratched, black frame, 19″ × 27″ **75.00**

Plank Seed, North English, Iowa, landscape with sheep, small, framed **67.00**

Print block, John Deere, leaping deer, 1″ square **10.00**

Puzzle

Coe's Fertilizer, "Use Coe's Fertilizer - 45 Years in Use Throughout the Country," 99 wood pieces, 8″ × 8″, 1909, no box **40.00**

Premiums, De Laval Cream Separators, die-cut lithographed tin, Guernsey, 5½" × 3" cow and 2½" × 1¾" calf, printed advertising on back, "De Laval" on front of cow, calf reads "Skim Milk for Me," with printed envelope (Country Hearth, Lexington, IL), 175.00

"Hood Farm Puzzle Box," three double sided, die cut cardboard puzzles with twenty pieces each are 7¾" × 10½", show farm scenes and mother administering Hood's Sarsaparilla to children, 1905 ....**60.00**

New Idea Implements, farmyard scene, 1950s **60.00**

"Pratt's Foods - Fed Throughout the World - Greatest Animal & Poultry Regulators," 10 double sided cardboard pieces, Uncle Sam and world map, 6¼" × 9", paper envelope, 1905 ....**35.00**

Rack

"International Harvester McCormick Deering Farm Machines," IHC logo at center, enameled, holds ten catalogs and ten pocket folders, stands or hangs, 25" × 16¼" **150.00**

Oliver Plows, countertop display, holds brochures, tin, excellent decal, c. 1900 ....**125.00**

Ruler

Hector's, Sirenia, Grant's whips, folding, celluloid **35.00**

"Plant Lime - The Key to Fertility," folding, wood, 24 inches **10.00**

Song book, The Sharples Separator Co., 50 pages, color cover, taped binding, worn (Antique Mall of Chenoa, IL), 14.00

Salesman's sample

fencing, galvanized, 4″ roll, paper label reads "U.S. Poultry Fence" **40.00**

harrow, horse drawn, wood and iron, 7½″ **100.00**

hog trough, wood slats, "Lyons Perfect Hog Trough - Feb. 28, 1902," 4½″ × 6½″ **245.00**

horseshoe, "Snowcleat" **45.00**

threshing machine, wood, galvanized metal, and cast iron, hand crank, red with illegible black stenciling, 13½″ high **425.00**

waffle iron, "Super Maid Cookware," aluminum with wood handles, 7½″ **65.00**

washtub and wringer, wooden tub, "Relief Wringer" **175.00**

windmill, "Aero - OILON Bearing - Model No. 12-B - Mfd. by Aero Mfg.Co. - Geneva, Nebr." stenciled in red on tail, 1940s, 17″ tall **175.00**

wringer, "American Wringer Co.," 11″, wood and metal **150.00**

Salt and pepper shakers, pair, Keen Kutter, plastic **200.00**

Scoop, tin, cylindrical

"Bingham Feed and Grain - Meecher, Iowa - Poultry, Eggs, Hides," 11″ × 5″ **12.00**

painted gray with yellow lettering, "Secor Elevator Company, Secor, Illinois" **17.50**

Sign

"Case Farm Machinery - Est. 1842," eagle on globe logo at left, red, white, and black, rust spots, 72″ × 30″ **300.00**

Case Threshing Machines, tin, 1880s, 14″ × 20″, slightly rusted, chipped corners **1200.00**

"Crib Filler Seed Corn Dealer," rusted tin, red, yellow, black and white, 17½″ × 23″ **25.00**

"Collins Axes - The Axes of the World are Collins - The Best is the Cheapest," cardboard, color, pictures two globes and ax, 10″ × 19½″ **58.00**

Conkey's Feed, "It Pays to Feed Conkey's Feed," red on yellow, painted masonite, 18″ × 12″ **15.00**

DeKalb, masonite base, red, green and yellow winged ear of corn, 32″ wide **30.00**

DeKalb, porcelain over tin, winged ear of corn, yellow, green, and white, 26″ × 16″ **40.00**

De Laval, "Sooner or Later You Will Buy a De Laval Cream Separator - sold by Hamilton Cook Hdwe Co.," heavy paper, black and gold, 36″ × 5¼″, very good condition **22.00**

De Laval Local Agency, separator with two buckets catching cream and milk, porcelain on metal, white background is chipped, 14″ × 20″ **80.00**

"De Laval Cream Separators - The De Laval Separator Co.," 1910, tin, red background, ten colors, each corner pictures a milkmaid, cow, and separator, oval at center pictures milkmaid with arm around cow's neck, 21″ × 30″ self-framed **1750.00**

De Laval, "We Use the De Laval Cream Separator," yellow on black, 12″ × 16″ **75.00**

De Laval, "We Use the De Laval Milker," 16″ × 12″, tin **35.00**

Embro Corn, tin, shows colorful ear of corn, 13″ × 11″, 1940s **30.00**

Ford, "This Modern Farm Uses Ford Tractor Ferguson System," pressed wood, yellow and black, 20″ × 12″ **45.00**

Fordson Tractors, metal, multicolor paint, 36″ × 12″ **395.00**

Gale Plows, "This Gale Plow was Exhibited at the Centennial, Philadelphia 1876 & at the Paris Exposition 1878," metal sign with rolled in edge, red with black lettering outlined in yellow, approximately 30″ × 22″ **325.00**

International Stock Foods, "Three Hogs Dressed," 10″ × 13″ **45.00**

International Stock Foods, "3 Feeds for One Cent," double sided **40.00**

International Stock Foods, World Milk Record, Animal Tonic **70.00**

John Deere, porcelain over metal, leaping deer, yellow on green, approximately 40″ × 32″, 1950s **245.00**

John Deere Farm Implements, enameled

metal, deer logo at center, black, yellow and red, 9′ × 3′, several chips, wood frame **650.00**

"Long Bill Post Everlasting For Lifetime Fences - Pressure Creosoted Southern Yellow Pine," enameled metal, yellow, white, and black, picture of fence posts, 19″ × 13″, rusted **9.00**

Massey Harris, tin, "Another Proud Owner - Massey - Harris Better Built Farm Machinery," yellow, red, black and white, 20″ × 9½″ **45.00**

"Masterpiece Fertilizers," tin, orange and black, 20″ × 14″, 1930s **25.00**

"Moco Feeds for Turkeys," tin, white on red, 24″ × 6″ **25.00**

Monarch Poultry Feeds, wood, figural crowing rooster, 22″ × 34″ **750.00**

Myers Hay Tools, embossed metal with wood base, 20″ × 4″ **50.00**

Nears, "We Use Near's Livestock and Poultry Products," porcelain over metal, black on yellow, 10″ × 14″, chipped **25.00**

Nutrena, "Feed Nutrena - It Pays," on 42″ round metal sign, yellow, red, white and black, rusted **48.00**

Ohio Sulky Cultivators, "Use Famous Ohio Sulky Cultivators," metal, black with white raised letters, 13½″ × 6½″, slightly rusted **50.00**

"Oliver Farm Implements - Plowmakers for the World," porcelain, globe **345.00**

"Oliver - Finest in Farm Machinery - Kohler Farm Equipment Co. - Bloomington" in red shield, metal, green background with yellow, red, and white, 1950s, 24″ × 24″ **85.00**

Phoenix Horse Shoes, paper, framed, 1909, 15″ × 23″ **150.00**

"Producer's Clear Tag Field Seeds - Exclusive Dealer," red, white, and blue, porcelain over metal, fair condition ..**30.00**

"Procal - Always a Difference - Western Soils Co. - Waterloo, Iowa," blue and yellow, bent and rusted, 17″ × 11½″ **22.50**

"Professional Feeds," metal, red, white and blue, 20¼″ × 8″ **15.00**

"Sharples Tubular Cream Separators," tin, self framed with wood grain finish and gold reserves with lettering, color lithography, mother and child at separator at center, 23″ × 29″ **2500.00**

"Smith Great Western Endless Apron Manure Spreaders," in yellow on red, wood, 120″ × 13″, slightly faded **245.00**

"Standard's Quality Premixes," "FEED" on red barn with silo, sign is shaped like a barn, red, white and yellow, Standard Chemicals Mfg. Co., Omaha, Nebraska, 22″ × 11½″, excellent condition **55.00**

"State of Maine Potatoes - As Only Maine Can Grow 'Em," cardboard, life sized boy in straw hat and overalls seated on box of potatoes, color **65.00**

"Stull Hybrids," porcelain over metal, two ears of corn crisscross with picture of man in hat in center **60.00**

"Surge - Cleaner Milk - Faster Milking," tin, 12″ × 19″, orange, white, and navy, 1940s **25.00**

"Tracto Motor Oil - Reduces Friction - Saves Wear," metal, blue and red on yellow, barn and oil derrick, 35½″ × 11″ **45.00**

True Fit Overalls, cardboard, picture of overalls, 18″ × 6″ blue and white, faded, ...**25.00**

"Turkeys - Robt. Yordy & Sons - Oven Ready," hand painted turkey, gold with red, gray, and black, wood Deco style frame, 84″ × 40″, worn condition **65.00**

"We Buy Our Chicks from Zimmerman Hatchery - Milford, Ill.," yellow with black lettering, metal, 18″ × 12″ **28.00**

"We Use Sharples Cream Separator," wood with black lettering, made from side of shipping box, 50″ × 12″ ..**24.50**

Skillet, miniature, nickel-plated iron, "Anchor Stoves & Ranges - Louisville, Ky." embossed in bottom **20.00**

Song book, The Sharples Separator Co., 50 pages, color cover, taped binding, worn **14.00**

Spoon rest, Coal City Locker Co., red plastic embossed "Spoon Holder," c. 1950, 5" × 2½" **2.50**

Stickpin

Case, brass, 1" eagle on globe logo on bent pin **27.50**

Case, brass, eagle on globe swivels on pin **25.00**

"IHC," brass **18.00**

John Deere, deer leaping over plow **75.00**

"P & O Plow Co. - Canton, Il.," brass, 1" **45.00**

Tag, celluloid, Missouri Egg & Poultry Shippers, Kansas City, Feb. 1928, egg-shaped **18.00**

Tape measure

Farmers Grain Co. - Piper City, metal, gold with red lettering **12.50**

John Deere, celluloid with leaping deer logo **35.00**

John Deere, celluloid, "He Gave the World the Steel Plow - 7/10/17" **75.00**

Lewis Lye, celluloid **35.00**

"The Mitchell Wagon - Mitchell Lewis Motor Co. - Racine, Wis.," illustration of wagon wheel hub, red, white, and gray **65.00**

Myers Crop Service, 1970s **4.00**

Tearsheet, New Idea Spreader, framed two page ad from *Country Gentleman*, color **30.00**

Thermometer

framed picture of Purina Chows building and elevator, inset thermometer, Capron & Kornmeyer Grain Co., Cramer and Farmington, 6" × 8", c. 1950 ....**22.50**

"John Deere Quality Farm Equipment Made Famous by Good Implements," plastic lens over green and yellow back, 14" diameter **22.00**

Keen Kutter, round **115.00**

metal, yellow, red and black, "Productionized Seasonized Laying Feeds - Quality Kent Feeds," stylized chicken, 14" × 4½", very good condition **40.00**

metal, "Join Your Farm Bureau - It's Doing the Job - Illinois Farm Bureaus, IAA Ser-

vice," yellow with red and black, working thermometer left of logo, 9" diameter **45.00**

mirror with thermometer at right front, "Gainesville Livestock Market - South's Finest Building - Phone FR2-3442 - Gainesville, Florida," picture of market, 22" × 12", c. 1950 ....**30.00**

silhouette, woman knitting in front of arched window, winter scene, Voorhies Co-Op Grain Co. 6" × 8" **25.00**

Tin, Dr. LeGear's Gall Salve, red and black, 2 oz, 3" round **15.00**

Tip tray

"Dowagiac Grain Drills," wood grained background **35.00**

"De Laval Cream Separators - The World's Standard," woman and child, cows outside door, 1905, 4⅜" diameter ..**150.00**

International Harvester, gold center with green edge, advertising front and back, 4½" × 3¼" **95.00**

"Voss Bros. Mfg. Co. - Ocean Wave Washer," stamped aluminum, picture of wooden washing machine, 5" × 4" **28.00**

Towel holder, white enameled metal, "Woodhull Grain Elevator Co. - Grinding & Milling All Feeds - Woodhull, Ill." in red, red flower at top, 3½" × 5", c. 1950 ....**20.00**

Trivet, printed Dutch boy on pressed fiber, octagonal, "If You are Hunting for the Best, Forget the Rest, and See Emory Snakenberg - Case Quality Farm Machinery Sales and Service - Phone 618M - Fairfield, Iowa" **10.00**

Umbrella, for tractor

"Case - Winamac Sales - Winamac and Francisville," white with red lettering, poor condition **175.00**

"McCormick Deering Machinery Sales and Service - C.A. Dabe and Sons - Sabina, Ohio," holes at top, wood pole **150.00**

Watch fob

All Crop Farming, A.C. Member, embossed combine **45.00**

"Allis Chalmers Industrial Traction Division," pictures girl **20.00**

Allis Chalmers, harvester **50.00**

Aultman Taylor, brass, embossed rooster **65.00**

"Avery Tractor," bulldog **95.00**

"Case" embossed below tractor, c.1915 ....**65.00**

Case Centennial, tractor with plow **65.00**

Caterpillar Holt, brass **200.00**

De Laval, blue enamel on brass, rectangular **70.00**

De Laval, enameled red, white, and blue, on strap **90.00**

"Dowden Potato Digger - Prairie City, Iowa" **75.00**

"Fordson Tractor" **110.00**

Fred Mueller Saddle, Denver, Colo., working man's saddle **165.00**

Gaar Shoot Co. Richmond, Ind., embossed early tractor **65.00**

Globe Scratch Feed, celluloid, laying hen in front of globe **40.00**

Grand Island Horse & Mule Co., Nebraska, 1917 ....**80.00**

Hameley Roundup Saddle, Pendelton, Oregon **125.00**

"Huber Farm Machinery," with spinner **55.00**

Indianapolis Saddlery Co., saddle and harness **80.00**

International Harvester, two globes and cornstalks **55.00**

International Harvester, red and black **45.00**

"Iron Age Potato Machinery - Farquhar Co., York, Pa.," cast iron, potato figural with bug **45.00**

John Deere, blue enameled, oval ..**150.00**

John Deere, mother of pearl, on matching strap **160.00**

John Deere, centennial 1837–1937, silver chain **55.00**

Kansas Livestock Co., horse and horseshoe **55.00**

Keen Kutter, logo shape **75.00**

Levi Strauss Overalls, celluloid with mirror **175.00**

Massey Harris Farm Equipment **75.00**

McCormick Deering, porcelain **80.00**

Missouri Livestock Show, buffalo, 1899 ....**95.00**

"Missouri Wholesale Dealers - Eggs and Poultry - Kansas City - 1914" **47.00**

Ogden Union Stockyards, figural hog, brass **35.00**

"Planter's Fertilizer - New Orleans" **35.00**

Plano, embossed grain, silver colored metal **100.00**

"Purina, Keeps Mules Up and Feed Bills Down", figural key **55.00**

Salvet Worm Destroyer **60.00**

Sharples Cream Separator, Westchester, Pa., separators and milkers **80.00**

Standard Horseshoe Co., horse in shoe **30.00**

Stewart Horse Clipping, silver **100.00**

Success Manure Spreaders, brass, picture of spreader and lion on front, back reads "The Success Manure Spreader - Mfd. by Kemp & Burpee - Syracuse, NY," on brass chain, $1'' \times \frac{3}{4}''$ **70.00**

Tractomotive **35.00**

Wallis, embossed tractor **75.00**

Welcome Western Livestock Commission, Denver, Colo. **50.00**

Woodbury Whip Co., Rochester, N.Y. **75.00**

Whetstone

"Compliments of the Pike Mfg. Co., Scythe Stones," razor hones, etc, pocket size **20.00**

"Cudahy's Blue Ribbon Meat Meal - 60% protein - Makes Big Strong Healthy Hogs," blue with red and white, picture of pig, 2" diameter **27.50**

"Griggsville Elevator Co. - Phone 268," red and gold, celluloid over metal, 2" round **15.00**

Montgomery Ward & Co., red and blue advertising, 2" round celluloid top **50.00**

"Ox Guanos Produce Money Making Yields," picture of ox, round celluloid back, pocket size **40.00**

Pine Tree Farm Seeds, E.C. Crosbly, Danby, Vt., round celluloid back, picture of pine tree, pocket size **12.00**

"S.E. Mattison, Grocer, Agt. Adams Express Co., Rock Island Plow Co. - Phone Line 59, Osborn, Ill.," white, 8" long tapered each end **6.00**

Sears Roebuck, guarantee and picture of Liberty with scales, 2½″ oval celluloid top **75.00**

Yardstick

Caterpillar, sliding, wood, two 18″ sections **14.00**

"Hoblet Seed Farms - Atlanta, Illinois," thick **15.00**

"Vitamineral & Cod-O-Mineral - The Original Vitamine Mineral Feed - Peoria, Illinois,"¾″ square rod **10.00**

Collectors' Clubs and Newsletters

Bees and Trees

International Society of Apple Parer Enthusiasts, c/o John Lambert, Utica, Ohio

Wind and Weather

Crown Point (lightning rod ball newsletter)
884 Lulu Avenue
Las Vegas, NV 89119

Windmiller's Gazzette
P.O. Box 507
Rio Vista, TX 76093

Kitchen

Blue and White Pottery Club, 224 Twelfth Street NW, Cedar Rapids, IA 52405

Collectors of Illinois Pottery and Stoneware, c/o David McGuire, 1527 East Converse Street, Springfield, IL 62702

Griswold and Cast Iron Collectors Association, c/o Joan Baldini (814) 459-2503 or Sally Swanson (814) 838-1866

Kettles 'n Cookware (monthly newsletter), David G. Smith, Drawer B, Perrysburg, NY 14129

Kitchen Antiques and Collectibles News (bimonthly newsletter), c/o Dana and Darlene DeMore, 4645 Laurel Ridge Drive, Harrisburg, PA 17110

KOOKS, Kollectors of Old Kitchen Stuff, c/o Carol Bohn, 501 Market Street, Mifflinburg PA 17844

Red Wing Collectors Society, Inc., Ken and Dee Gorgan, P.O. Box 124, Neosho, WI 53059

Needlework

The Continental Quilting Congress, P.O. Box 561, Vienna, VA 22183

Machinery

International Harvester Collectors, Box 237, Royal Center, IN 46978

Early American Industries Association, PO Box 2128, Empire State Plaza, Albany, NY 12220

Farm Toys

The Toy Farmer (newsletter), Toy Farmer, Ltd., HC 2 Box 5, La Moure, ND 58458

Patent Numbers and Corresponding Dates

The U.S. government began to grant patents to inventors in 1836. Patents protected the rights of the inventor against use of the invention by other parties for 17 years. Often patent numbers can be found on hardware; locks; springs; hinges; and mechanical parts of tools, furniture, and kitchen utensils. These patent numbers can be used for dating items or for identification with further research in government patent publications.

The patent numbers listed in the second column below represent the last number issued in that year. If an item bears a number that was issued in 1882, you can be sure that item was produced after that year. Remember that patent numbers protected ideas for 17 years and were used for many years after their issuance.

1836	1	1851	7865
1837	110	1852	8622
1838	546	1853	9512
1839	1106	1854	10358
1840	**1465**	**1855**	**12117**
1841	1923	1856	14009
1842	2413	1857	16324
1843	2901	1858	19010
1844	3395	1859	22477
1845	**3873**	**1860**	**26642**
1846	4348	1861	31005
1847	4914	1862	34045
1848	5409	1863	37266
1849	5993	1864	41047
1850	**6981**	**1865**	**45685**

1866	54784	1906	808,618
1867	60658	1907	839,799
1868	72959	1908	875,679
1869	85503	1909	908,436
1870	**98460**	**1910**	**945,010**
1871	110,617	1911	980,178
1872	122,304	1912	1,013,095
1873	134,504	1913	1,049,326
1874	146,120	1914	1,083,267
1875	**158,350**	**1915**	**1,123,212**
1876	171,641	1916	1,166,419
1877	185,813	1917	1,210,389
1878	198,733	1918	1,251,458
1879	211,078	1919	1,290,027
1880	**223,211**	**1920**	**1,326,899**
1881	236,137	1921	1,364,063
1882	251,685	1922	1,401,948
1883	269,820	1923	1,440,362
1884	291,016	1924	1,478,996
1885	**310,163**	**1925**	**1,521,590**
1886	333,494	1926	1,568,040
1887	355,291	1927	1,612,700
1888	375,720	1928	1,654,521
1889	395,305	1929	1,696,897
1890	**418,665**	**1930**	**1,742,181**
1891	443,987	1931	1,787,424
1892	466,315	1932	1,839,190
1893	488,976	1933	1,892,663
1894	511,744	1934	1,941,449
1895	**531,619**	**1935**	**1,985,878**
1896	552,502	1936	2,026,516
1897	574,369	1937	2,066,309
1898	596,467	1938	2,104,004
1899	616,871	1939	2,142,080
1900	**640,167**	**1940**	**2,185,170**
1901	664,827	1941	2,227,418
1902	690,385	1942	2,268,540
1903	717,521	1943	2,307,007
1904	748,567	1944	2,338,081
1905	**778,834**	**1945**	**2,366,154**

1946	2,391,856	1951	2,536,016	1956	2,728,913	1961	2,966,681
1947	2,413,675	1952	2,580,379	1957	2,775,762	1962	3,015,103
1948	2,433,824	1953	2,624,046	1958	2,818,567	1963	3,070,801
1949	2,457,797	1954	2,664,562	1959	2,866,973	1964	3,116,487
1950	**2,492,944**	**1955**	**2,698,434**	**1960**	**2,919,443**	**1965**	**3,163,865**

City Slickers' Picture Glossary

The items pictured in this glossary are presented to help anyone unfamiliar with common farm tools to identify them. The value assigned to each is the value for the example pictured and does not represent a value for all similar pieces. Unusual forms of the same tools may command higher prices. More information about each item can be found in the chapter that corresponds to the item or its function.

Corn nubber, *cast iron, "S-118 - Patt. Applied for," 4" × 2½" (Illinois Farm Bureau photo/Busch collection),* **45.00**

Corn knife, *15" × 2¾" blade, 6" handle (Ted Diamond photo/Eisele collection),* **10.00**

Barley fork, *three wooden tines cut from one piece of wood, one tine attached at iron joint, 68" (Illinois Farm Bureau photo/Busch collection),* **120.00**

Corn dryer, made from one piece of iron, 19" × 5" (Illinois Farm Bureau photo), **12.00**

Cow kickers, 2" × 3½" ends on 22" chain, **10.00**

Corn sheller, weathered wood, 50" high, **60.00**

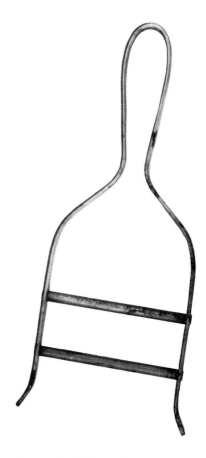

Device to hold horse's mouth open when giving it medicine, chrome, 9¾" × 4½" (Antique Mall of Chenoa, IL), **5.00**

Fanning mill, "Clipper Grain, Seed and Bean Cleaner - A.T. Ferrell & Co.- Saginaw, Michigan," *worn red paint and black stenciling, black and yellow line painting, "The Clipper" on hopper, 54" × 30" × 44", electric motor,* **125.00**

Fodder squeezer, iron, black paint, rope around shock of fodder was tightened by lever action of tool, 5" (Illinois Farm Bureau photo/Country Hearth, Lexington, IL), **10.00**

Grain scoop, 11½" × 8½" scoop, 3" handle (Ted Diamond photo/Eisele collection), **12.00**

190

Grain sieve, *bentwood frame, 18" × 4" (Country Hearth, Lexington, IL),* ***25.00***

Grass seeder, *horse drawn, iron with wooden hopper that is painted red with yellow lettering (Wilkey Auction, El Paso, IL),* ***125.00***

Hanging scales, *brass face, (left to right) chicken scale, "Chatilon's Balance No. 2 - New York," weighs to 25 pounds, bent corners, unpolished, 5"-long face, missing hook,* **12.00;** *reproduction, "Fisherman's Mate," 5½" face,* **5.00;** *butchering scale, cast iron with brass number plate, weighs to 200 pounds, 14" long,* **22.00** *chicken scale, weighs to 24 pounds, brass number plate, 10½" long, (Illinois Farm Bureau photo/Eisele collection),* **12.00**

Hay grappling hook, *(Williams collection),* **85.00**

Hay harpoon, iron, 35" (Illinois Farm Bureau photo/Busch collection), **28.00**

Hay hook or cotton hook, 10", wooden handle (Country Hearth, Lexington, IL), **12.00**

Hay knife, 34", red blade, two wooden handles, "Lightning Hay Knife - Patent 1871, reissued 1886 - Noah Wayne Tool Co. Oakland, Maine" on gold and blue label (Busch collection), **17.50**

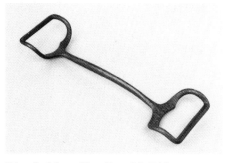

Hog holder, *"Pat Dec. 29 74," cast iron, 15½" × 4¾" at larger end (Illinois Farm Bureau photo),* **15.00**

Planter box, *"Moline Champion Combined Corn Planter Check Row Drill - Moline Plow Co., Patented June 16 & Sep. 15, 1885" on cast iron lid, yellow wood box with red stenciling, 10" × 10" × 12" (Mays collection),* **45.00**

Rake, *wood, two rows of teeth, top row had 22 teeth, lower hinged row had 21, iron support, missing 5 teeth, 53" × 24" (Illinois Farm Bureau photo/Eisele collection),* **95.00**

Pulley, *wood wheel in cast iron frame (Sandy's Surplus, Lexington, IL),* **8.50**

Reaping hook, *18" × 12½", c. 1850 (Illinois Farm Bureau photo/Busch collection),* **45.00**

194

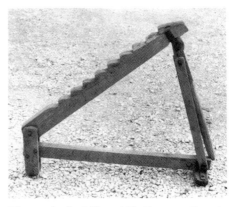

Rope maker, *wood and iron, "Pat Nov 12, 1901," 13½" × 5" (Illinois Farm Bureau photo/Busch collection),* **85.00**

Weed scythe, *slightly curved rectangular handle, side handle is mortised into main handle, 20" blade, 57" long, c. 1850 (Illinois Farm Bureau photo/Busch collection),* **75.00**

Wagon jack, *38" × 30" (Country Hearth, Lexington, IL),* **35.00**

Wire twister, *wood handle, iron hook swivels, "St. Regis Paper Co. - New York - Patented 1,365,649 - A-232" imprinted in handle, 5½" (Illinois Farm Bureau photo/ Busch collection),* **6.50**

195

Bibliography

Adams, Bob. "Lightning Rod Ornaments: Bright Baubles for Prairie Roofs." In *The Encyclopedia of Collectibles: Lalique to Marbles*. Alexandria, Va.: Time-Life, 1979, pp. 36-45.

Barlow, Ronald S. *The Antique Tool Collector's Guide to Value*. El Cajon, Calif.: Windmill, 1991.

Brackman, Barbara. *Clues in the Calico: A Guide to Identifying and Dating Antique Quilts*, McLean, Va.: EPM Publications, 1989.

Bruner, Mike, and Rod Krupka, eds. *The Complete Book of Lightning Rod Balls with Prices*. Ortonville, Mich.: Author, 1982.

Clark, William H. *Farms and Farmers: The Story of American Agriculture*. Freeport, N.Y.: Books for Libraries Press, 1945.

Courter, J. W. *Aladdin Collectors Manual and Price Guide Nine 1983*. Simpson, Ill.: Author, 1982.

Crilley, Raymond E., and Charles E. Burkholder. *Collecting Model Farm Toys of the World*. Tucson, Ariz.: Aztex, 1989.

Dennis, Lee. *Warman's Antique American Games: 1840-1940*. Elkins Park, Pa.: Warman, 1986.

Dinelli, Carol and Jerry Dinelli. "Even on Toys, Wheels, Tires Can Tell the Maker's Story" [Carol & Jerry on Antique and Collectible Toys]. *AntiqueWeek*. June 1, 1992, pp. 12-13.

Drepperd, Carl W., and Marjorie Matthews Smith. *Handbook of Tomorrow's Antiques*. New York: Crowell, 1953.

Evanoff, Betty. "The Lure and Lore of Hooked Rugs." *Antique Trader Annual of Articles* 11 (1979-1980): 286-87.

Farm Toy Price Guide: The Blue Book of the Hobby. Paradise, Pa.: Nolt Enterprises, 1993.

Force, Edward. *Dinky Toys*. West Chester, Pa.: Schiffer, 1988.

Hankenson, Dick. "Old and New Cast Iron Trivets." *Spinning Wheel* June 1962, p. 16.

Hawk, Dale. "Farm Machinery: Ingenious Implements to Till the Land." In *The Encyclopedia of Collectibles*: *Dogs to Fishing Tackle*. Alexandria, Va.: Time-Life Books, 1978, pp. 109-125.

Hobson, Anthony. *Lanterns That Lit Our World*. Spencertown, N.Y.: Golden Hill Press, 1991.

Hothem, Lar. *Collecting Farm Antiques: Identification and Values*. Florence, Ala.: Americana, 1982.

Hurt, R. Douglas. *American Farm Tools: From Hand Power to Steam Power*. Manhattan, Kans.: Sunflower University Press, 1982.

Johnson, Laurence A. *Over the Counter and on the Shelf: Country Storekeeping in America, 1620-1920*. Rutland, Vt.: Tuttle, 1961.

Jones, R. Duane. "Hoosier Cabinets: Kitchen Helper of the Early 1900's." *Antique Trader Annual of Articles* 12 (1980-1981): pp. 208-14.

Levy, Marion I. "There's Fascination in Apple Parers." *The Antique Trader Annual of Articles* 11 (1979-1980): 22-25.

McNerney, Kathryn. *Blue & White Stoneware: An Identification and Value Guide*. Paducah, Ky.: Collector Books, 1981.

Mergenthal, Bill. "Fool Me Once." *AntiqueWeek* (Central Ed.), February 22, 1993, p. 8.

Morykan, Dana Gehman, and Harry L. Rinker. *Warman's Country Antiques & Collectibles*. Radnor, Pa.: Wallace-Homestead, 1992.

Robacker, Earl F. *Old Stuff in Up-Country Pennsylvania*. Cranbury, N.J.: A. S. Barnes, 1973.

Rupp, Becky, "Sleigh Bells." *Early American Life* December 1985.

Russell, J. Almus. "Cheese Making Artifacts of Long Ago." *Antique Trader Annual of Articles* 9 (1978–1979): 126–29.

Simpson, Milt. *Windmill Weights*. Newark, N.J.: Johnson and Simpson, 1985.

Smith, David G. "Cast-Iron Cookware Has Its Share of Reproductions." *AntiqueWeek* (Central Ed.), October 26 1992, p. 12.

Springer, Lois. "Horse-Swingers." *Hobbies*, September 1966.

Swedberg, Robert W., and Harriett Swedberg. *Country Store 'n' More*. Radnor, Pa.: Wallace-Homestead, 1985.

Thuro, Catherine. *Oil Lamps: The Kerosene Era in North America*. Radnor, Pa.: Wallace-Homestead, 1992.

Williams, Anne D. *Jigsaw Puzzles: An Illustrated History and Price Guide*. Radnor, Pa.: Wallace-Homestead, 1990.

Index